Penelope Fitzgerald

Preface by Hermione Lee, Advisory Editor

When Penelope Fitzgerald unexpectedly won the Booker Prize with *Offshore*, in 1979, at the age of sixty-three, she said to her friends: 'I knew I was an outsider.' The people she wrote about in her novels and biographies were outsiders, too: misfits, romantic artists, hopeful failures, misunderstood lovers, orphans and oddities. She was drawn to unsettled characters who lived on the edges. She wrote about the vulnerable and the unprivileged, children, women trying to cope on their own, gentle, muddled, unsuccessful men. Her view of the world was that it divided into 'exterminators' and 'exterminatees'. She would say: 'I am drawn to people who seem to have been born defeated or even profoundly lost.' She was a humorous writer with a tragic sense of life.

Outsiders in literature were close to her heart, too. She was fond of underrated, idiosyncratic writers with distinctive voices, like the novelist J. L. Carr, or Harold Monro of the Poetry Bookshop, or the remarkable and tragic poet Charlotte Mew. The publisher Virago's enterprise of bringing neglected women writers back to life appealed to her, and under their imprint she championed the nineteenth-century novelist Margaret Oliphant. She enjoyed eccentrics like Stevie Smith. She liked writers, and people, who stood at an odd angle to the world. The child of an unusual, literary, middle-class English family, she inherited the Evangelical principles of her bishop grandfathers and the qualities of her Knox father and uncles: integrity, austerity, understatement, brilliance and a laconic, wry sense of humour.

She did not expect success, though she knew her own worth. Her writing career was not a usual one. She began publishing late in her life, around sixty, and in twenty years she published nine novels, three biographies and many essays and reviews. She changed publisher four times when she started publishing, before settling with Collins, and she never had an agent to look after her interests, though her publishers mostly became her friends and advocates. She was a dark horse, whose Booker Prize, with her third novel, was a surprise to everyone. But, by the end of her life, she had been shortlisted for it several times, had won a number of other British prizes, was a well-known figure on the literary scene, and became famous, at eighty, with the publication of *The Blue Flower* and its winning, in the United States, the National Book Critics Circle Award.

Yet she always had a quiet reputation. She was a novelist with a passionate following of careful readers, not a big name. She wrote compact, subtle novels. They are funny, but they are also dark. They are eloquent and clear, but also elusive and indirect. They leave a great deal unsaid. Whether she was drawing on the experiences of her own life – working for the BBC in the Blitz, helping to make a go of a small-town Suffolk bookshop, living on a leaky barge on the Thames in the 1960s, teaching children at a stage-school – or, in her last four great novels, going back in time and sometimes out of England to historical periods which she evoked with astonishing authenticity – she created whole worlds with striking economy. Her books inhabit a small space, but seem, magically, to reach out beyond it.

After her death at eighty-three, in 2000, there might have been a danger of this extraordinary voice fading away into silence and neglect. But she has been kept from oblivion by her executors and her admirers. The posthumous publication of her stories, essays and letters is now being followed by a biography (*Penelope Fitzgerald: A Life*, by Hermione Lee, Chatto & Windus, 2013), and by these very welcome reissues of her work. The fine writers who have provided introductions to these new editions show what a distinguished following she has. I hope that many new readers will now discover, and fall in love with, the work of one of the most spellbinding English novelists of the twentieth century.

By the same author

PENELOPE FITZGERALD

The Knox Brothers

with an introduction by Richard Holmes

Edmund 1881–1971
Dillwyn 1884–1943
Wilfred 1886–1950
Ronald 1888–1957

FOURTH ESTATE • *London*

Fourth Estate
An imprint of HarperCollins*Publishers*
77–85 Fulham Palace Road
Hammersmith
London w6 8jb

www.4thestate.co.uk

This Fourth Estate paperback edition published 2013

5

Previously published by Flamingo, an imprint of HarperCollins*Publishers* in 2002
Previously published by the Harvill Press in 1991
First published in Great Britain by Macmillan in 1977

Series advisory editor: Hermione Lee

Penelope Fitzgerald asserts the moral right to be identified as the author of this work

A catalogue record for this book is available from the British Library

ISBN 978-0-00-711830-4

Set in Goudy and Bernhard Modern

Printed and bound in Great Britain by Clays Ltd, St Ives plc

MIX
Paper from
responsible sources
FSC   **FSC® C007454**
www.fsc.org

FSC™ is a non-profit international organisation established to promote
the responsible management of the world's forests. Products carrying the
FSC label are independently certified to assure consumers that they come
from forests that are managed to meet the social, economic and
ecological needs of present and future generations,
and other controlled sources.

Find out more about HarperCollins and the environment at
www.harpercollins.co.uk/green

Contents

Illustrations

(With one exception, noted below, the photographs are from the personal collections of the author and her family.)

Genealogy

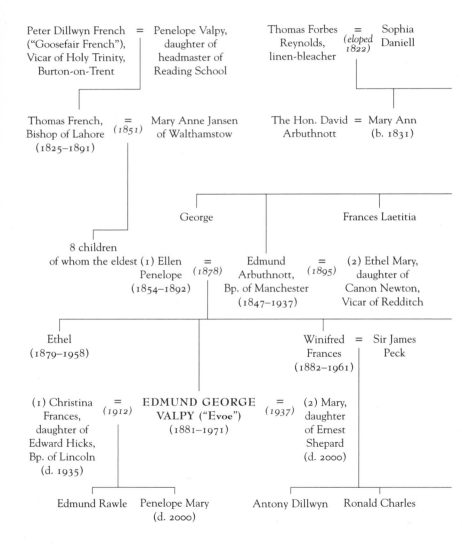

Peter Dillwyn French ("Goosefair French"), Vicar of Holy Trinity, Burton-on-Trent = Penelope Valpy, daughter of headmaster of Reading School

Thomas Forbes Reynolds, linen-bleacher = (*eloped 1822*) Sophia Daniell

Thomas French, Bishop of Lahore (1825–1891) = (*1851*) Mary Anne Jansen of Walthamstow

The Hon. David Arbuthnott = Mary Ann (b. 1831)

George

Frances Laetitia

8 children of whom the eldest (1) Ellen Penelope (1854–1892) = (*1878*) Edmund Arbuthnott, Bp. of Manchester (1847–1937) = (*1895*) (2) Ethel Mary, daughter of Canon Newton, Vicar of Redditch

Ethel (1879–1958)

Winifred Frances (1882–1961) = Sir James Peck

(1) Christina Frances, daughter of Edward Hicks, Bp. of Lincoln (d. 1935) = (*1912*) **EDMUND GEORGE VALPY ("Evoe")** (1881–1971) = (*1937*) (2) Mary, daughter of Ernest Shepard (d. 2000)

Edmund Rawle   Penelope Mary (d. 2000)

Antony Dillwyn   Ronald Charles

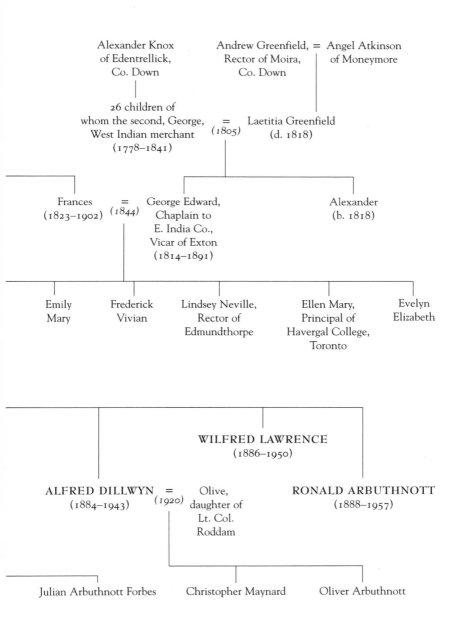

Introduction
by Richard Holmes

PENELOPE FITZGERALD'S MARRIED NAME, the name under which she became loved and celebrated as a novelist, subtly disguised her true inheritance. For Fitzgerald was really a Knox, and this marked her invisibly – or perhaps, indelibly – all her long life, and especially in her later and astonishingly creative years.

As a Knox, she was descended from one of the great intellectual, Anglo-Catholic clans of late Victorian England. She was born Penelope Mary Knox in December 1916. Her great-grandfather had been the missionary Bishop of Lahore; her grandfather was Bishop of Manchester; one uncle was the writer and translator of the Bible Monsignor Ronald Knox (like Newman, a Roman Catholic convert); and her father was for sixteen years the much-admired editor of *Punch*, at a perilous time (1932–1948) when the magazine was still a great institution of national identity, like *The Times* or Speaker's Corner or Harrods (and shared some of the attributes of each).

The Knox Brothers is her remarkable tribute to this family inheritance. It is a strikingly original group biography, and a highly engaging piece of family history, written with extraordinary wit and shrewdness: a funny, tender, clever book. But it is very much more than that. One might call it a study in a vanished civilization, and I am sure that it is destined to become a twentieth-century classic.

Its place in Penelope Fitzgerald's work is intriguing. The biography first appeared in 1977, when she was sixty. But because of her unusual, late-flowering literary career, it was in fact one of her earliest books, and seems intimately connected with her self-discovery as a writer. In taking the measure of her formidable family background (and this is hardly a work of pious memorial), Penelope Fitzgerald found a narrative style, a fascination with human character, and a series of moral preoccupations which seemed to release the whole flow of her fiction.

Her late start as a novelist was something Penelope Fitzgerald was frequently, and often wistfully, quizzed about – for instance at the Hay-on-Wye Festival of 1994. She was famous for the modesty of her replies, and one explanation was that she had simply been too busy with life, until she happened to enter a Ghost Story competition organized by *The Times* in Christmas 1974, when she had just turned fifty-eight.

(Her winning story, 'The Axe' was published in *The Times Anthology of Ghost Stories* in 1975, and subsequently collected posthumously in *The Means of Escape*. Its victim, an ancient and – one might say – an almost *disembodied* office clerk called Singlebury, is introduced with a gentle but slightly unnerving irony, that is already recognisably hers. 'Singlebury had, however, one distinguishing feature, very light blue eyes, with a defensive expression, as though apologizing for something which he felt guilty about, but could not put right. The fact is that he was getting old. Getting old is, of course, a crime of which we grow more guilty every day.')

More searching interviews (such as that by Hermione Lee, for BBC Radio 3, in 1997) revealed how directly her first novels drew on a mass of autobiographical material, stored up over forty years, and awaiting a moment of release. The pattern of her life suggested a long, slow period of imaginative and intellectual assimilation, in preparation for a literary career that she had always hoped for, but never quite expected.

Tantalizing glimpses of her as a teenager appear in later chapters of *The Knox Brothers*. But, characteristically, she always refers to herself in the third person, as 'the niece' or 'the daughter'. If you blink, you will miss them. From these we learn that she was largely brought up in literary London, in Hampstead and Regent's Park, with an elder brother, and her father's circle of brilliant acquaintances such as Belloc and AP Herbert. She attended (unhappily, one gathers) Wycombe Abbey, near Oxford, one of the most academically demanding of public schools for girls. This too appears in a wonderful, single-paragraph cameo in chapter seven.

In 1935, when she was still only eighteen, her mother died of cancer, which devastated the household. She writes characteristically of her father, Edmund Knox, at this time of overwhelming grief. 'It was many years before Eddie could bring himself to mention her name directly, even to his own son and daughter. At the time, he asked the proprietors of *Punch* for a short leave of absence, and an understanding that he would not be writing any funny pieces for the paper that year.' She says not a word of her own ('the daughter's') feelings, but only notes that her uncle Ronald, when attending the Anglican funeral, being a Catholic insisted on kneeling alone in the aisle. (p. 208)

Penelope Knox took a First at Somerville College, Oxford. She then worked in a series of institutions, great and small (the wartime BBC, a children's drama school, a Suffolk bookshop) having married Desmond Fitzgerald, a lawyer, in 1941. The family was mildly bohemian, in the Knox tradition, and were happy to live on a Thames barge, while taking occasional summer holidays in Italy and one memorable winter holiday in Russia. All of these experiences appear, transformed but recognisable, as settings for her later novels.

In 1976, the year following the ghost story, her husband Desmond died after a long illness. Penelope Fitzgerald never wrote directly about this time. But it was now, in amazingly rapid succession, that she produced in just five years, no less than six books which must have been, in some sense, bursting within her. The fascinating thing is that the first two were not novels, but biographies.

She had been working for some time on her life of the pre-Raphaelite artist Edward Burne-Jones (1975), perhaps as a distraction from her own immediate pain and unhappiness. It was inspired, she said, by Burne-Jones's stained-glass window of the Last Judgement, in St Philip's, Birmingham. 'No agitation here, the dwellers on the earth simply stand waiting for their sentence. The whole effect depends on the late afternoon sun slanting through the glorious red of the massed angels' wings. It is a window for Evensong.' (p. 271) The biography is lively, engaging, and well-researched, with a particularly striking picture of Burne-Jones's domestic life. But it also has the slight narrative stiffness, the uncertain deployment of materials, and uneven emotional tone, of a first book.

Nothing could be less true of *The Knox Brothers*, which appeared just two years later in 1977. Somehow, an artistic transformation has taken place. From the very first chapter, with its amazing and moving tale of her great-grandfather the missionary Bishop, sailing calmly out to his lonely death from Muscat, 'in a fishing boat, under a blazing sun, with his book-bag', the biography is pitched with a narrative assurance, a gentle irony, and a delight in curious anecdote, which proved to be the hallmarks of Fitzgerald's clear and silvery style.

Reading *The Knox Brothers* now, some twenty-five years after it was written, one is delighted by its period charm, its playful narration, and its barely repressed sense of mischief. But one is also struck by its technical ambition. For Fitzgerald, the obvious choice was to write mainly about the two famous literary figures of the family: her father Edmund and her uncle Ronald. Here were two well-known, but nicely contrasted brothers, who provided a perfectly balanced biographical subject, of great interest and wide appeal.

But in fact, of course, there were four Knox brothers. Penelope Fitzgerald took the daring (and indeed characteristically loyal) decision to write about all of them, and all of them equally. The biography thus has a highly unusual and almost musical form: a string quartet. The brothers' individual stories are not presented separately as four static portraits (perhaps the obvious biographical method). Instead, they are carefully interwoven and developed, with a novelist's sense of their growing individuality and changing fraternal alliances.

Their story begins in a country rectory deep in rural Leicestershire of the 1880s: the 'blue remembered hills' of arcadian childhood. (p. 15) As Penelope Fitzgerald later said, in an interview for the Highgate Institution Newsletter, in 1997: 'They were a vicarage family and vicarages were the intellectual powerhouses of nineteenth-century England.' But soon, as the four brothers grow up in Edwardian England, each alarmingly clever with strong but increasingly distinctive personalities, Penelope Fitzgerald starts to switch her narrative from one to the other, obtaining penetrating effects of emotional contrast, suppressed rivalries and shifting loyalties.

These transitions are wonderfully well handled, as for example in their very different experiences in the First World War. One brother is in the trenches, another in Naval Intelligence, the third working as a priest in the East End, the fourth writing books of spiritual comfort (chapter five). There is a wonderful scene in which they all manage to meet up, for one evening in 1917, in Gatti's restaurant in Mayfair, and drown their sorrows in champagne. (p. 139)

These contrasts immensely enrich and deepen the human scope of the biography. Though it remains a work of family history, it becomes something much broader. It is partly the vivid, humorous evocation of a lost England. But it is also a study in different kinds of human intelligence, and different kinds of virtue. One of the many things we learn, is that intelligence and virtue are not the same qualities at all. Another is that neither is very comfortable to live with. A third is that both may frustrate happiness.

The oldest, and the longest-lived brother, was her father Edmund Valpy Knox (1881–1971). Fitzgerald draws the portrait of a clever, handsome, clubbable man, a brilliant journalist, a light-verse writer, a survivor of Passchendaele, a legend in Fleet Street, universally and fondly known by his curiously perverse and un-pronounceable pen-name – 'Evoe' of *Punch*. This was meant to be in the tradition of Lamb's 'Elia', at the *London Magazine*. But Eddie used to complain that people were always referring to him as 'Heave-Ho'. He was unfailingly generous and encouraging to young writers.

But Fitzgerald also hints shrewdly at a disappointed, and perhaps embittered man, driven in on himself by the early loss of his own mother, difficult and saturnine as a father, secretly feeling that his ambition to be a poet was never fulfilled by his ephemeral Fleet Street glories. The editor of *Punch* thought that real humour 'lay not in ingenuity, but incongruity, particularly in relation to the dig-nified place that man has assigned to himself in the scheme of things.' (p. 264) Years later his daughter, in the interview with Hermione Lee, would describe herself as 'a depressive humourist, or a depressed humourist, which comes to the same thing.'

In strongest contrast was the youngest brother, her affectionate and even cleverer uncle, Monsignor Ronald Knox (1888–1957). Fitzgerald presents him as a conscious celebrity, the widely-read essayist, detective-story writer, Catholic apologist, Biblical transla-tor and (significantly) pipe-smoker. He emerges as an odd mixture of childlike unworldliness, and powerful social ambition. He is the poverty-stricken socialite, the shabby chaplain visiting the great country houses of England, the golden friend of the Waughs and the Lovats and the Asquiths, who also lives in tiny, freezing, antiquated rooms at the Oxford University chaplaincy.

For some years Knox was considered by many to be the intellec-tual heir to Cardinal Newman in England. But in Fitzgerald's won-derfully funny, but faintly subversive account he is always 'Ronnie', never Monsignor Ronald Knox. Ronnie 'did not have Newman's musical ear, nor his pastoral touch with ordinary people.' Ronnie was always slightly in danger of being spoilt, or self-dramatising, or taking up poses (kneeling alone in the aisle). He ultimately played

safe with his translation of the Bible, sticking close to the unin-
spiring Catholic Vulgate instead of returning to the original Greek
and Hebrew texts, and so rendering 'Peace on earth, good will
towards men' as what Fitzgerald calls the much more grudging
'Peace on earth to men of goodwill.' (p. 241)

Of course Ronnie was witty, intelligent, charming, modest to a
fault. He was the greatest popular asset to English Catholicism of
his generation. He was always ready to write engaging, religious
articles for the newspapers (quickly to be turned into a never-end-
ing stream of books). These articles, writes Fitzgerald carefully,
'introduced an exceedingly brilliant person whose reasoning mind
was able to accept the contradictions of Christianity. At the same
time they showed that a normal, pipe-smoking, income-taxed
Englishman, not a Jesuit, not a mystic, no black cloaks, no sweeping gestures, could become a Roman Catholic priest. The *News* and
Standard columns, with their wide readership, brought very many
people to think rather more favourably of God.' (p. 166)

The final, softly ironic landing of that last sentence suggests that
Fitzgerald, in exploring the subtle ambiguities of Ronnie's character,
had quickly begun to find her mature style. This she would carry
directly over into the humorous, subtle, understated portraits of her
fiction. Indeed Ronnie Knox, himself an ironist and prose stylist
of great finesse, seems to have inspired Penelope Fitzgerald by
example.

Writing of his uneasy sojourn as the Catholic chaplain at Oxford
in the 1930s, we find her entering into his persona, and imitating
his voice, in a way that is perhaps closer to fiction than traditional
biography. 'He regarded himself, he said, as medieval rather than
middle-aged, a man who refused to fly or go to the cinema and
whose idea of the last really good invention was the toast-rack.
Oxford, of all places, was prepared to tolerate such an attitude.'
(p. 210) It is fascinating to compare this with the much blander and
more respectful accounts of Evelyn Waugh (1959), or Father
Thomas Corbishley SJ (1964).

Next among the brothers, the closest in age to Eddie but the

shortest lived, was Dillwyn Knox (1884–1943). In some ways he is
the most enigmatic, and fascinating of all the Knoxes. He is the
eminence grise behind the family, the austere Mycroft to Ronnie's
glamorous Sherlock. Fitzgerald unfolds his character slowly,
expertly, appreciatively. First we become familiar with a tall, be-
spectacled, fiercely clever and donnish young man, with a biting
wit and distant manner, who seems both withdrawn and imperious.
His standard response to anything vaguely emotional or wrong-
headed is, sharply, 'Why do you say that?' (p. 221) He is the dry,
atheist scholar of Greek texts, a Fellow of King's College,
Cambridge, an aloof friend of Maynard Keynes and Lytton
Strachey.

But as it turned out (and unknown even to his own family)
Dillwyn was also a brilliant cryptographer. Recruited by the
Admiralty to its top secret 'Room 40' in 1915, he broke the German
naval flag-code in World War I; and in World War II he helped to
'find the way in' to Enigma at Bletchley Park, even as he was dying
from cancer. Fitzgerald clearly admired this work and dedication
enormously. It arose from a different kind of unworldliness,
oblivious to praise or recognition, hugely conscious of duty and a
different kind of virtue. She explains his cryptography at great
length, and has brilliant perceptions of the kind of superb intelligence, hovering between poetry and mathematics, that it involved.

In Fitzgerald's portrait, Dillwyn also slowly reveals an oddly
romantic side to his nature, a natural grace and shy gallantry. He
unexpectedly falls in love and marries one of his wartime secretaries
from Room 40. Twenty-five years later, he somehow finds himself
surrounded by particularly tall and pretty girls at Bletchley Park. He
is instinctively kind to, and protective of, 'the niece' when she is an
awkward teenager, unhappy at her school. Fitzgerald presents this in
a brilliantly funny paragraph, rich with tenderness and ironies, and
ending in a characteristically provoking epigram. (One needs to
know that 'Dilly' loved cars, but was an appalling driver.)

'The fates did not give Dilly a daughter, before whom, very likely,
he would have been as helpless as he was without his spectacles. To

his niece, confined for what seemed an eternity to a boarding school at nearby High Wycombe, where the girls, although their anatomy made it impracticable, were obliged to play cricket, Dilly was the kindest of visiting uncles. Agitated at having brought her back late in the Baby Austin, which seemed to spring and bounce along the road like a fawn, he bravely entered the precincts, blinking in the bright light, confronting the outraged housemistress, who said, "Rules are made to be kept," with the answer: "But they are defined only by being broken."' (p. 191)

Finally there was Wilfred Knox (1886–1950), in some ways the most obscure, humble and unworldly of the brothers, yet also the most unbending and emphatic. Wilfred inherited the burning missionary zeal, but none of the Victorian pomp, of his bishop forebears. He was an Anglo-Catholic priest in the East End, a dedicated socialist, a fearless motor-bike rider, a welfare worker, an eccentric recluse and just possibly a saint.

He remained closest, not to the other priest in the family, Ronnie; but to the most worldly of his brothers, Edmund. He always came for family Christmas, when 'the niece' was there, and consumed huge helpings of brandy butter, the famous Knox 'hard sauce'. He loved to go trout fishing in the summer with Eddie in Wales, his one other sensual indulgence. Fitzgerald shows a man of great spiritual honesty and simplicity; but also one of harsh impatience, extreme loneliness and cruel abruptness. Religious doctrine had divided him from Ronnie, and Fitzgerald guesses that the loss had damaged him emotionally for life. She quotes a fellow priest: 'he somehow communicated with everyone a deep love from a broken, unloving man . . . Looking back now one realises how deeply he had been hurt, and how he hid behind his wit and apparent tartness.' (p. 235)

Despite all this, or because of it, Wilfred finally became a Doctor of Divinity, a Fellow of the British Academy and an influential wartime university chaplain at Cambridge. He proved a natural pastor among the young. 'The attendance in chapel, which a priest watches as carefully as an editor watches the circulation, went

steadily higher.' His demeanour, 'a curious mixture of briskness and
spirituality', was so striking that one undergraduate recalled that
the very sight of Wilfred silently wheeling an old bicycle through
the Pembroke College gate, 'helped me grow in the Christian faith.'
(p. 238)

So Penelope Fitzgerald builds a memorably rich, composite
portrait of these four brilliant and unusual brothers, which is both
moving and compelling. We are left with the tantalizing question:
which one of the brothers was Penelope Fitzgerald's favourite? It
cannot be assumed that it was her own father, Edmund. It might,
for example, have been Dillwyn. For beneath her bright, witty
narrative, the biography allows for large areas of shadow, leaving
deliberate zones of mystery, and moments of discretion. For
instance, we only discover in passing asides, that Ronnie was
actually disinherited by his father the Bishop; that Dillwyn's marriage was unhappy; and that Edmund became 'haunted' and
depressed by having to write his weekly article for *Punch*.

We are told that among the characteristics that they all shared,
was the terrible 'Knox Temper'. But perhaps we are slightly shield-
ed from the causes of this, and how exactly it manifested itself –
shouting? sulking? silent furies? It was known to terrify colleagues
(Dillwyn's), alarm fellow priests (Wilfred's), and even drive the
family dog out of the sitting room (Eddie's). The reader can use-
fully consult the Index under 'Knox Brothers: Collective
Characteristics', which also included love of pipe-smoking, Greek
poetry, and steam-trains.

We never learn much of the two Knox sisters, Ethel and Winnie,
though Winnie in particular clearly played a vital part in her
brothers' emotional lives. This reminds us that it is essentially the
picture of a male world, and among Penelope Fitzgerald's imaginative triumphs are the evocation of particular closed, long-lost,
masculine societies: the Edwardian Cambridge of MR James,
Housman and Lytton Strachey; the boisterous Fleet Street of the
1930s; the tense, cocoa-drinking, war-time nightlife of Bletchley
Park. (p. 229)

In fact it is now clear how the Knox biography seemed to open the door directly into Fitzgerald's own imaginative world, taking her from history to fiction. In the same year of its publication came her first novel, a murder mystery, *The Golden Child* (1977), followed almost immediately by *The Bookshop* (1978, using the Suffolk experience, including a poltergeist that she always claimed was genuine); and then *Offshore* (1979, using the Thames barge) which won the Booker Prize; and then *Human Voices* (1980, using the wartime BBC). In five years she had established herself as a major fiction writer. Afterwards, she only once returned to biography, in an intriguing life of the reclusive Victorian poet Charlotte Mew (1984).

Over a decade later, in her last two novels, Penelope Fitzgerald seemed to return to fictional versions of her Knox inheritance. *The Gate of Angels* (1990) is set precisely in an Edwardian Cambridge like Dillwyn's, and begins with the incident of a bicycle accident that is close to a 'romantic encounter' described there by Ronnie. (p. 77–8) Moreover, its theme of the battle between intellect and emotions, one very close to Fitzgerald's heart, is central to her picture of the Knox family. There are similar echoes in *The Blue Flower* (1995) – her wonderful last novel about Frederick von Hardenberg, the Romantic poet Novalis. The picture of the close-knit, brilliantly clever family of the Von Hardenbergs, although they are late-eighteenth-century members of the German aristocracy, bears considerable resemblance to the Knoxes.

It was this last book that bore an epigraph from Novalis himself, which Penelope Fitzgerald said she had come to love. 'Novels arise out of the shortcomings of history.' But perhaps it could also be said, that novels sometimes arise out of the impulses of biography.

Foreword

IN THIS BOOK I HAVE DONE MY BEST to tell the story of my father and his three brothers. All four of them were characteristically reticent about themselves, but, at the same time, most unwilling to let any statement pass without question. I have tried to take into account both their modesty and their love of truth, and to arrive at the kind of biography of which they would have approved.

When I was very young I took my uncles for granted, and it never occurred to me that everyone else in the world was not like them. Later on I found that this was not so, and eventually I began to want to make some kind of record of their distinctive attitude to life, which made it seem as though, in spite of their differences, they shared one sense of humour and one mind. They gave their working lives to journalism, cryptography, classical scholarship, the Anglican Church, the Catholic Church. Since I wrote this book twenty-three years ago all these professions, all these worlds, have changed. If the four of them could be reborn into the twenty-first century, how would it treat them? I can only be certain that they would stand by the (sometimes unexpected) things they said. Evoe, my father, muttered to me, on the way to my wedding, "The only thing I want is for everyone, as far as possible, to be happy." Dillwyn: "Nothing is impossible." Wilfred: "Get on with it"—also "Why should we not go on, through all eternity, growing in love and in our power to love?" Ronnie: "Do the most difficult thing." I miss them all more than I can say.

I should never have got any way at all without the help and encouragement of my family, and the notes, letters and photographs which they lent me. I should like to begin by thanking my step-mother, Mary Knox, for all that she did, my brother, Rawle Knox, and my cousins Christopher and Oliver Knox, Tony Peck and Julian Peck.

Lord Oxford and Asquith most kindly let me use the large collection of unpublished material collected by the late Evelyn Waugh for his biography of Ronald Knox; to that brilliantly discreet work, and to the collection itself, I owe a very great deal. The bibliography of Ronald Knox's published works, which he believed had grown too complicated even for the Recording Angel, has now been undertaken by Miss Patricia Cowan, who was good enough to lend me her copy.

I feel very real gratitude to Dr Alec Vidler, who found time to answer all my inquiries about Wilfred Knox, and to Professor Henry Chadwick, for his most helpful letter about Wilfred and *The Sources of the Synoptic Gospels*; to the late General Gustave Bertrand, who explained to me the early stages in the solving of Enigma; to Professor Gilbert Waterhouse and Professor W. H. Bruford, who told me about Room 40; to Mavis Batey, Helen Morris, Margaret Rock, and Peter Twinn, who most kindly and patiently re-created for me the strange world of Bletchley Park; to Richard Price, the historian of *Punch*; to Professor W. G. Arnott of Leeds University, and to Mr I. C. Cunningham, the most recent editor of Herodas; to the late Rev. Meredith Dewey, Dean of Pembroke; to David Kahn, the authority on codes and ciphers; to Malcolm Muggeridge, who knew all four of the brothers and was able to give me a detached opinion; to the late Dr A. N. L. Munby

and the staff of King's College Library, who let me read the unpublished autobiography of Nathaniel Wedd; to Mr P. J. Law, the
librarian of Corpus, who showed me Dr Fowler's letter-book, and to
Dr John Lake, who made mathematics seem simple.

I should also like to take the opportunity to thank the following
people, who, simply out of their affectionate memories of one or
other of the Knoxes, wrote to me and helped me in many different
ways: Canon Jack Bagley, O.G.S., Mr Ian Bailey (Manchester
Grammar School), the Hon. Mrs Vera Birch, Canon Henry
Brandreth, O.G.S., Mrs Susan Brooksbank, Mrs Patricia Chambers,
Mrs Dorothy Collins, Mr John Cooper (Trinity College Library),
Mr J. J. Creaven, the Very Rev. Horace Dammers, Dean of Bristol,
Mr Robin Denniston, Mr Humphrey Ellis, Mr Laurence Elvin
(Lincolnshire History and Tennyson Collection), Professor Herbert
Farmer, the Rev. John Gillings, Mr Harry Golombek, Mrs Bridget
Grant, Mr J. Green (Borough Librarian of Newham), Canon
George Handisyde, Professor and Mrs Edgar Lobel, Canon Murray
Macdonald, Mr Iain Mackenzie, Mr Leslie Marsh, Mr Hugh Mead
(Librarian of St. Paul's School), Miss Dionys Moore, Mrs Elsie
Moseley (who remembers being chased round the lawn at
Edmundthorpe by my uncles when they were all very small chil-
dren), Dr Joseph Needham, the Rev. J. C. Neil-Smith, Mr Bernard
Palmer (editor of the *Church Times*), Mr Pepys-Whiteley (Deputy
Keeper, Magdalene College Library), the Rev. Richard Rawstorne,
Mr Gilbert Spencer, R.A., Canon Robert Symonds, O.G.S., Canon
George Tibbatts, O.G.S., Mr George Wansbrough, Mr Auberon
Waugh, Mr Patrick Wilkinson. I am most grateful to Richard
Garnett of Macmillan, who helped me through so many difficulties.

Finally, for this new edition I should like to thank Christopher
Carduff for his energy, inspiration and patience.

Penelope Fitzgerald
15 March 2000

The Knox Brothers

Beginnings

THIS IS THE STORY OF FOUR BROTHERS who were born into the family of a Victorian vicarage. When, seventy years later, the eldest was asked to consider writing his life, he declined, but suggested the title: *Must We Have Lives?* If we must, and if we want to understand them, we need to go back two or three generations.

The family was descended from landed settlers in Ulster, the Knoxes of Edentrellick, Rathmullen, Moneymore and Prehen. At the end of the eighteenth century the head of the Edentrellick branch, Alexander Knox, surrounded by his twenty-six children, set his face firmly against change. Although he and his descendants were Presbyterians, and suffered from the same political disabilities as the Catholics, he disapproved profoundly of the United Irishmen, who were hoping, by means of a somewhat amateurish rebellion, to establish a republic. Several of the family were implicated in the rising, and were wounded, disgraced, disowned, or, as the old man put it, "lived to be hanged". But one of the sons, George, steered clear of trouble altogether, and went to try his fortune in the West Indies. This George was to become the great-grandfather of the four Knox brothers.

Having a hardheaded Ulster business sense, George acquired a
sugar plantation and later recommended himself to the Governor,
General Nugent, who was of illegitimate birth and always ready to
help those who helped themselves. He returned to Ireland only once
in the next ten years, to marry Laetitia Greenfield, the daughter of
Angel Atkinson, of the Moneymore branch. Angel, who wrote that
she was "waiting till it was God's pleasure to dismiss her soul from
its frail habitation", was sickly, and George no doubt hoped, when
she died, to inherit some more of the Knox property. Back in
London, he set up as a merchant in Henrietta Street. The next
prospects were to be the begetting of a numerous family, and the
Moneymore inheritance. But everything went amiss: the property
passed to a cousin, and Laetitia proved as delicate as her mother.
She bore two sons—George in 1814, Alexander in 1818—then
died, a few days later, of childbed fever.

To the four-year-old elder son it was a cruel shock. One of his
books survives, a little leather-bound Tasso from his schooldays,
with a Latin inscription: "This book was my mother's, my loved, my
long-lost mother's." The words come as something of a surprise in
the history of the shrewd and so far dislikeable family. With poor
Laetitia, the Knoxes acquired the beginnings of tenderheartedness.

Against all expectation, young George's father turned away from
him and lavished all his affection on the second son, who had inno-
cently caused his mother's death. What was left of the West Indian
properties was settled on Alexander; everything was for Alexander.

Tempers blazed high when George refused to sit under a
Presbyterian minister. His mother had been an Anglican, and so
would he be. He went on to read for Holy Orders, and in 1837 was a
totally penniless curate when General Nugent kindly intervened
once again, and offered him a chaplaincy in the service of the East
India Company. Once arrived in India, George asked for no further
patronage or "interest". Even though the great John and Henry
Lawrence were his cousins—their mother was a Laetitia Knox from
Prehen—he never applied to them, believing, in the words of John
Bunyan, that "every tub should stand on its own bottom".

His calling in Madras was not that of a missionary, but of chaplain to the English community. At first he inspired fear, a "black" Ulsterman, forceful as a soldier, whose heart was kept hidden. It was thought that he was more than fortunate to meet and win his future wife, Frances Reynolds.

Frances was of Quaker descent. The Reynolds family were reputable linen-bleachers at Beddington in Surrey, pious, discreet and thriving; but her father, Thomas Reynolds, was not a successful business man. He was drawn to impracticable schemes. As a very young man he had been sent to Paris by George IV to fetch back a mysterious "Miss Jones", supposedly the daughter of Mrs Fitzherbert, who spoke much of her "rights", and bequeathed to the Reynoldses a tiny pair of "royal" scissors. Later on Thomas eloped to Gretna Green with his bride, Sophia Daniell, after bribing her maid with the present of a workbox. After his marriage he gave up the bleaching business altogether and went to Cambridge to study medicine, though with no intention of practising. The result of all this airy dreaming was that his two daughters felt obliged to go out as governesses. To avert this fate the Curzons, who were distant connections, offered to take them to India, but the girls refused, "fearing the worldliness of the society into which they would be thrown." "There were very tender consciences," Frances's son wrote, "in the borderland where Quakerism and Evangelicalism met." Eventually the Daniells paid for the passages to India, and Frances and Mary Ann set off, their boxes full of dove-grey and sober brown dresses. They took with them, also, a copy of Keble's *Christian Year*, something more intensely and romantically devotional than the Meeting House could offer.

Mary Ann might have been supposed to do the better of the two, for she eventually married the Hon. David Arbuthnott; but in later years she horrified her family by announcing that she and all her children were to be received as Roman Catholics. This meant that the sisters could never meet or communicate again, and both of them accepted this, in spite of the intense grief it caused. It was a division sharper than the sword.

In 1844 Frances Reynolds was a girl of twenty, short, slight and dignified, with fair hair and complexion and a sweet smile of a kind unknown among the gloomy Ulster farms and linen-sheds, a smile which she bequeathed to her descendants. George Knox, on the other hand, was the kind of Irishman who, like Samuel Beckett's Watt, "had never smiled, but thought that he knew how it was done." They were married that winter, in the church at Cuddalore, a handsome couple whose charm and influence were long remembered in Madras. In 1855 they returned to England, bringing with them a "fine family" of four sons and three daughters.

George had no intention of returning to Edentrellick, and for a while they were travellers, passing from one curacy to another. York was the place the children remembered best, and how their father, preaching at St John's by candlelight, put all the candles out, during a flight of eloquence, with a sweep of his pudding-bag sleeve, so that the church was left in darkness. In 1857 he was appointed Association Secretary of the Church Missionary Society, and they settled at Waddon, then a village, near Croydon. The house was not really large enough. The three elder boys slept together, the youngest, Lindsey, downstairs in the pantry. Edmund, the second son, who showed early scholastic promise, had to "get up" his lessons in the corner of his mother's room, and witnessed, in fear and reverence, his mother's daily prayers, as she struggled out loud to submit her will to God. But if there was overcrowding, nobody had time to worry about it. Everyone was hard at it, family and servants alike; if nothing else offered, there was sewing and poultry-keeping, though half the eggs had to be set aside to sell for the Missions. "There was no talk of slavery," Edmund wrote. "Industry was the normal condition of rational beings, and idleness a dangerous sin. That principle ruled throughout the household."

After her eighth confinement, it is true, Frances took to the life of a semi-invalid, but from her sofa she supervised every detail of the housekeeping. Between Ulster thrift and Quaker sobriety the economy was amazingly narrow. Only one piece of bread-and-butter was allowed—after that, dry bread only. Clothes were the subject of the deepest embarrassment. The boys were dressed in tartan tunics of seemingly indestructible material, handed down from one to another, or "a shapeless garment intended to represent a lounge coat." The girls could only pray that fashion would come round full circle so that people would not laugh at their appearance in the street. Fortunately, perhaps, they went out very little, and at the neighbours' parties they had to leave before the dancing, passing, with glances of acute regret, the loaded supper-table. The Knoxes, who for years had led the spacious social life of mid-Victorian India, now "kept no company". Neither did they take seaside holidays, or, indeed, any holidays at all. Books were severely restricted, novels forbidden, and the father, who chose all his sons' school prizes, would not hear of Ruskin, who tended to unmanly self-pity.

If George was becoming as tyrannous as his own father before him, it was out of an obsession which his whole family understood. At all costs, he must save them from hell-fire, and keep them on the narrow path of Low Church Anglicanism where he himself walked. Parents in those days did not dispute in public, and whatever Frances suffered when she heard, at a distance, the savage discipline and floggings that went on behind the study door, she was never seen to disagree with him. The boys, in time, made their own protest. Frederick, the third son, bit his father through the hand during a whipping, whereupon George, the eldest, threatened to run away unless the punishment stopped. But hardship never destroys a family if the parents share it, and all the children did well. The girls, it is true, never had much opportunity to meet any company and never married, but Ellen, without opposition from her father, won her way to Oxford and became Principal of Havergal College, Toronto. And as their parents grew old the children, as a natural thing, and without resentment for their hard upbringing, helped to support them.

Edmund, the industrious second son, who was to be the father of the four Knox brothers, was a stoutly built boy, with a native cheerfulness which was difficult to subdue. Of all the family he was the most profoundly influenced by the spiritual life of his mother. Her

Quaker gift of prayer remained with him as he was gradually drawn towards the Evangelicals; what that meant, he has explained himself. First and foremost, the conviction that God loved him, "as an actual fact, that must take first place in my life." There was no real division between the unseen and the seen. Secondly, to look at the Bible as a personal message from God to the individual soul, "and to read it daily with a resolve to hear what God had to say to me that day—I must find words that were meant for me." Thirdly, to value the Sacraments of Baptism and the Lord's Supper, which was celebrated by the Evangelicals only rarely, perhaps once a month. This faith survived even the natural doubting-time of adolescence. "When the testing came, and when I heard the question put to my soul, 'Wilt thou also go away?' I was able to see that unfaith could not satisfy my deepest needs."

Meanwhile, Edmund was determined not to be a "burden". He was justifiably proud of the fact that (apart from the railway fares and the indestructible clothing) his education cost his father only one shilling. This was for the tip traditionally given to the porter by a new boy at St Paul's School. Once this shilling was paid, scholarships covered everything. In later years he became a stout supporter of free education.

Edmund, entering in 1857, was an excellent classical scholar, but although the discipline at St Paul's was considered mild—largely owing to the absent-mindedness of the High Master—every boy had to expect to be beaten every day. The beatings were administered on both moral and social grounds: the "old Adam" had to be driven out of them, and they had to be "hardened" to face a competitive world. For the same reason, Latin and Greek were made doubly difficult because the grammar-books themselves were printed in Latin. At St Paul's there were no organized games, no "team spirit" to assist in the hardening process. The boys' free time was spent in the streets or on the muddy foreshore of the Thames.

After "hardening" came "forming", when the University was supposed to give a young man's character its final shape. When, in 1865, Edmund went up to Corpus, Oxford was spiritually in low water. The loss of Newman was still felt, and the aftermath of Tractarianism lingered. "Several other combatants of the great fray," he recalled, "were familiar in the street and at University sermons— the ferret-like Dr Hawkins, the elephantine Ben Symons, the statuesque Plumtree, the dapper Wynter, the caustic and ingenious Mark Pattison." But even these alarming figures, even Pusey himself, seemed weary; and the vacuum created was in danger of being filled by a liberal spirit of anti-clericalism, determined to remove power, once and for all, from the hands of the Church. This did not frighten young Edmund. If the new spirit meant that fellowships would be open to everyone, if it blew into musty corners, then he welcomed it. If it denied God, he would fight it.

Corpus itself was a pious and respectable college. It was nothing for the men to study, as Edmund often did, from four in the afternoon till two in the morning, sustained by cups of strong tea, and be ready, after a cold bath, for chapel at seven-thirty. On Sunday they put on black coats and top hats for their walk in the country. At first, to be sure, Edmund felt somewhat lonely, sitting, uncouth and penniless, in his room, hearing the steps of visitors go up the stairs, never for him. But, being naturally sociable, he looked out, and made friends. The company of his mother and sisters he certainly missed, and he went so far as to give up a course of lectures on the Greek Testament to go every week after evening service to a professor's drawing room where he could spend a precious hour "in the society of ladies". But he had much to do, and had found a firm ally in F. J. Chavasse (later the great Bishop of Liverpool), "a little man, almost deformed", but full of inward fire. With Chavasse, he could make headway, in the name of Evangelicalism, against the indifference of the University. "A dull life, do you say?" he wrote. "Well, we did not find it so." In his second year he told his father that he wished to be ordained.

George Knox had not forgotten how he fought this battle on his own account, but his concern for his children's success, as well as their salvation, by now amounted to a mania. If Edmund was to enter the Church, he must start as something better than a curate;

he must either get first-class honours, which would lead to a University appointment, or renounce the idea, and go into the Indian Civil Service.

All turned on the final examinations, Greats in 1868, Law and Modern History in 1869. While he waited for the results, he wrote to his sister Emily, "visions of every conceivable class came before me, and I was absolutely wretched." The results came, and Chavasse wrote: "Thank God, thank God, dear old boy, that you have got a First—the sight of the class list took a load off my heart. I was dreaming all night that you had got a Third. I feel now how faithless I had been to mistrust God . . . I am glad for your father's sake—above all I am glad for the sake of Evangelical religion in Oxford. No answer is needed: I should not expect a letter—*nay I shall be vexed if I get one.*" The President of Corpus offered Edmund the Cobbe Prize of £3 5s, "if I cared to take it, which of course I was not loth to do." It enabled him to buy "a new suit of clothing" to receive his honours.

Edmund was ordained in 1870, by which time he had already been elected a Fellow of Merton. He was assured of three hundred pounds a year for the rest of his life, as long as he did not acquire extensive landed property (a very remote contingency), and as long as he did not marry.

Hard work, academic success, faith, endurance—these were the keys to the future. But Edmund had inherited from the Reynolds family something quite beyond his father's capacity—the ability to enjoy himself. With his round parson's hat at the mercy of the winds, he took to tricycling and spun across the Christ Church Meadows; on vacation in Scotland he learned to love the Highland scenery, never, as far as he could remember, having seen mountains before; "croquet," he wrote, "had but a passing hold on me; it came in while I was still a boy," but he introduced *jeu de paume* and lawn tennis, both of which he played pretty badly, into the quadrangle at Merton. On weekdays, too, he began to read novels—Jane Austen and Trollope. And he was living in one of the oldest and most picturesque colleges in Oxford, "its Common-room panelled with oak, lit by candles in silver candlesticks, heated by a noble fire." These things were luxury, but he could not avoid the feeling that it was wrong for a man to have them at the start of his life. They should be earned and worked for, and nothing that he had done so far seemed enough. As Tutor, and later Dean, of Merton, he threw his considerable weight into the battle for sobriety and wholesome religious instruction. For example it had become, as he put it, "the habit of the idle to smash the windows of the new buildings with stones or with small loaves left over from meals." From his method of dealing with this and other problems he became known as Hard Knocks. At the same time, he took on an unpaid curacy in the poorest parish in Oxford. He was in sole charge there, one long hot summer, when smallpox raged through the district. He improvised as best he could. There were no hospitals in Oxford then for infectious diseases.

But what about "the society of ladies"? The young Tutor who was not permitted, by statute, to marry, and who had contemplated, though not taken, a vow of celibacy, found that he had fallen in love. A new rector had come to the church of St Ebbe's, near Christ Church Meadows—a missionary who was recuperating, somewhat unwillingly, in England from illness and over-fatigue on his Indian journeys. His name was Thomas French, and Edmund had met him before, when he had come for a time to Croydon. The eldest daughter, Ellen Penelope, was twenty years old, delicate in health and appearance, with elegant straight features. She was well educated, musical, seemed never to think of herself—but then, nor did anyone else in Dr French's household. Almost at once Edmund "formed an attachment".

He was returning from a summer parish outing. There were roses for sale on the Oxford station platform. On an impulse he bought one, and offered it to Ellen. If she accepted it, he would try his fate. Ellen took it. He did not know that on her first morning in Oxford she had felt a premonition when she had seen him, quite by chance, walking up Keble Terrace. She had thought, "That is my future husband."

Thomas Valpy French was a saint, holy in the noblest sense of the word, and as exasperating as all saints. A poor judge of character, he always believed the best of everyone, in spite of repeated disappointments, and was so generous that his friends did not dare mention their wants, for fear of his ruining himself. Edmund Knox, in those Oxford days, "would gladly have sat at his feet". His wife yearned to have him at home more often, but could never regret his calling.

The Frenches were a family of Norman descent, originally the de Freynes, and Thomas's father, the Rev. Peter French, inexplicably known as "Goosefair" French, was a comfortable clergyman with good connections. His mother had been a Dillwyn from Wales, and he had married the daughter of Dr Richard Valpy, the headmaster of Reading School. The Frenches lived in the spacious vicarage of Holy Trinity, Burton-on-Trent, with a prosperous brewery round the corner. How did their son, with easy prospects in front of him, come to end his life in a lonely sand-strewn grave at Muscat, "on the edge of nowhere"?

At Rugby, Thomas French was a fine classical scholar, who had had "much to bear" during his schooldays because of his lack of guile. There was in fact a terrible simplicity about him. The urgent command of Christ, at the end of St Matthew, to "preach the truth to all nations", came to him first at Oxford; then, like his contemporaries, he had to pray for a right choice between Africa, India and the new industrial cities. He went to India. From then onward his life was a reckless sacrifice of the body and a broadening of the mind. "The Padri Sahib," said the Punjabis pityingly, "wears himself out and leaves no water in the well."

French arrived in Calcutta in 1850, and began the intensive study of Indian languages which made him known as the "seven-tongued Padri". But the swarming poverty struck him like a blow. He gave away his stipend, cut down his meals to a handful of rice, and "set his face" against being dressed by a bearer.

His first appointment from the Church Missionary Society was to St John's College, Agra, a Christian school which he founded himself. He knew perfectly well that his unruly Hindu pupils only attended in the hope of getting Government jobs, and at first was pained by the "power of repulsion" they showed, but gradually their minds opened to him. They found that their headmaster was a fakir—like St Paul, as he pointed out—who could be seen after school in the marketplace, seated on a heap of melons, taking part in disputes and preaching contests, or reading the Bible among lepers. After a while, he was admitted without opposition wherever he went. He was a holy man.

In 1851 his betrothed, Miss Mary Anne Jansen, courageously came out to Calcutta to marry him. She was the daughter of a merchant of Dutch origin who had married one of the Quaker Lloyds of Birmingham, the faithful friends of Charles Lamb. The Jansens were wealthy, which of course was of no importance at all to Mary Anne's husband, but, since he was never likely to save a penny, it was just as well. Their first children were born in India, the fourth one in the garrison at Agra during the Mutiny. Mrs French watched the furniture of the British community floating downstream by the light of their burning houses; the Professor of English Literature was shot, and his horse and carriage flung into the compound. Thomas French, however, refused to enter the fort unless he had permission to bring his native Christians in with him. When this was granted he appeared carrying a large bag, which contained, not valuables, but his Arabic dictionary.

It was the end of his work in Agra, but in 1862 he returned to India, shrunken, ill, leaving his wife and children behind him, but unable to feel at peace in England. "The more I am borne away from you, the more my thoughts travel towards you," he wrote to Mary Anne as his train left London Bridge, but there were more tongues to learn and untold millions to reach, even though in the Moslem regions to which he was bound he was lucky to make five converts in a year. His appointment was now as Principal of the college at Lahore, but in the vacations he travelled tirelessly over the mountains, first to the wild districts of the North-West Frontier, then to

Kashmir, studying Hebrew and Pushtu on muleback, arriving with his shabby books and luggage, often too weak to wind up his own watch. He had become deeply interested in both Hindu and Moslem asceticism, his ambition now being to understand the mind of Indian religion and to present Christianity "without losing a grain, yet measuredly and gradually as the people can bear it." At the same time, he had become increasingly impatient of the doctrinal quarrels within the Church itself. Small wonder that the Church Missionary Society were growing somewhat doubtful of their broad-minded servant.

Why did he do it? The Jansens pressed him to come home to his family, and "I must feel the objections of my father-in-law," he wrote, "but I *could not* abandon the work without a farther trial of it." Today he would certainly be asked: why not leave these people to their own beliefs? Why press on them something they did not ask for and do not want? To this his reply would be: "The viewing of the unseen world instead of the visible things of time—this cannot be a shallow matter; it *must* be deep or not at all—no halves in such a business."

French's only vanity was in the management of his tea-things on his journeys; when his mule fell and broke the cup, he taught himself to drink out of the spout. The study of languages was not vanity, but a way of bearing witness. It was his ambition to revise the Urdu and Hindustani Prayer Books, and to translate the Scriptures into Pushtu. This work was in hand when, after a terrible attack of fever, he returned to England and to Oxford in the spring of 1874. In June, Edmund Knox offered the rose he had bought on the station platform to Ellen.

No one among his Ulster forebears would have offered the rose, which was a measure of how much sentiment and heart could now find expression in the Knox family. It must have been with some misgivings that Ellen, with her sister as chaperon, went to pay her first visit to Edmund's parents, but this, fortunately, was less formidable than it would have been a few years earlier. George and Frances Knox, with their four unmarried daughters, had moved to the vicarage of Exton, in Rutland. Although the children of the parish were told "always to think what Mr Knox told me not to do", his habitual fires had sunk, and Frances had quite reverted to the easy ways of her girlhood. She sat in her room, the Lavender Room, still dressed in Quaker grey, but wrapped in Indian shawls, serene, and much loved by the neighbourhood. Edmund and Ellen were allowed to walk in the garden by themselves, and, according to Edmund's diary, "had a profitable talk in the summer-house".

Two years later, in 1876, Merton amended its statutes to allow four married fellows, and the wedding took place in the spring of 1878. Dr French, though with much regret, could not be present; he had been appointed Bishop of Lahore, a diocese of some twenty million souls, with only a thousand native Christians. Letters arrived from snowy hills and mud huts, from the famine area, from the battlefront of the Afghan War, where he refused to call the Afghans God's enemies, and aroused criticism after our defeat at Maiwand by praying for "friends, lovers, orphans and widows". "I did strike out 'lovers,' " he said, "but put it in again." But it was not till he received a telegram in April 1879, telling him of the birth of his first grandchild, Ethel Knox, that he began, for the first time, to feel old.

In 1884 Edmund and Ellen left Oxford for their first parish, Kibworth in Leicestershire. By that time they had four children, and two more were born to them there. Ethel was followed by Edmund George Valpy (1881); Winifred Frances (1882); Alfred Dillwyn (1884); Wilfred Lawrence (1886); and Ronald Arbuthnott (1888). Family affection dictated all the names. Dillwyn was the name of Frances's grandmother, Lawrence was Bishop French's younger brother, Arbuthnott recalled the sister from whom Frances had been so cruelly divided when she joined the Church of Rome.

Kibworth Rectory might have been designed and built to bring up a large family. All the children were so happy there that in later years they could cure themselves of sleeplessness simply by imagining that they were back at Kibworth. They had their own cow in the pasture, their own rookery in the elms, and, best of all, the railway ran past the bottom of the garden, and the dark red engines of the Midland line could be observed five times daily. The Knoxes were passionate railway children. True, people said that the drains were bad at Kibworth, but who cared? They were completely safe in the large nursery at the top of the back stairs, looking down into the kitchen garden, where in memory it was always summer, with the victoria plums ripening on the south wall. Their father mounted his stout horse, Doctor, to set off on his parish visits, and their dearly loved mother waved from an upper window.

The pack of children fell into distinct groups: the girls, said by their brothers to be an inferior species, but holding their own; the elder boys, dark, charming, dangerous-looking, with a disposition to fight each other to the death under the nursery table on some point of honour; the "little ones", fair, Quakerish and much more manageable. All, except poor Ethel, who was somewhat slow and stunted, were clever. All were tenderhearted, but, after babyhood, only Winnie was able to express her feelings with no inhibitions at all. "Enter Winnie, and kisses everybody" was a sardonic stage direction in one of Eddie's first plays.

The girls were in an ambiguous but familiar position. If the elder brothers regarded them as things of naught, unable to throw a ball overarm or crack nuts with their teeth, yet in times of trouble the boys were eager to champion and comfort them and help them down to the last coin in their pockets. This meant that the girls, readily reduced to tears, were perpetual winners in the war between the sexes.

A singular characteristic of the boys was their insistence on games of which they invented or changed the rules, with the object of making them as difficult, and therefore as worthwhile, as possible. Any one of them who had a birthday was entitled to make his own rules, though these lasted only till the next morning. A game is a classic method of bringing life to order by giving it a fixed attainable objective, so that even if we lose, we are still in control. As time went on, the brothers would try to bring increasingly large areas—logic, ethics, poetry—into the same field as billiards or ludo—ludo, that is, under the Knox rules. Cheating was instantly detected. It was cheating to show fear, cheating to give up. A monstrous rule, superimposed on all the others by Dilly, was that "nothing is impossible". But, inconveniently enough, the emotions are exempt from rules, and ignore their existence.

They were distinguished, even in a late-Victorian Evangelical household, by their truthfulness. Wilfred—with one possible exception, which will be discussed later—never told a lie at all. Ronnie told his last one in 1897, when he was nine. Social necessity would drive Eddie and Dilly to evasions, but they hated them. Honesty can scarcely, however, be counted a virtue in them; it was simply that they never felt the need for anything else.

Eddie was his mother's favourite, and this was not resented by the other children, not even by the baby, for he was their favourite, too. Among a courageous group, he was the most daring. It was he who rode Doctor, he who climbed higher and higher, feeling that it would be a glorious death to plunge head-foremost through the tops of green trees, scattering the branches, he who fell off the jetty into deep water on holiday at Penzance. "It was a sad scene," Winnie wrote, "as for some reason it was considered necessary for the whole party to return home . . . so out of the sea we were all bidden, five pairs of moist sandy cold feet stuffed into black stockings, five pairs of boots buttoned or laced on, and back the sad procession made its way." "You'll never live to be old, Mr Eddie," threatened the nurse. But Eddie was not born predictable.

Eddie's fall was known as The Accident. It was not thought that he took it seriously enough. It was known that one of Bishop French's daughters, their Aunt Ethel, had died because she did not change her wet stockings after the monsoon. But the outing to Penzance, one of many seaside holidays, shows how anxious Edmund Knox was to give his children this new source of happiness and disaster which he had never known. George Knox, indeed, had never looked up a train in his life, but simply went down to the station and complained to the stationmaster if one was not ready for him. Edmund struggled valiantly with the difficulties of early starts and missed connections. As a result of one of these the family, with mountains of luggage, were stranded for hours at Bristol, and Eddie and Dilly seized the opportunity to study the master timetable in the office. Its complications appealed to their ingenious small boys' minds, and *Bradshaw's Railway Guide* joined Macaulay's *Lays of Ancient Rome* as a favourite recitation. As soon as humanly possible they taught it to their little brothers. At the age of three, Wilfred, when called upon to recite in company, could reel off the stations between Kibworth and Birmingham and the times of goods and cattle trains, adding

> And wounded horses kicking,
>   And snorting purple foam:
> Right well did such a couch befit
>   A Consular of Rome.

Life for the children at Kibworth was disturbed only when Bishop French came on leave, and impetuously swept his relatives together on holiday, wishing to see them all at once. "It was no small privilege to be his guest," Edmund wrote, "and to hear him as he discoursed on Scripture, on the Fathers, or the antiquities we were to visit." The children did not altogether agree. They were embarrassed by the old man's habit of saying "a few seasonable words" to everyone they met, by his old-fashioned Rugby slang, mixed with phrases of classical Persian, and by his tendency to disappear entirely. On the day when they visited Lindisfarne it rained in torrents, and Edmund Knox thought it right to order a carriage, but "at the time of starting it was discovered that the Bishop had slipped away unnoticed." Some three or four miles onward they overtook him "in his shirt-sleeves, dripping wet, his coat over his arm, trudging gallantly onwards." He had forgotten everything in his desire to be at the scene of the ministry of St Aidan. Worse still, he refused to calculate where, at the end of the day's walk, they could get tea. The simple people of the country, he said, in the goodness of their hearts, would provide. This sometimes meant no tea at all. And yet it is something to have a saint in the family.

French resigned his bishopric, for reasons of ill-health, at the age of sixty-four. To the C.M.S. he was a "grand old campaigner" more in danger of going native than ever, a man who had friends among both Franciscans and Quakers, and who, during a recent tour of the Middle East, had shared an altar with a Chaldean priest. The Jansens still wondered whether unworldliness could not be carried too far, and were heartily thankful to hear of his retirement in 1889. Even French wondered "if perhaps my dear Lord and Master has no more need of me." But in the following autumn, after much thought and prayer, he knew he must venture again. The Jansens were appalled to hear that he had been up to London to look at an exhibition of Stanley's African medicine chest, so that he might choose the same brands himself. With little more than these and his book-bag, which he had carried himself over deserts and mountains and up the stairs at Kibworth Rectory, the old man set out in the November of 1890. He had no authority or backing. His destination was the whole Arab world, simply to tell them, even if no one accepted it, that Christ loved them and had died for them.

In this spirit he reached the holy city of Kairouan, where, dressed as a mullah in cloak, burnous and shawl, he sat down to teach at the outer gate of the Mosque. The Bishop of Jerusalem urged him, for his own safety, to move to Cairo. There he met a young missionary, Alexander Maitland, whom he had ordained himself, and who gave up everything to be with him and to accompany him to the Red Sea coast. They lived on dates and early oranges, and French took a quantity of Bibles in the folds of his burnous, to distribute where he could.

In February they reached Muscat, the capital of Oman, a little gap in a sea-wall of sheer rock, rising to six thousand feet. In that scorching climate, the Arabs say, the sword melts in the scabbard. The British India Company's steamers called only once a fortnight. French and Maitland were not expected and knew nobody. The consul begged them to leave. They had to take refuge in two dirty rooms over a Portuguese grog-shop, and there they read and prayed together, and Maitland managed as best he could. "Don't misunderstand me," he wrote to Mrs French. "I was *glad* to wash plates for the Bishop."

Maitland had the heavy responsibility of the old man, who disappeared, as he had done at Lindisfarne, without warning, to preach in the bazaar. Because of the danger of violence and stoning, he would not let his young friend accompany him there. After a month Maitland, who was consumptive, was overcome by the heat and had to go back to Cairo. The servant he had hired soon deserted, and French was left quite alone.

"As a villager told me the other day," he wrote to his wife, "I am no Englishman but an Arab! I shall be in danger of becoming an alien, not to my *own* children I trust even then, and grandchildren. With a tanned and dyed skin, however, and added wrinkles, even Ethel and Eddie might fail to recognise grandpapa. . . . So Eddie has begun his schooldays! May they be days he will look back upon with happy thankfulness and joy hereafter . . . "

The ink dried, he added, before he could put pen to paper; he was living "like a sparrow on the housetops". Occasionally he found a listener, who would stay for a reading of the gospel. He was trying to lay in a little store of biscuits "so as not to be at the mercy of the people I may be amongst".

It was true that schooldays had started at Kibworth. While their sisters studied with a governess, and lay down every day on a blackboard to give them a good posture, Eddie and Dilly walked over to Mr Rogers's school in the village. Eddie had begun on Kennedy's Latin grammar; there were more inexplicable runes for Wilfred to repeat in the nursery: "Caesar adsum jam forte—Caesar had some jam for tea."

Dilly was the mathematician, to the amazement of his father, who had not been able to make head or tail of the Merton College accounts. Dilly could not balance his accounts (twopence a week pocket-money) either, but he did not have to "do" sums, he "saw" them.

Meanwhile, the tender messages from their grandfather had ceased. No more letters came from Muscat. It was only later that they were able to follow his last wanderings, from Muttrah up the coast to Sib, from which place he hoped to journey into the interior. He had set out in a fishing-boat, under the blazing sun, with his book-bag. Agents of the Sultan, who deeply respected the strange old fakir, were deputed to keep watch over him, but they could do nothing when they found him insensible, still with a book in his hand. When they picked him up to bring him back to Muscat they found he weighed almost nothing. He died on 14 May; his body was prepared for burial by a group of Goanese Catholics, who had heard of him and his mission, although he did not know them.

"God had not left him the measure of strength he hoped to have," Maitland wrote to Mrs Knox, "but that could only be proved by experience." He arranged for the burial in the northernmost of the two coves of the Bay of Muscat, at the foot of the cliffs. It was wild and barren, but a kind of shrub with pink flowers grew there. He painted on the gravestone the words: *He endured as seeing Him who is invisible*. French's biographer noted that "the grave is under the protection of a British gunboat, so there is little likelihood it will ever meet with neglect."

At Kibworth the children were put into black clothes, and a new game—Caves in Arabia—was added to the nursery, played by any one of them who wanted to get away from the others. The effect on their mother of her father's lonely death was profound. It led directly to an upheaval and to the end of their first happy period of childhood.

II

1891–1901

The Sterner Realities of Life

EDMUND KNOX HAD TAKEN ORDERS because he felt God called him to do so. But to enter the mid-Victorian Church meant both more and less than this. "The plain fact is," his son Ronnie wrote, half a century later, "that while England led the world, and the Church of England was the expression of its national life, there was a monumental quality about the partnership which, do what you would, laid hold of the imagination. Anglicanism fitted into the landscape, was part of the body politic."

To become one of its ministers was to join a legal establishment which influenced those who governed, to take responsibility for the souls of a great empire, and to make effective judgments in peace and war. That might mean a disputed loyalty. Knox, the scholarship boy whose education had cost one shilling, was a passionate supporter of free education, but a stout opponent of the government's long-drawn-out attack on the Church schools. Again, when he became rector of Kibworth, it was assumed that, as a mild Tory, he would settle down comfortably in that heavy clay country and become a squire's parson. But nothing of the kind happened.

Edmund's heart sank when he saw the farm-labourers, in their smocks and tall hats, waiting outside the church so that "the quality" could go in first. He did not feel at ease with such a system, and longed for a wider scope, if not abroad, then in one of the great industrial cities. In 1891 he received from the Trustees of Aston-juxta-Birmingham (who were mostly Evangelicals) an offer of preferment. Aston was a huge, built-over, crowded industrial district, known to the world only through its football team, Aston Villa.

On a preliminary visit he found the vicarage, after making a number of inquiries, "in a dark and narrow street, set in a maze of smoke-begrimed small houses." Edmund was more than doubtful about what the effect of the "air", to which nineteenth-century doctors and patients attached so much importance, would be on his wife's health. She had never quite recovered from the birth of Ronnie, when she had had a long and difficult labour. But Ellen was not afraid of the sulphur-laden air of Birmingham. She was her father's daughter, and his last lonely mission had inspired her to do something, no matter how little, that would be worthy of him. She herself had never been to India, and had followed all his wanderings through his frequent letters to her. In the very last of them, written from Muscat two weeks before his death, he had congratulated them both on their resolution to take on the new difficult work. His only sorrow was that "I shall never be able again to offer to take a Sunday for you and set you free for needed rest." "Your children will miss the beautiful lawn and the pleasant strolls in the country," he added; "they have to enter on the sterner realities of life."

If forty-two thousand souls of Birmingham's workforce could live in the smoke and darkness of Aston parish, so, obviously enough, could their priest. Edmund threw himself into organization and visiting, Ellen into work for the schools—Sunday schools, reading classes for adults, and what were still called the Ragged Schools. They were full of confidence. When they left Kibworth a well-wisher, looking at Edmund's solid form, had said: "Those shoulders are broad enough for anything."

The six children had arrived at Aston with the girls in tears at parting with Doctor and at the sight of the tiny, soot-blackened garden. The boys, however, were stopped in their tracks by the sight of a new and instantly attractive form of transport, trams. "I was early fascinated by those gigantic steam-kettles in two sections, which used to ply between Aston and Birmingham," Ronnie wrote. The cable past Snow Hill, where you could peer down a slit at the endless cable, gave the brothers the concept of perpetual motion. The trams were kings of the road; in Lancashire they were known as "cars". Bicycles skidded on the lines, one breakdown held up the whole system, and old ladies were marooned in the middle of the street and had to be rescued. The years to come were never to bring any form of transport that they loved quite so well. They became trammers from that first day.

One advantage of Aston was the schools. By tram the girls could go to Edgbaston Ladies' College, and Eddie and Dilly to day school. Edmund Knox did not like boarding schools, which he considered unnatural, and he wanted to undertake the family religious instruction himself, at home. Here a certain unevenness of response had already appeared. The girls were devout, so were the little boys, Ronnie in particular; dressed in Ethel's pinafore for a surplice, he conducted the funerals of pet birds in the grimy flower-beds. On Eddie, as he put it himself, "Church did not seem to rub off properly," though he conformed for his mother's sake. Dilly held his counsel.

Leaving the question of doctrine aside, all the instruction they received from their parents was positive and humanitarian—not so, however, the grim warnings of Nurse and Cook, whose villain was that horror-figure, the Pope, "always laying snares," Winnie remembered, "in far-off Italy to entrap our nursery in especial, and in general, into the evil lures of his superstition." Old Nurse said she could smell a Papist a mile off, and was much preoccupied with the imminence of the Last Trump, which she hoped might come when they were all at prayer, and if possible in clean underclothes. But the children were born with the power of discrimination. Even the girls were able to discount Old Nurse, and "in such homes as ours," Winnie thought, "we surely experienced something of the clear light crystal world of the earlier ages of Faith."

The vast parish was responding well, and Aston was now divided into seven districts, with willing helpers in each of them. But a few days after Christmas 1891, in the thick of the Christmas work, Ellen Knox caught influenza. She did not seem to be able to pick up. For the next eight months she had to be sent to one nursing home after another, the last one being at Brighton, "for the air". Aunt Emily, Edmund's kind, but harassed and ineffective, sister, came to keep house. She had no imagination, was not used to children, and had no idea what to do. There was an atmosphere, so frightening to children, of things not being quite right, and of discussions behind closed doors. The news from Brighton was worse. They were sent for, and although on this occasion their mother recovered, they never forgot that Aunt Emily had refused to let them travel, because it was Sunday. The immediate danger was said to have passed. Then, at the end of August a letter came from their father, addressed to all of them: "My dear, dear children." Their mother had died that morning.

The blow to Eddie was such that in the course of a very long life, he, like his grandfather before him, never quite recovered from it. It gave him, at twelve years old, a spartan endurance and a determination not to risk himself too easily to life's blows, which might, at times, have been mistaken for coldness.

For a year he remained alone at Aston with his father and Aunt Emily, while the others were distributed among relations. Edmund Knox could find relief from his misery only by working all day and half the night, so that the small boy was intensely lonely. He was old enough now to go to King Edward's School; during the long miserable evenings he went up by himself to the box room and comforted himself by devising his own tramway system. It had to be horse-drawn, because he could not think how to represent the steam engines.

There was a large kitchen table in the box-room [Eddie wrote]; I cut
the tramlines with a penknife and burnt them out to make them
deeper with a knitting needle heated on a candle. The system was
fairly accurate and I bought some little tin engines and Stöllwerk
chocolate horses to pull them. These were very cheap, and lasted till
they melted. The grown-ups found out, of course; they didn't punish
me, nor did they praise my industry.

Winnie, Ethel and Dilly were packed off to Eastbourne. Their
broken-hearted father hardly knew which way to turn, and was prepared to accept any reasonable offer. The relative at Eastbourne was
a widowed great-aunt, a sister of George Knox's, who made it clear
that by offering them a home (she was in fact being paid for their
board and lodging) she was exceeding herself in Christian charity.
Her Protestantism was of the "black" variety. When Dilly, shy and
unmanageable, was told to kneel down and "give himself to Jesus"
he took refuge in the coal hole. He had to go to an uncongenial
preparatory school where he too rapidly learned all that they could
teach him, and he was suffering the frustration of a natural athlete—
there was no one at school who could play his spin bowling—and
what sort of practice can you get in a coal hole? His sister describes
him at this time as "brusque and cutting beyond endurance to the
uppish or conceited, but kind beyond belief in one's troubles."
Therefore although Dilly, like Eddie, had made a promise to himself
not to care too much about anyone or anything again, he was
obliged to break it every time the girls cried, or were given arith-
metic homework.

The little boys, Wilfred and Ronnie, were far more fortunate.
They were sent to their father's younger brother, Uncle Lindsey, the
vicar of Edmundthorpe, near Grantham, in Lincolnshire. It was a
small country parish where life went by placidly, and on Sundays
even the old horses in the fields knew what day it was and did not
come down to the gate to be harnessed. The grandmother, Frances
Knox, now widowed, occupied one of the rooms, and was so much
respected that when she drove out, still in her Quaker cap and
shawls, the whole village stood at their doors to see her. She was

able to give a good deal of discreet financial help to the family (it was she who had paid for the Knox children's seaside holidays) and "did much good", as the saying went, locally. Three of the unmarried daughters also lived at the vicarage, and Lindsey, who had never married either, had very little say in the household. He lived a life of untroubled contentment. The ladies gave all the orders and told him what to say and do; sometimes he would forget, and wander off into the fields, returning with a hatful of mushrooms. This absent-mindedness was in part a self-protection, perhaps, but Uncle Lindsey had no grievances. He cared deeply for the welfare of his little flock. When a visitor's carriage was ready to drive away he would emerge tremblingly on the front steps and cry: "Beware! Beware the parting pot!" The Parting Pot was, as it turned out, a public house at the crossroads from which his parishioners often came out in a confused condition and in danger of being run over. Farther than this ten-mile distance he rarely ventured. Some things which he saw in the newspapers he could hardly believe, and he put them out of his mind, which had room only for belief.

When Wilfred and Ronnie arrived they were told to pay particular respect to the stationmaster, because he had refused to put up Liberal posters during the election of 1886. "Conservative" was far too weak a word to describe the politics of Uncle Lindsey and the Aunts. Their lack of understanding of industrial and social problems was absolute.

On the other hand, they were most successful as hosts to young children, perhaps because they had never left childhood behind. The atmosphere at Edmundthorpe was quite unlike Waddon or even Kibworth; it was a sweet and primitive Evangelicalism, where Christ was felt as "the unseen guest" at every meal, and to be distressed if your umbrella was missing was "a sin of angry thought". When Ronnie won fivepence at ludo—which, in a sense, was gaming—he felt it was tainted money, and put it in the collection. There were no harsh words; the motive power was always love. And Uncle Lindsey, like Mr Dick, had quite definite ideas as to what to do with a small boy, if one came his way: amuse it; wash it; feed it. With their uncle they collected honey, made bonfires of autumn leaves and jumped over them, and slid on the ice in winter. He also conceived the idea of starting their education, and crammed into his small nephews, aged six and four, an amazing quantity of Latin and Greek. He saw no difficulty in this, and in fact there was none. Ronnie was an exceedingly bright little boy, and Wilfred, who in some ways had the better brain of the two, was gifted with an exceptional memory. He could read through the *Times* leader once, shut his eyes, and re- peat it word for word.

Ronnie accepted the régime in a less critical spirit than Wilfred, who had a sharper temper than his brother. But both of them were happy, and, above all, happy with each other. They shared all their games, all their confidences, and grew up, Winnie thought, "in ab- solute dependence on each other". It was an alliance against fate, which, it seemed, Time would never have power to break.

It was during the four years at Edmundthorpe that Wilfred told, or rather implied, his only lie. While Ronnie and he were ambush- ing each other in the garden they had the bad luck to break off a branch of the flowering Judas tree. Wilfred dared not confess—not for fear of punishment, for there was none at Edmundthorpe, but because the Aunts were so fond of the tree. By bedtime he had still said nothing, and that night there was a storm, which scattered twigs and branches everywhere. All the damage was put down to the wind, but Wilfred's conscience ached.

During the school holidays the children all went back to Aston for a noisy reunion. Different backgrounds had made them adjust differently, and they quarrelled, but at the approach of authority, all made an impenetrable common front together. Eddie and Dilly were particularly glad to see each other—"I can't think what I'm going to do without you, you lazy hound," Eddie wrote to Eastbourne—and disagreed particularly fiercely. Their father, coming home to uproar, was driven distracted. "It was specially painful to me," he recalled, "to feel increasingly as each holiday came round the bereavement that I had sustained." The doctor suggested a visit to the seaside, even if it could only be a shadow of their happiness at Penzance.

Aunt Emily, protesting feebly, embarked with them to Brid-
lington. They immediately escaped from her care, rushed down to
the sea (which the doctor had forbidden), and for the first time in
their lives saw a theatre, or rather a nigger minstrels' fit-up, where
Uncle Sam was clacking the bones, and inviting the audience to
join in singing

> Can't get away
> To marry yer today—
> My wife won't let me!

When their father arrived he could hardly credit the vulgar gaiety, so different is the measure of heartbreak in adults and children.
He hastily inaugurated new amusements—cricket on the sands, as
far as possible from Uncle Sam, and expeditions to neighbouring
churches. The next year Aunt Emily's nerves and health failed, and
he had to take them himself to the Isle of Man. "But of course," he
wrote, "it was evident that while I might be able to manage a parish,
I was a poor hand at controlling the high spirits and caring for the
costumes and manners of so charming and irresponsible a party.
'Garters' I remember as a special trial. They were always missing!"

Although Knox's pastoral work flourished, the rectory at Aston grew
more seedy and neglected with every passing month. The furniture
was engrained with soot, the drawing room shut up, the cupboards
full of mislaid or broken articles. The boys were beginning to resem-
ble savages, speaking Latin and Greek. There was no help for it, the
home would have to be broken up. At this point the Bishop of
Worcester, Perowne, an old friend of Bishop French, sent for Knox
and offered him a new appointment—the parish of St Philip's,
Birmingham, with the post of Bishop Suffragan of Coventry.

It would be a considerable responsibility—another vast district, a
diocese with only one minister to every five thousand of the popula-
tion. In his own words, "it became evident that I must marry again."
The whole rich supporting background of Victorian churchgoing—
the parish workers, the lay readers, the churchwardens, the Gospel

Temperance meetings, the missions, the men's Bible classes—everyone, up to the Bishop himself, knew that Knox could not go on without a wife.

She would have to be vicarage born and bred, or she could hardly face the huge city diocese, administered from Coventry, as Knox knew, "by the most charming of old-fashioned clergy, whose interest in Birmingham was, to say the best, tepid." All the work and duty would be his. As a husband, he was now a man of forty-seven, growing bald and very stout, his natural geniality under a cloud, barely solvent as a result of his many charities and building activities, and chronically overworked. He would never marry without love and respect, and that meant respect, also, for his uncouth children. Many, however, were undaunted. Out of the unmarried lady church workers of Aston, few would have refused the new Suffragan Bishop. Here was another difficulty. From this aspect, Edmund Knox was in need of rescue.

Through Bishop Perowne, he was invited several times to meet Canon Newton, the Vicar of Redditch—a kind of vicar quite outside Knox's experience, because he had inherited an absurdly large sum of money and had not given it away, but lived in comfort, even luxury. Horace Newton went deer-stalking every year on his own moor in the West Highlands, travelling from Glasgow on his own steam-yacht; he built a vast holiday mansion there, Glencrippsdale, and, since the vicarage was much too small for him, another one at Redditch. This house, Holmwood, had been designed for him by Temple Moore at the beginning of his career as an architect.

At Holmwood there was ample room for his six daughters and his long-wished-for son, and the handsome family moved like the Shining Ones in this appropriate setting. In Scotland the girls rode and fished, but always gallantly and high-heartedly, enjoying risk, but not taking it seriously. As vicar's daughters, and sincere Christians, they undertook the parish duties, but admitted frankly that they found them very boring. They remained serene, never pretending. They had style.

The eldest of them, Ethel Mary, was a graceful and handsome

young woman with blue eyes, an airily penetrating blue gaze before which affectation collapsed. Her uncle, Richard Wilton, a minor Victorian poet, wrote a sonnet on her photograph:

> Since through the open window of the eye
>   The unconscious secret of the soul we trace
> And character is written on the face,
>   In this sun-picture what do we descry? . . .

Courage, certainly. Wilton also refers to "the gentle current of thy days", but this was soon to be interrupted.

In 1894 Ethel was twenty-seven, with many admirers, one of them a wealthy cousin. She could certainly have "looked above" Edmund Knox. This was in spite of the fact that Canon Newton settled no money at all on his daughters when they married. Why should he? His own wife, their mother, had been penniless, and they were perfectly happy. He did not give the girls any formal education either. They were taught music and languages, spoke French, and picked up the rest of their knowledge from the books in the library. Ethel had learned classical Greek, but simply because she wanted to.

Was it possible that she would consider marriage with Edmund? Not much less romantic than the day when he bought the rose on the station platform, he decided that if Ethel accepted an invitation to his consecration at St Paul's Cathedral, that would mean that she had given him encouragement to hope. "It proved," he wrote, "that I was right, to my own unspeakable gain."

But would it be a gain for Ethel? She had not yet met the children, to whom, after all, she must be stepmother. Determined to risk everything, Edmund Knox arranged to bring the whole lot of them to Holmwood for the New Year of 1895.

The Newtons, meeting them at the station, gave no sign of dismay, for that would have been unkind, and they were never unkind. The Knox children looked like scarecrows, or remnants from a jumble sale, the girls in all-purpose black frocks, two sizes too large to allow for growth, Ronnie and Wilfred in grotesque black suits, hand-

sewn by their grandmother's maid at Edmundthorpe. The six of
them clung together awkwardly, too shy to find the right words.
They had known them at Kibworth, but had forgotten them since.
For their part, they stared almost in disbelief at the house to which
they had been brought. Holmwood was in the highest style of the
Arts and Crafts movement, with stone-framed lattice windows and
steep slate roofs, the haunt of doves in summer, now deep in snow.
Once inside the white-painted hall they saw shining floors, Gimson
furniture, Morris chintzes, and a staircase sweeping upward to the
glass dome of the house. A blazing wood fire drew out the scent of
hothouse plants. And where did the light come from? None of the
children had ever seen electric light in a house before. When
Wilfred and Ronnie were put to bed they sat in their nightgowns,
taking strict turns, as they always did, to turn it on and off, and nobody told them to stop.

At dinnertime, under the glowing lights, the Newton girls wore
Liberty gowns of velveteen; they were beautiful, the house was beautiful—in the boys' terms, "awfully jolly". Faced unequivocally with
beauty, the older children recognized at last a starvation they had
never known by name. It was strange territory. They felt humiliated
most of all when, as they usually did at home, they began to quarrel,
punching and pulling each other's hair to emphasize their points.
The Newtons said nothing in reproach, they simply went away; no
one ever quarrelled, or even raised their voices, at Holmwood.

"It never occurred to me," Winnie wrote, "for we had no idea why
this treat had come our way, that upstairs slender forms in satin
dressing-gowns were slipping in and out of their charming bedrooms
to murmur to my future stepmother: 'Ethel, darling, you can't *possibly* face that family.' But luckily for us expostulations were useless."
Ethel would never have given Edmund Knox encouragement if she
had not intended to carry off everything in her stride. She wanted
to do this, just as she had wanted to learn Greek. The family never
let her forget the entry she made in her diary on her wedding day.
Finished the Antigone. Married Bip.

All that could be done in the way of improvement she did, rapidly and tactfully. Her first task was the decoration of St Philip's Rectory, a good large house in the very centre of Birmingham, but with no garden, only a small backyard. This was a further restriction for the children, and a real sacrifice to the Bishop, an expert gardener. As to the rooms, St Philip's would never be much like Holmwood, but it could be painted white, and hung with Morris's Blackthorn chintz, and good pieces of furniture could be recovered from the shambles at Aston; she added things of her own, china, silver, watercolours, poetry books, French literature. Some of the Knox possessions she never managed to get rid of, the Indian bedspread, for example, brought back by Mrs French, embroidered with tigers in gold thread with looking-glass eyes, and a steel engraving of "God's Eye Shut Upon the Heart of the Sinner", which she finally banished to the lavatory. All the Newtons' prophecies were falsified. The home was reestablished and the whole family reunited. In the evening Ethel coaxed her dreaded charges into the drawing room and read aloud to them—Stevenson's *Will o' the Mill* and *The Wrong Box*, Edward Lear's *Nonsense Rhymes*—undisturbed by the boys who were winding up their clockwork engines behind the sofa. To them it was keenly interesting that one of the main railway lines ran into the station from a tunnel actually underneath the house. Very well, their stepmother accepted this, just as, to begin with, she accepted everything, except the annual seaside lodgings; instead of these, she hired vacant rectories, in different parts of England and Wales, for their summer holidays. Here she adapted gallantly to the demand for high teas and to long cricket matches, during which Dilly was not allowed to make more than a hundred and fifty runs, and little Ronnie, quite ignoring the game, picked bunches of wild flowers in the deep field and brought them, as an admiring tribute, to his new mother.

The little ones, naturally, were the first to be won over and the most dear to her; the girls had begun to turn to her from the first evening at Holmwood. The older boys, Eddie in particular, were a challenge. She saw that the trouble lay partly in names, and told them to call her Mrs K. But a slight barrier remained. She was reluctant, for example, to discuss health matters, her own or anyone else's. Eddie's nervous indigestion was dismissed as "the gulps". He could not quite lower his defences, even when she took him to Glencrippsdale, and taught him to fish.

The civilizing process had to be gradual. In the main, it was assumed in those days that it was sufficient amusement for brothers and sisters simply to be together. So, indeed, it was. But Mrs K. would look into the schoolroom and note that all was well, the girls banging out a duet on the piano, the little boys quietly playing, Eddie and Dilly sarcastically reading to each other out of Smiles's *Self-Help,* then be summoned urgently a few minutes later to find *Self-Help* sailing out of the window, Eddie and Dilly locked in a death grapple, Wilfred and Ronnie cowering in corners with their hands folded over their bellies to protect their most valuable possession, their wind. At other times the boys disappeared completely for long periods to avoid being made to "pay calls".

On the subject of education—perhaps because her own had been so casual, partly perhaps because of the maniacal scenes in the schoolroom—Mrs K. stood firm. The boys must go to boarding schools. Their father was still doubtful and would have liked to keep them at home, but was induced to agree. Of course, they would have to win scholarships or the fees could not be met, and it would be a mistake for those nearest in age to compete with each other, so Eddie and Wilfred were entered for Rugby, and Dilly and Ronnie for Eton.

Meantime, Eddie was sent to a distant preparatory school, Locker's Park, in Hemel Hempstead; Dilly went, at the age of eleven, to Summer Fields (then still called Summer Field), near Oxford. Mrs McLaren, the formidable manager, was, it appears, unwilling to admit him at such a late age, for she liked to catch them young, but changed her tune when she heard that Ronnie, already reading Virgil at the age of six, would soon be joining him. Dilly needed only a year's coaching to take his Eton scholarship. As for Ronnie, the little boy who had been asked at four years old what he liked doing and had replied, "I think all day, and at night I think about the past," was already a natural philosopher. He made a docile and friendly pupil, saved from any temptation to vanity by his relentless elder brothers.

Neither he nor Dilly remembered Summer Fields with much pleasure, except for the chance to swim in the river under the willow trees on sunny afternoons. In middle age, Ronnie used to recall deliberately what it was like to be beaten for having an untidy locker, to remind himself "how much better it is to be forty than eight". The preparation of the children for scholarships was so intensive as to be only just over the borderline of sanity. Before the Eton exam Dr Williams, the headmaster, used to take a room in the White Horse Hotel in Windsor and walk the candidates up and down to steady them while he crammed in a few last showy bits of information. Many of them never reached such a high standard of learning again. Fortunately Ronnie's sparkling intelligence, and Dilly's dispassionate view of adults, enabled them both to survive.

In 1896, the year that Ronnie arrived at Summer Fields, Eddie won his scholarship to Rugby. Thomas French had been there in the days of Arnold, although he had been quite unmoved by the great Doctor, whose teaching was "not the Gospel as he had been accustomed to receive it." The headmaster was now Dr H. A. James, known as The Bodger. In comparison with Eton it was a rougher, more countrified, more eccentric, more rigidly classical, less elegant and sentimental establishment. There were the usual bewildering regulations, much more binding than the official rules; only certain boys, the "swells", could wear white straw hats, all first-year boys must answer to a call of "fag" and run to see what the "swell" required, it was a crime to walk with your hands in your pockets until your fourth year, one hand was allowed in the third year, and so forth, proscriptions being multiplied, as in all primitive societies. The younger boys got up at five forty-five and took turns in the cold baths. Eddie, who was in School House, could consider himself lucky to get a "den" at the end of his first year, overlooking the seventeen green acres of the famous Close.

Divinity was taught by The Bodger himself, a short, squarish man with a luxuriant beard, concealing the absence of a tie. "Dr James walked up and down," as Eddie remembered him; "if it was the Upper Bench, round and round, because it was a turret room. He walked like a Red Indian, placing one foot exactly in front of the other. He kept a small private notebook in which he put favourable remarks about a boy, but a quotation from the *Lays of Ancient Rome* would gain at least five marks a go." This was fortunate for the Knoxes, reared since nursery days on the *Lays*. The finest scholar on the staff, however, was Robert Whitelaw, Rupert Brooke's god-father, who taught classics to the Twenty, the form below the VIth. He is described as looking like a bird of prey, and was unable to cor-rect examinations without listening to the music of a barrel organ, which he hired to play underneath his window. "I don't think I ever felt so grand," Eddie thought, "as when we were set to translate a poem of Matthew Arnold's into Latin, and I hit on the same cou-plet as Whitelaw." Eccentrics scarcely disturbed the late-Victorian schoolboy, who, however, had a rare sense of quality, and recognized the expert.

Undoubtedly Rugby could claim to "harden". The boys worked an eleven-hour day, with two hours for prep. Hacking, scragging, mauling and tripping were supposed to have disappeared under The Bodger's rule, but the prefects punished by making a wrongdoer run past an open door three times while they aimed a kick at him. Ribs got broken that way. At breakfast, rolls flew through the air and but-ter was flicked onto the ceiling, to fall, when the icy atmosphere had thawed out, onto the masters' heads. There was a strong faction in favour of the Boers during the South African War, and strikes against the horrible food; to counter them, Dr James was obliged to eat a plateful, in furious indignation, in front of the whole school, but then, furious indignation was his usual attitude. All the notices he put up ended with the words THIS MUST STOP.

The tradition of Arnold was continued with frequent compul-sory chapels, but Eddie, and later Wilfred, were less influenced by these than by another boy in School House, "a rotund, ridiculous, good-natured boy, who had from the start the sort of quiet purpose that earned respect—rather grudging, I suppose." This was Billy Temple, the future Archbishop of Canterbury.

Eddie liked Rugby well enough and accepted its routine, though he particularly enjoyed the moments when it was interrupted. One midday a boy threw a squash ball which exactly struck the hands of the great clock that set the time for the whole school, and stopped it. Masters and boys, drawing their watches out of their pockets as they hurried across the yard, to compare the false with the true, were thrown into utter confusion. It turned out that the boy, who confessed at once, had been practising the shot for two years. The Bodger called this "un-English". Eddie did not agree. The patient, self-contained, self-imposed pursuit of an entirely personal solution seemed to him most characteristically English.

At St Philip's, Mrs K. was undismayed by the routine of the diocese. She taught herself shorthand to deal with her husband's correspondence, gave heart to the shy chaplains, charmed the ordinands, and managed surprisingly well on an inadequate stipend, though the housekeeping was somewhat haphazard, and the wine was cheap and sometimes undrinkable. Perhaps only Mrs K. could have tamed Alice, the cook (though in those days it was assumed that all cooks were ill-tempered), but charm, energy and devotion carried all before them. With such a wife, it was clear that Edmund Knox would soon be more than a Suffragan Bishop.

The holiday expeditions continued, but now with much wider range, with the advent of bicycles. A Coventry firm presented a machine to the Bishop; Mrs K., although as a horsewoman she mistrusted the contraption, learned quicker than her portly husband, who was, he said, "an ardent devotee, until, one day, the bar snapped and let me down"; the children all followed, teaching themselves on Raleighs paid for by old Mrs Knox. Eddie and Dilly were soon rapidly skimming through the Birmingham traffic, the girls pedalling gamely along in hats and white cotton gloves, the little boys doing the best they could, before the days of freewheel, their short legs turning rapidly. Rules were immediately invented, and it became a point of honour among the four brothers never to get off even up the steepest hill. Pale with fatigue, Wilfred and Ronnie toiled upward, Eddie describing wide circles around them, until he brought them to a halt by the wayside, with the words THIS MUST STOP.

Ronnie sometimes stayed behind. He had become fascinated with dictionaries. He threatened, in spite of a rule that no one must speak a language that the others did not understand, to learn Sanskrit and Welsh. "I can still see Ronnie," Winnie wrote, "on the seat by the Welsh driver of the waggonette which conveyed us all to church, making out a Welsh Bible with the aid of this friend, while the horse wandered along unnoticed, and my father predicted we should all be late for the service."

At home, Eddie took charge of the family newspaper, *The Bolliday Bango*. It was the voice of Scholesia—their name for the world of the shabby schoolroom. Eddie levied the contributions, sometimes by force, copied them out in ink, and did the illustrations. There are action pictures of the bicycles, of a peculiar form of football played in the tiny yard, and, more fancifully, of a synod of bishops playing billiards with their crosiers, and hanging up their mitres on the pegs. It was Eddie's first venture into journalism, and in its handwritten pages Dilly produced his first document in cipher (though the editor refused further instalments), and Ronnie, at the age of eight, his first Latin play.

In time, however, the editor and sub-editor became interested in other things. Developing a keenly critical spirit, they detected a number of inaccuracies, even downright contradictions, in the Sherlock Holmes stories, and sent a list of them to Conan Doyle in an envelope with five dried orange pips, in allusion to the threatening letter in *The Adventures of Sherlock Holmes*. Eddie acquired photographs of a number of music-hall actresses who had appeared, or were appearing, on the Birmingham stage. Then he and Dilly acquired pipes and tins of Tortoiseshell Mixture. Clouds of smoke began to float round Scholesia, already frequently plunged in darkness while Wilfred tried to develop his photographic plates. Mrs K. heroically avoided noticing the haunting whiffs of tobacco. *The Bolliday Bango* ceased publication, and Ronnie, still in his sanctum underneath the table, tried to produce a magazine on his own, but the impetus was gone as he became the last one left in childhood.

His consolation was a book—not one of the borrowed dictionaries, but the first book that had ever been truly his own, not to be touched by any of the others without his permission. It was a present, and the pencil mark inside showed that it had cost five shillings: *Natural History*, by the Rev. J. C. Wood.

The influence of this book, which gave him his first glimpse of independence, was disproportionate. From the first picture (of a man raising a bottle to his lips, contrasted with a noble lion, and titled: "Between man and brutes there is an impassable barrier, over which man can never fall, or beasts hope to climb"), Ronnie was as if hypnotized. When, sixty years later, he went to Africa, he judged both flora and fauna by the steel engravings in Wood. He knew the whole book by heart, and professed to believe it all; the animals were all graded by their usefulness to man, which meant that the Labrador came top ("many must have perished but for its timely aid"). Yet, as he said himself, in spite of the years at Edmundthorpe, outside the book he could not tell a bullfinch from a chaffinch.

Absurd though it may seem, Wood had an even deeper effect on Ronnie; this was because of his praise of reason. "It were an easy task to prove the unity of mankind by scriptural proofs," Wood wrote in his introduction, "but I thought it better to use rational arguments." This went deep. Ronnie told Eddie that there were "rational arguments" why he should be allowed to join the brothers' inner group—the St Philip's Pioneering and Military Tramway Society; they were not accepted, he had to pass the set tests, but Ronnie remained convinced of the supreme saving power of reason.

Ronnie could not help knowing that he was clever for his age, and that much was expected of him, and he hoped not to disappoint anybody. Meanwhile his elders, the fixed stars of his firmament, sometimes praised him, and sometimes took him to a football match; for sheer quality of happiness, he did not think one could beat the moments when Aston Villa won at home, and his brothers allowed him to wave a flag.

The Bishop's tasks multiplied. Queen Victoria did not take kindly to Evangelicals, and tried to exclude them from high responsibilities until they were too old to give trouble. Knox was an exception. Rejecting, to the relief of his family, the offer of the bishopric of Madras, he fought on until "dignified Worcester and placid Coventry began to look upon Birmingham as something more than a rather heathen shopping town." In 1896 the last of the lovely Burne-Jones windows were installed at St Philip's, and the church was worthy of becoming what it now is, the Cathedral of Birmingham.

Preoccupied as he often was, deep in church affairs to the exclusion of all others, he remained a family man, confident of his children's support. He could be, and often was, exceedingly angry with them, and sometimes cuffed the elder boys all the way round his study, but he was perfectly tolerant of their jokes at the expense of his dignity. One Sunday his private chapel was mysteriously full of the scent of Popish incense; once, when he was on a visitation, he found that his hostess had been told (by Eddie) to be sure to supply him with a bottle of whisky—"the Bishop could not do with less"— and with a pair of black silk stockings, in case he had forgotten his own. Once a representative of the press called at their holiday rectory, and since there were no servants and Mrs K. felt that the family might be considered too informal, Winnie and Ethel obligingly did duty as cook and parlour maid; only Eddie told the reporter that both of them were deaf and dumb, and could be addressed only in sign language; this caused Winnie to drop the soup. The Bishop marvelled, thinking of his own industrious and obedient boyhood, at where such ideas could come from.

St Philip's Rectory never became completely settled territory. There was always an unpredictable element. But the boys were going ahead unchecked, maintaining their early promise. All were winning prizes and scholarships, and their father was accustomed to measure progress by such things. As soon as it was dark, wherever they were, there was a cry, as though from the Inferno, for lamps and candles, so that the children could get down to their studies. Beyond his knowledge, however, there were stirrings, intimations of nature and poetry and human weakness, which could never be confided either in him or in Mrs K., who, in Eddie's phrase, in spite of her sterling qualities, seemed to them "rather drawing-roomy". There were certain aspects of sea and cloud and open country that brought to them, as it did to Housman's Shropshire Lad, "into my heart an air that kills"—certain poetry, too, that would always have the power to bring them together, *Sylvie and Bruno,* Catullus, Matthew Arnold, Housman himself, Cory's epitaph:

> They told me, Heraclitus, they told me you were dead,
> They brought me bitter news to hear, and bitter tears to shed.
> I wept when I remembered how often you and I
> Had tired the sun with talking and sent him down the sky.
>
> And now that thou art lying, my dear old Carian guest,
> A handful of grey ashes, long, long ago at rest,
> Still are thy pleasant voices, thy nightingales, awake;
> For Death, he taketh all away, but them he cannot take.

They knew that this was nothing more than an inaccurate translation from the Greek, made by an Eton schoolmaster to help out his class; later, they knew that the schoolmaster had had to leave Eton under a cloud, and take a different name. But the power of the two verses to remind them of each other, across time and space, was beyond this, and indeed beyond "rational argument".

Still, every morning, at family prayers, the whole household knelt down together, while the ancient coffee-machine simmered ferociously in the background, and the unity and peace, like that of England itself, seemed unlikely to be broken.

III

1901–1907

"We imagined other people might think we were peculiar"

ON THEIR SUMMER HOLIDAY OF 1900, the last year of Queen Victoria's reign, the Knoxes lost their holdall, containing all their waterproofs, umbrellas, fishing rods and tweed coats. Mrs K. believed, with a serene optimism which the years never dimmed, that it would turn up, perhaps on the next train. The boys, with their inborn melancholy and natural relish for disaster, declared that it would not, and it did not.

The holiday that year was in a large house on the desolate fringe of Dartmoor. "We should have been warned," Winnie wrote, "by the low rent demanded, but this my father held was due to its being in so remote a spot, so far from any railway station." They arrived in two open waggonettes through the Devonshire lanes thick with honeysuckle, all of them drenched with rain, Ronnie with a pitiful cough on which he had decided to write a treatise. In the damp house itself, mice ran over the girls as they knelt at their evening prayers, and Ronnie, still coughing, had to meow like a cat (he had a talent for animal imitations) to keep them at bay. In the morning spirits revived, and Eddie and Wilfred went down to the rushing stream to fish, but there was a sensation, not to be shaken off, of something coming to an end. The family was dividing into children and those whose childhood was past.

Eddie was nineteen, Dilly seventeen, two pipe-smoking, Norfolk-jacketed young men. The sight of them, both unattached, was maddening to local hostesses in this remote district; "calls" had to be paid and returned. But Ronnie at twelve still clung to childhood, while Wilfred, fourteen, imperturbably arranged his Bits of Old Churches. These were souvenirs, stones and chippings which must genuinely have fallen off and been honestly picked up, otherwise they did not "count", though Eddie and Dilly sometimes assisted with a good hard blow at the church wall which Wilfred never suspected. Dilly handed over to Ronnie his collection of 231 railway tickets; they no longer interested him.

In the autumn Eddie would be going to Corpus and Ronnie to Eton. In this family which breathed the air of scholarship, but had constant difficulty in making ends meet, education was the key to the future, and the Bishop believed that he could look forward with sober confidence. Although it was clear that Ethel, increasingly deaf and much slower than the others, would never leave home, Winnie was destined for University and, surely, for a brilliant clerical marriage, the three elder boys for the Civil Service, Ronnie for the Evangelical ministry. The Bishop was exceedingly busy, both with his pastorate and with the immense task of raising £100,000 for church extension. It is probable that he did not notice certain disturbing undercurrents, and that Mrs K. did not like to mention them. Neither Eddie nor Dilly felt certain any longer about the truth of Christianity. Their bookboxes contained not only classical texts but also *The Golden Bough*, *The Ballad of Reading Gaol* and George Moore's *Esther Waters*. On the other hand Winnie, dreamily adolescent when she was not energetically bicycling, escaped into Malory, into William Morris and the stained-glass colouring of the Ages of Faith, and, safe in the airing cupboard, read aloud to Ronnie from the poems of Christina Rossetti.

The family were still conscious, if threatened, of a solid front against intruders. "We imagined other people might think we were peculiar, and yet we were quite sure that our family standpoint on almost any question was absolutely and unanswerably right." No passage of time would ever destroy this feeling, but neither would it ever bring back the unity of 1900.

For the dimensions of earthly happiness, Ronnie always had to turn back to his childhood, and in particular to Eton. From the moment he arrived in College, was gowned and told "Sis bonus puer", he gave the school his wholehearted devotion, and it offered him in return the certainty, the sense of belonging, and the discreet respect for brilliance which he so much needed. This was so in spite of the early days of bewilderment, which were not made much easier by Dilly, descending, when he remembered, like a vaguely amiable god, from his room to see how his "minor" was doing.

Sept 23 1900

Dear Mother,

I don't quite understand the way the forms go, but Dilly says I am in the bottom division of Fifth Form as a matter of course. I hope this letter will reach you early, but I am only writing at 18 3/4 minutes past 8 p.m. . . . Yesterday I played in a game of Eton field game. I was put to hold a person up on one side, then someone threw the ball in among us, and by the time we were all sitting on top of one another the ball was far away.

We won apparently by three to none. I am very happy here. My love to Winnie,

your very sleepy son,
R. A. Knox

P.S. Floreat Etona.

He was possessed by a kind of pleasurable anxiety to do the right thing, and yet not to waste money at home, asking diffidently for a Liberty's armchair for his room "to get something in accordance with the rules of taste. Mr Goodhart [the Master in College] is always calling chairs 'horrible!', because he makes little expeditions into one's room just as one is getting into bed, and remarks on pictures and things. He told me the picture of Rembrandt was the sort of thing you could look at for hours. I've never tried." But if Ronnie was eager to conform, he felt free to be happy at Eton. The romantic in him, the inconvenient love of mystery and beauty—inconvenient, that is, to one who thought he mistrusted enthusiasm and only valued a reasonable faith—began to spread its wings. He felt a devotion to Henry VI, the Sorrowful King, the Founder of Eton, which merged, in his thirteenth year, with his feeling for the poetry of the Rossettis and for the splendour of the west window at St Philip's, the Burne-Jones window through whose ruby-red glass the light streamed in at evensong.

To outward appearances he was still the brilliant, dutiful and rather delicate prizewinner, petted by the Matron in College and still kept firmly in order by his brothers. As the cold of winter approached, Wilfred had "borrowed" his gloves, Dillwyn his cherished new overcoat, which he had christened Alitat, the name of a goddess in Herodotus. Alitat was returned, but Ronnie was often in the sickroom. He meditated anxiously on his resources. "I have bought all my birthday presents, expending 10/- on the whole lot," he wrote home in June 1902. "I shall have to send Eddie his to-morrow; I have got him a knife-sharpener and strop combined, and also a little pendant for his watch chain."

Eddie's departure to Oxford meant that the first of the Bishop's sons was at University, and he could not help recalling his own achievements there and Bishop Chavasse's letter to him: "Thank God, thank God, dear old boy, that you have got a First." Might not this very real triumph be repeated, in four years' time? Corpus was the Bishop's own college, and the President, Dr Thomas Fowler, was an old friend. Fowler was one of the great men of the University, a grammar-school boy from Lincolnshire who had become Professor of Logic, but valued philosophy principally as a means of training character; in his famous "private hours" he drew out his young men, and made them apply thought to conduct. To parents he made the terrifying observation, that if they failed to give their children a good education they were no better than the parents in primitive societies, who were permitted to put their children to death. He was both conscientious and sympathetic, and the terrible responsibility of choosing undergraduates for commissions for the Boer Wars was said to have shortened his life.

Eddie went up to Corpus not only as a good classical scholar, but as an Edwardian elegant. He had never bought any clothes for himself before he was sixteen. Mrs K. made large orders at the drapers and outfitters as required, while in the "girls' room" Winnie pinned and sewed, with Dilly intervening to adapt the sewing-machine to steam power. But the Bishop, who had suffered himself from reach-me-down clothes and "boots heeled, and, I think, tipped with iron—in vain did I attempt to deaden the hateful noises that attended my movements"—was sympathetic to his own boys, all of whom, except the lounging Dilly, had the instincts of a dandy. Eddie was made an allowance of a hundred pounds per annum, to be deducted from his share of the money left in trust by their mother. To the awe of the younger ones, he opened an account with a Birmingham tailor and a cigar merchant, and indulged his good taste in eau-de-Cologne and silk handkerchiefs.

The Oxford to which he went up, on the other hand, was still a slumbrous place where the old eccentrics, whom Lewis Carroll had compared to caterpillars and fantastic birds, emerged from the "sets" which they had occupied for some forty years, complaining at the disturbance of young bloods. The University was still slowly digesting the Commission of 1877, aimed at diverting wealth from the colleges, to expanding the sciences and giving increased chances to poorer students. In 1893 the mighty Jowett had died, glad to have lived to interpret the ideas of Plato to the world, and Corpus itself, which up to 1850 had never had more than twenty undergraduates, had cautiously followed the times, and had expanded into Merton Street. The college remained small, all the members could be gathered at once on the secluded green lawn under the old mulberry tree, and the record of scholarship, as always, stood high.

The idea that a son of Bishop Knox could be "frivolous and extravagant" did not cross Dr Fowler's mind. But the President's regulations, even by the standards which Edwardian Oxford tried to impose, were strict to excess. He had a horror of even the mildest forms of gambling, and imposed penalties on the undergraduates for playing the dreaded new game of "Bridge" and for attending the theatre in gowns "on the pretext that they thought the play was by Shakespeare". Eddie could not conform. He stayed out late. The most difficult route for climbing in at night was across the wall from Merton, where the less agile were sometimes impaled on revolving iron spikes; he became an expert, only damaging his wrists during the last few feet when his friends dragged his light weight across the windowsill.

With these friends, and in particular with Alan Barlow, later Secretary of the Treasury and Trustee of the National Gallery, Eddie passed golden hours. He was the unobtrusive wit of the dining clubs, organized races in hansom cabs, and introduced Miss Mabel Love, a music-hall performer, into the college. But he was aware of a document headed *Communication to Mr E.V. Knox, Scholar, after complaints by the Tutors on his Idleness*, and of the bitter disappointment that this was likely to cause at home. The summer of 1901 was spent at Glencrippsdale, where in the course of damp picnics and fishing expeditions Eddie fell into the melancholy which lay in wait for all the brothers. In an elegant version of the *Greek Anthology*, not the less true because it was a commonplace, he wrote,

> Leaf and bud, ah quick, how quick returning
> > Here is visaged immortality;
> Freshly from the dark soil sunward yearning
> > Lifts the ageless green; and must I die?

The natural confidante for these moods would be a young woman, in this case a girl called Evelyn Stevenson, who was also staying at Glencrippsdale, a spirited creature who played billiards and tramped over the heather in an "artistically simple" outfit from Liberty's. "Do you know, I actually read your letter right through?" she wrote to him. "Awfully good of me, wasn't it? I hope you are taking a generally less gloomy view of life and things in general . . . it's really easier than one thinks to go on living—at least it seems to me to be so." She also advised him "not to get too clever". But on his return to Oxford Dr Fowler informed him, in a spirit of anxious justice, that his scholarship had been suspended.

To retrieve himself he must come back in September and take an examination on the whole of Herodotus and the whole of Plato's *Republic*, with a fine to be paid if he did not pass, "which I fear would fall on your father rather than on yourself"—and Dr Fowler would be unable to supply him with testimonials of any kind. As a threat this would have had no effect on Eddie, but as an appeal to his affection it could and did. He gave up his "habitually late hours" (the records by now refer to him as "Mr Knox's case"), spent only eightpence a week on bread and beer in Hall, and he passed his Honour Mods. A further letter from the Doctor recalls the pastoral atmosphere of Edwardian Oxford:

Dear Mr Knox,

I sincerely hope that our relations may be more pleasant in future, and that the discipline you have been under, and will continue to be under, in a modified form, this term, may turn out to be for your good, not only by teaching you the useful lessons of obedience and submission to authorities, but also by procuring for you more opportunities of reading undisturbed by callers, during the solitary hours in your rooms, as well as by leading you to reflect on, and I trust to repent of, the folly of some part of your conduct in the past.

If all goes well for the rest of the term, I shall regard your present punishment and the spirit in which you have received it as purging your offences of the past, and, I trust, giving me the opportunity of speaking well of you to any one who may make enquiries as to your character.

Those who were expected to make enquiries were the examiners for the Indian Civil Service, for which Eddie was destined. But now he knew—and, indeed, he had told Miss Stevenson—that he was going to be a writer, and one good enough to justify his choice of career to his father. He never took his final degree, but spent his last two years at Oxford training himself as a debater, essayist and poet by practising, as an apprentice has to do, in the styles he admired most—Swinburne, A. E. Housman, the young W. B. Yeats, the later George Meredith. Confined to his rooms by nine-fifteen every evening, he wrote alcaics:

> I am dumb to-night, I cannot sing your praises,
> Only feel this cool sweet-smelling silence,
> Between leaf-lattices, upward and upward . . .

Wilfred was left stolidly behind at Rugby, working towards his turn for a scholarship. He was not very interested in school teams, and not very successful in getting prizes. But the placid exterior was deceptive, for Wilfred, like his brothers, had to come to terms with an inner struggle between reason and emotion, and between emotion and the obligation not to show it. From his letters it appears that his solution, for the time being, was a strange fantasy life entirely of his own devising. He refused to join the school debating society, "as if one who has spoken in all the Parliaments of Europe would condescend to speak at a petty school society!" When his box arrived and the Railway Company had demanded four shillings and ninepence he had "flung the minion out of the window for his presumptuous demands." The heat had been appalling for October and during a rugby match several players melted into pools of water, drowning one of the onlookers, "a double tragedy which has cast a gloom over the whole community." The Bishop complained about his spelling, and was told that "as soon as my friend Joseph Chamberlain has finished with Free Trade I shall instruct him to introduce a bill for spelling reform." No alterations were to be undertaken at St Philip's Rectory until Wilfred had come home to direct the workmen with a few well-chosen words, and if too many visiting clergymen arrive, he advises that it will be best to poison them with white arsenic.

In contrast to this, Wilfred showed the humility of the "in-
between" child in a large family when he insisted that he doesn't
need a new bicycle—the old Raleigh will do quite well "for something I have always rather wanted to do, ride back from Rugby to
Birmingham," and his only request for new clothes is when the time
comes for him to sit for his University scholarship.

The problem which had begun to occupy Wilfred's inmost
thoughts was moral and social, rather than religious. It was the question of poverty, which concerned him at the simplest and perhaps
the only important level: is it tolerable that anyone should be truly
poor? At Edmundthorpe he had asked Aunt Fanny whether it was
right that the village children should be lifting potatoes until it was
too dark to see, and had received the reply, "Nonsense, Wilfred! It
will teach them habits of industry!" Since then he had seen the
frightening slum poverty of Aston, where the women gathered
round the stalls on Friday nights to fight for scraps of bone and offal.
He did not, of course, underestimate his father's tireless work in the
grimy parish, but the Evangelical Movement, with all its wonderful
record of service to humanity, did not go as far as Wilfred wanted.
He felt that a new century needed a new direction.

Of all the older boys at Rugby, the one who had impressed him
most had been Billy Temple. Temple, even as a schoolboy, had
steadfastly refused to discuss "the Christian solution" for any specific problem; there was only one solution, and that was a total
change of heart in society. From this idea, for which he had an un-
grudging respect, and from what he had read of Ruskin and F. D.
Maurice, Wilfred, at the age of seventeen, began to arrive at his own
vision of the socialism of the future. In March 1903 he wrote to
Ronnie about the Woolwich by-election in which Will Crooks,
brought up in the workhouse, had just won the seat for Labour in
what had always been considered a safe Conservative stronghold.
Ronnie was not sure whether to rejoice or not. He was struggling,
for his part, with a "Sunday Question" on the subject "What do you
understand by Socialism and by the doctrines of Nietzsche?"

Ronnie's suggestion was that the poor and habitually unemployed might be shipped to Canada "or other places". "This would only be applicable to the young," Mr Goodhart wrote in the margin.

In the August of 1903 Wilfred and Ronnie were sent abroad together on a trip down the Rhine in the perennial hope of parents that they would "improve their German". They were to photograph the churches and to keep a *Tagebuch*. They began by drawing up elaborate rules and regulations for calculating the number of lemon squashes consumed and the probable weight of the very stout German ladies on the boat. The tramway systems were, they thought, unimpressive, but they dutifully did the sights. Cologne was "clean but papistical"—and Ronnie, very much the junior, was made to sew on Wilfred's buttons. The diary soon became light-headed:

> *August 5:* Wilfie asks for beer at Gurzenich restaurant. Thrown downstairs. [Ronnie] . . . Ronnie evicted from St. Somebody's by sacristan for sitting on tomb and intoning from Baedeker during mass. [Wilf] . . . W. excommunicated by Archbp. of Cologne for photographing him in Compline. [Ronnie] . . . Pulled Archbp's mitre about his ears and beat him with a beadle's bargepole. [Wilf] . . . Got W. out of military prison on plea of insanity. [Ronnie] . . .

As the trip went on, however, Ronnie grew serious. Not very sensitive, in later life, to the language of painting, he was touched, during those hot summer days, by the unmistakably direct appeal of what religious pictures he saw. On 16 August he wrote: "We went to the church of Notre Dame in Bruges, where there is a glorious Van Dyke Crucifixion with a very dark background and no one else except Our Lord in the picture. It makes one feel terribly lonely." Although Ronnie, as he wrote in *A Spiritual Aeneid*, "then as always dreaded the undue interference of emotion in religion," he bought a small silver crucifix in Bruges which he put first on the wall, then on his watch chain, then round his neck. Such an object had never been seen before at St Philip's Rectory. He found himself responsive also to the metaphysical poets of the seventeenth century. "I should like books for presents; obscurer English poets, esp. before and just after the Revolution," he wrote to Mrs K. He was still very ready to become a finished product of Eton; he still valued highly the power of Etonian understatement. (The best reproof for a violent offender, A. C. Benson tells us, is "I believe, Smith, we do not see you quite at your best today.") Ronnie's heart was given to Eton, but it was also open to the poetry of Henry Vaughan and his emblems of light and "dazzling darkness", the night-time when "spirits their fair kindred catch". He read for the first time, and memorized, Vaughan's "Peace":

> My soul, there is a country
>   Far beyond the stars,
> Where stands a wingèd sentry
>   All skilful in the wars . . .

But the book which moved him most at this time was a present from his sister Winnie, a volume of unashamedly sentimental short stories, Hugh Benson's *The Light Invisible*, a book abounding in wise, tobacco-stained old priests, one of whom tries and fails to save a child in danger of being crushed by a cart: an angel appears and gently guides the child, not away from, but underneath the wheels. This story particularly struck Ronnie. We have no idea what God intends for us; we have no right to ask for safety, perhaps we do not even know what it is. A lifelong enthusiasm for unpopular causes awoke in him. He borrowed a history of the Tractarian Movement, and, as he put it, "trembled for Newman, mourned for him as lost to the Church, and rose with the knowledge that somewhere, beyond the circles I moved in, there was a cause for which clergymen had been sent to prison and noble lives spent; a cause which could be mine." To his father, to all the Evangelical homes of his childhood, the Tractarians were traitors from which English Christianity must be rescued. Ronnie's changing views were "known at home, and doubtless regretted", but he was only sixteen, the favourite child, the youngest, and these notions of his would surely pass.

Meantime the Bishop's field of activity grew even wider when he was appointed, in the autumn of 1903, to the see of Manchester. He accepted by return of post, knowing that Balfour's ministry might fall and the offer might not be repeated by a new Prime Minister less favourable to the Evangelicals. The bishopric had been constituted only fifty years earlier, and covered a huge district of east and central Lancashire, caring for three million souls. The great Lancashire battle to keep its own religious education, of which the Bishop was to be a staunch champion, had only just begun. There were unshepherded multitudes in Blackpool, where in Wakes Week the landladies let their beds for half the night, then put in a new relay of holidaymakers while the first lot were turned out in the backyard. Manchester, with God's help, would be a worthy opportunity for his energy and splendid powers of organization.

Ronnie, who had rather expected "fatal opulence", as though the Knoxes were entering a new chapter of *Barchester Towers*, was a little dashed to be told by Mrs K. that "it wouldn't make much difference; it would make much more if we all got scholarships." Perhaps even she was disconcerted by a moving day of such formidable proportions—it was during this move that Wilfred's Bits of Old Churches were finally dispersed—and still more by the sight of Bishopscourt, the family's new home in Manchester.

Dear Father [Ronnie wrote],

I told you that I didn't want us to be *better off*, but only *not worse off*, so I am quite happy. Besides, you speak as if keeping a carriage was a necessary expense without any remuneration; but if we have a carriage we save cab-fares. Again, if we keep a garden, no more (or at any rate a little less) need to buy vegetables; even extra hospitality always has its remains; with charity the gain is purely moral. So we are practically better off.

About the house sounds more serious. But I am quite ready to

. . . let my childish eyes
Distort it into paradise . . .

(this is not a quotation but a thing I have just made up à propos). Anyway there is a walled garden which has a small dogs' graveyard in it. And whatever it's like, I shall be ready to be happy there.

Bishopscourt, behind its forbidding gateway and under its mask
of soot, was about two miles north of the Cathedral; an electric tram
passed within about thirty yards, but you had to be adept—as all the
boys were by this time—at jumping off at the right place. There
were three acres of garden, "the soil of which," the Bishop recalled,
"was, on the whole, waterlogged, and the surface blackened with
coal-dust and fog." The rooms were ill-arranged, and the butler, who
"went" with the house, was offended to find the chaplain working
next door to his pantry in a kind of cupboard. "My Lord," he said,
"what is to become of my dignity?" There was, however, plenty of
room to entertain visitors on a large scale, from the Ragged School
children to the justices of Assize, and to put up ordination candidates; the Bishop was satisfied. Two bathrooms were put in, and the
drainage improved, and although the curtains were still being hung
in the front rooms as the first Examining Chaplain appeared in the
drive, Mrs K. was immediately her charming, welcoming self. Alice,
the grumbling cook, and Richmond, the parlour maid, retreated
into the cavernous kitchen, and the Bishop entered upon a further
twenty years of selfless hospitality.

"What one chiefly remembers of Manchester," Eddie wrote, "is
the great dray-horses bringing loads of cotton to be bleached; they
made a tremendous noise, and struck sparks, because of the stone
setts." When they were not at large in the roaring city, the boys took
possession of a darkish, dampish study on the ground floor. If they
wanted to smoke, they climbed up on to the roof and sat on the top
of the glass dome of the entrance hall, where a false step meant a
broken neck. The Bishop was unaware of this, and also of some of
the scurrilous and wide-ranging discussions in the "boys' room".
where the brothers could disagree just as fiercely as in the days when
they had punched one another in the wind. "In polite and educated
circles," Dr Fowler of Corpus had written, "physical blows are replaced by sarcasm and innuendo, but this refined mode of warfare
may give an equal amount of pain." The brothers, who loved each
other, could not resist the temptation to hurt each other at times.

Dilly, when roused, was particularly arrogant, always taking, in argument, the extreme position.

The Bishop had understandably determined not to send his second son to Corpus, or even to Oxford. Dillwyn, who seemed equally attracted to classics and mathematics, should try for Cambridge, and sit for a scholarship to Eton's sister foundation, King's.

In the December of 1902 the Bishop had received a letter from Canon Bowlby, at Eton, which began: "I cannot imagine a better Christmas present than the report on your two boys." But the delight and astonishment in young Ronald's progress became somewhat clouded when he turned to the perplexing Dillwyn, who in his Cambridge exam had done two brilliant papers, one in maths and the other in Greek verse, and had left all the others unfinished. "It is not known whether he has any taste for philosophy or archaeology." Perhaps Dilly had been asked, but had not replied. The Canon's letter now takes on the tone of a racehorse trainer as he adds: "As to the Newcastle [scholarship] one can never be sure what D. will do. Only two boys are left who might beat him in classics, Swithinbank and Daniel Macmillan. They are a dangerous pair, no doubt, as they have been improving at the same time as he has." One feels he might go on to recommend more oats and regular exercise, as, indeed, an Edwardian schoolmaster would not hesitate to do. But Dilly would not compete where he was not interested. His friend Maynard Keynes, who had beaten him the year before in the Tomline Prize, wrote to his father that Knox showed up his work "in a most loathsomely untidy, unintelligible, illegible condition," forgetting to write down the most necessary steps, and "even in conversation he is wholly incapable of expressing the meaning he intends to convey." Yet he respected Dilly as a mathematician, and perhaps, as Sir Roy Harrod suggests in his biography of Keynes, "it was precisely the shower of irrelevant ideas impinging on a brain of the very highest quality that produced such successful results." We recognize the description of genius. So, too, did Nathaniel Wedd, the King's admissions tutor in classics; he recommended Dillwyn for a scholarship, and said that he "appeared to be capable of indefinite improvement". This was fortunate for Dilly.

In a certain sense, he had left home already. During his last half at Eton, Dilly had become a ferocious agnostic. He had postponed a confrontation with his father for the familiar reason—not fear, but the fear of giving pain. God once dismissed, Dilly and Maynard Keynes had calmly undertaken experiments, intellectual and sexual, to resolve the question of what things are necessary to life. Pleasure, like morality and duty, was a psychological necessity which must therefore be accepted, but without too much fuss; and just as Dilly had eaten cold porridge at Aston, because the pleasure of eating consisted of the pleasure of filling your belly, so now he declared that one should drink only to get drunk, and that women (to whom he was always timidly and scrupulously polite) existed only for sex. True pleasure came from solving problems: "nothing is impossible". Happiness was a different matter; it was suspect, as being too static.

Dilly's Cambridge was liberating in quite a different sense from Eddie's Oxford. In 1903 it was still a small East Anglian market town with shopkeepers anxious to supply to the great colleges, and not without its share of Victorian eccentrics; old Professor Newton, in his top hat, walked between the rails of the horsetrams and refused to give way to oncoming vehicles. But the spirit of the University was the exposure of truth at all costs, and in that atmosphere, under that remorseless light and in the cold winds of the Fen country, Dilly's mind was condensed into a harder crystal. By compensation, he developed even wilder notions and a tenderer heart, and made there the friendships of a lifetime.

His rooms, like most of those allocated by King's to its freshmen, were in The Drain, a row of cramped buildings without running water, and connected with Chetwynd Court by a kind of tunnel. He was obliged to buy crockery and furniture from the last occupant, but, as he wrote to Mrs K., "they look solid, and may last for years . . . I am doing the room mainly in green," he added, rather surprisingly, but one could never tell what Dilly would, or would not, notice.

King's at this time had only a hundred and fifty undergraduates and thirty dons, all unmarried; it was a little world within a world, self-regarding, self-rewarding, and doubtful about how far life outside the boundaries of King's was worth undertaking. The college finances were depressed, the food uneatable, and Hall so crowded that waiters and diners were in constant collision, but the prevailing air was one of humanism and free intellect, and many felt, as Lowes Dickinson had described it, that "the realisation of a vast world extending outside Christianity was like a door that had once or twice swung ajar, and now opened and let me out." But across the way their magnificent chapel stood in all its beauty, a perpetual reproach to them.

The Provost, in 1903, was the mighty Henry Bradshaw, the "don's don". Bradshaw, a man of ferocious integrity, once faced a visiting preacher who had said that the loss of Christian faith must mean a loss of morals with the words: "Well, you lied, and you know it." This was the last year of his provostship; in 1904, he was found dead in his chair, with an open book in front of him. Nathaniel Wedd, Dilly's first tutor, seemed to many people an aggressive man, shocking with his red tie and open blasphemies, but, as his unpublished autobiographical notes show, he had hidden complexities. By origin he was an East Ender, raised in dockland, who had got to Cambridge the hard way; on the other hand, his hard-working cynicism was relieved by strange communications from the unseen world, to which, as time went by, he paid increasing attention.

But the greatest influence upon Dilly was the best-loved and most eccentric of the Fellows, Walter Headlam. Headlam, one of the finest of all interpreters of Greek thought and language, was a pure-bred scholar, descended from scholars. In 1902 he was thirty-seven years old, and seemed to have only a frail contact with reality. Travelling was difficult because he could not take the right train, and even when on horseback he rode straight into the pond at Newnham, saying doubtfully, "Do you think I ought to get off?" Letters were difficult, because Headlam chose his stamps only for the beauty of the colours. But his rooms in Gibbs Buildings were open to everyone who cared to come, and anyone who could make their way through the piles of manuscripts and bills was sure to be listened to and taught. The pupils' work was usually lost and rapidly disappeared under the mass of papers, but Headlam sat "balancing an ink-pot on one knee," as Shane Leslie described him, "and scribbling words into Greek texts, missing since the Renaissance, with the other. His famous emendations, in exquisite script, were allowed to float about the room until gathered for the *Classical Review*. A year later they became the prey of German editors."

Headlam taught both by night and by day, for both were the same to him. His knowledge of Greek literature was enormous and consisted quite simply of knowing everything that had been written in ancient Greek, down to the obscurest Rhetoricians; he had no need for a dictionary. But Greece, to him, was not a dead civilization. He taught the Eleusinian mysteries with reference to ghost-raising and *The Golden Bough*, Greek obscenities were collated with Burton's *Arabian Nights*, he strummed on a hired piano to illustrate the music of the tragic chorus, and, draped in his own beautiful faded crimson curtains, demonstrated how they should enter. Enthusiasm, however, combined with meticulous exactness. Headlam's vast learning told him infallibly what an author could not have written, his artist's eye helped him to supply missing letters. And only here, in matters of textual criticism, a battlefield of giants in those days when reputations were lost and won and German and English scholars faced each other in mighty competition, did Headlam make enemies. Confronted with an inaccurate text, his charming, sunny temperament disappeared and was replaced by a concentration of scorn. Afterwards he would be mildly surprised at the resentment of those he had called "idiotic pedants" and "illiterate amateurs"; a party had formed against him, even in King's itself. Meanwhile his own undertakings, and in particular his edition of Aeschylus, remained unfinished; his own sense of perfection made it impossible for him to finish anything.

Dilly did not find Dr Headlam's rooms unusual at all, or even untidy. They were exactly the kind of rooms he would have liked himself, and he responded at once to the problems of emendation, which, as Headlam wrote to Professor Postgate, "are, I suppose, empiric; what you call 'instinct,' I should rather call 'observation.' " The borderland where the mind, prowling among misty forms and concepts, suddenly perceives analogies with what it already knows, and moves into the light—this was where Dilly was most at home. And he was able to help Headlam to find his notes. They are, after all, always more or less where you left them last night, as long as no one is allowed to tidy them away.

As far as friends were concerned, the college, as E. M. Forster put it, was divided into the excluded and the included, and Dilly, as an Etonian, was included, though this was of singularly little importance to him. The prodigiously brilliant and impatient Keynes had arrived in The Drain a year earlier, and had made his classic comment: "This place seems pretty inefficient to me." With Lytton Strachey, who had already been up at Trinity for three years, he had taken readily to the Apostolic atmosphere of intense friendship and mutual criticism, based on a very natural desire to talk about each other's shortcomings, and on a convenient version of some of the notions of their captive philosopher, G. E. Moore. Moore, diffident and speechless himself, was confidently interpreted by the brilliant Kingsmen. His proposition that it is useless to discuss what is meant by "I've got sixpence," but useful to think what we mean by saying it, led to endless variations of "What do you mean by . . . ?" and "You don't really mean . . . ?" His recognition of goodness and beauty (Moore did not think they could be defined) as inherent qualities of things, in some ways like blueness or squareness, and his insistence that it was actually wrong to be in a state of contemplating ugliness, meant that those who could recognize beauty must be in a superior class apart, as, indeed, the Apostles already felt they were. This particularly infuriated Dilly. "Knox, of course, was highly enraged at anyone's writing such rubbish," Keynes wrote to Strachey, after a reading of his paper on Beauty. Furthermore, the search for beauty tended to become narrowed to a search for fresh-faced undergraduates with whom one could fall in love.

Homosexuality appeared in many shades in early-twentieth-century Cambridge, linking more than one generation, from the outrageous Oscar Browning, wallowing naked, though by this time decrepit, in the Cam, to the "charmed life", sometimes more a matter of imagination than of fact, of the Apostles themselves. Headlam himself had found, as he told Mrs Leslie Stephen, that "life is not simple for those who have to choose between conflicting tendencies," and had expressed this in the finest of his English poems, on the death of John Addington Symonds:

> I go mourning for my friend
> That for all my mourning stirs nor murmurs in his sleep . . .

Dilly regarded the subject with detachment, knowing that it explained why Lytton Strachey should at first dislike him violently and describe him as "gravely inconsiderate". Dilly never became an Apostle, although his name was more than once put forward.

But, in spite of his hesitations (one of his nicknames at home was Erm), he was a speaker much in demand at college societies. Of these there were many, including one organized by Lowes Dickinson (it was here that Keynes had read his paper on Beauty) which was known as the "As It Were In Contradistinction Society".

The adjective "noxian", applied to Dilly in *Basileon* (the irregularly appearing Book of King's), was said to mean "noxious and anti-Christian". It must be said that the loss of faith, now apparently final and complete, was a process far more painful for him than for his contemporaries. Thus, G. E. Moore had ceased to be a Christian simply from what he heard his elder brother say at table; Leonard Woolf, so he tells us, gave up God because He was not of much use if He did not produce rain when it was asked for; while Nathaniel Wedd had been told at the age of eleven, "Most people have some form of religion, but your father and I have none," and advised to find one for himself. But Dilly had been brought up with active Christianity around him, his stepmother's kindness and hope, his father's charity and energy. In exactly the same way as Ronnie, Dilly felt the need to justify his faith—since his refusal to believe was nothing less than a faith by an appeal to reason. His scepticism was not logical; it came to him in the form of blazing indignation, a vision of Christianity as a two-thousand-year-old swindle, inducing human beings to fear where there is nothing to fear, and hope when there is nothing to hope for. If the swindle could be proved, that would "save his reason", and Dilly always hoped that it might be. Yet his attitude was always to defy God for what He had done, or reprove Him for not existing, rather than ignore Him because He didn't. And, more treacherous still was the fact that Dilly, like all his brothers, could not forget or unlearn the words of the Authorized Version of the Bible, which had been interwoven since childhood with his daily life. He would never cease to be profoundly moved by "Son of Man, can these dry bones live?" or "Hast thou found me, O mine enemy?" or "Many waters cannot drown love," or simply by phrases like "clear shining after rain", or that strange description of a breeze, "a going in the tops of the mulberry trees". And Dilly could not forgive himself, because he had been betrayed by his emotions and was unable to keep his own rules.

At Cambridge he swam and rowed on the Cam ("Poor Cam!" said Walter Headlam, "it thinks it's a river! But rivers sing! rivers are transparent!"), bowled the slow spinners that nobody could play, and played cards at bridge that nobody could understand. Even Maynard Keynes, who allowed no one to hesitate during the game, paused in amazement at some of Dilly's leads, but Dilly, with only fifty-two cards to think about, was able to calculate the probabilities so rapidly that he and his partner usually won. His absent-mindedness, however, seemed to increase, and he had rather more accidents than Headlam, whom a special Providence apparently guarded. He acquired a motor-bicycle—it was just five years since the Hon. C. S. Rolls had ridden the first one in Cambridge down the Corn Exchange—and this caused difficulties, since Dilly was logically rather than mechanically minded, and insisted, in the face of all experience, however painful, that certain results *must* follow certain causes. On other occasions his habit of suddenly standing stock still, lost in thought, led to trouble—"Colbeck of Marlborough ran into me at a good pace, and fell on the pavement, but escaped with some bruises." On an impulse he went down to Eton to take Ronnie out to tea, but kicked a football over the wall "which landed on the floor of a carriage containing two ladies". In the summer of 1904 he burned himself badly in a fearful explosion, the result of adjusting an acetylene lamp on a motor-car. "As an invalid he is a gentle creature," John Sheppard wrote to Wedd, "though he tells me that when he first met me he thought me a doubtful character, and I gather he still does." This combination of mildness and downright rudeness was very like Dilly.

Mrs K. became alarmed, and wrote to both Ronnie and Wilfred to go and see what their brother was doing. She could not leave the Bishop, who was occupied with preparations for a great holiday mission on Blackpool sands.

At Eton, Ronnie by now, though still fragile and delicate, was swimming in a golden atmosphere of popularity and success. As Captain of the School, he was known as the cleverest boy within living memory; his recent operation for appendicitis had kept the whole school in suspense; he was getting ready his first book of poems, *Signa Severa*, for publication, and had just been given his gold Newcastle medal, "one of the oases," as he told Mrs K., "in the arena of my struggling existence." His friends, too, were those who seemed set apart, not only because they had been born into the governing aristocracy, but because they naturally did all things well. But at Cambridge, anxiously trying to find Dilly's tobacco and to be generally useful, he felt himself a small boy again. "I generally came to feel myself rather a fraud," he wrote home, "as Dilly quite suddenly got up and went out to dinner." Maynard Keynes, he added, had taken pity on him and showed him round the college, but, not unexpectedly, he had had to go to Evensong by himself. "King's Chapel is topping," he added.

Wilfred also came over to see Dilly; his comment was that he had already warned his brother that no good would come of messing about with motor-cars. "I don't know that Dilly liked this very much, but he had to admit I was right."

Wilfred was going up to Oxford in the coming autumn. The Bishop, although he did not know the whole extent of Dilly's agnosticism, knew enough about it not to risk another son at Cambridge, and Wilfred, without much remark from his family, had won a scholarship to Trinity, Oxford. His letters home were in his customary unruffled style. He told Mrs K. that the President of the college, Dr Blakiston, would make an excellent butler (there was a vacancy by now at Bishopscourt), "while his removal would confer a real benefit on the University." As cox of the Trinity boat, he had had several opportunities of shipwrecking the University crew, but had "decided to spare them". In the meantime, since Winnie had come up as a student to Lady Margaret Hall, the river had become a place of daily dread, being crowded with strange females whom he was required to take on picnics.

The Bishop did not fear idleness or dissipation from Wilfred, but he might, if he had known more, have feared something more serious, for this third son had gradually reached a state of mind in which he "didn't particularly believe in anything". He had lost the precious sense of communication with God, without losing the need for it. Wilfred had, however, a great capacity for clearing his mind, and for making it wait patiently for what might come. He did not want to waste time, and he was aware that—as he wrote many years later—in times of crisis "the weakness of the flesh will probably suggest to us that the laziest method is really most suited to our individual temperament." To avoid the dangerous empty moments when vacancy threatened, he set himself—when he was not working, or with friends, or at socialist meetings—a series of ingenious tasks. One of these was to establish, by a series of controlled experiments in the college gardens, whether tortoises really preferred yellow flowers. Wilfred always lifted the Trinity tortoise carefully, by the edge of its shell, to avoid putting it off its feed, and he made his notes the basis of an essay on the inductive method.

It was surely to the credit of the brothers that all four of them stood by their father when, in 1905, he organized a march to London in support of the Church schools. Even Dilly refused an invitation to go to Brittany with the artist Henry Lamb, whom he found totally sympathetic, to join, as he put it to Keynes, "10,000 Lancashiremen and that unprincipled ruffian, the Dean of Manchester," in the great demonstration. The Bishop described his feelings on the summer's day when, after weeks of preparation, he descended from his hansom at the appointed rallying-place and found himself alone. But the excursion trains soon came rolling in, and with the support of Lord Halifax, he led his procession, more than a mile and a half long, to a mass meeting at the Albert Hall. There were brass bands and waving banners, and Eddie in particular was delighted when the chosen hymn, under the swelteringly bright sun, was "Lead, kindly light, amid encircling gloom". But there was no mistaking the desperate earnestness of the occasion. Lancashire in those days was prepared to go to great lengths to maintain her in-dependence and her right, if she wanted it, to maintain her religious education. It also brought home keenly to the brothers how wide the gap was now between their interests and those of their father.

In the November of 1906 Dilly attempted a reunion of a different kind when he invited his father and brothers to the Amateur Dramatic Society's production of the *Eumenides*, which was in-tended to revive the glories of the classical play in Cambridge. Eddie and Ronnie came, and, sitting together, saw Rupert Brooke, in his first term at King's, come on stage as the Herald—"a vision of ideal beauty," according to the connoisseur of poetry Eddie Marsh, but, in the view of some of the undergraduates, "accoutred in a not very de-cent manner." Dilly himself was being apprehended as an object of beauty by Lytton Strachey, who was in the audience, and, after a change of heart, had begun to find his appearance "transcendent". Only Walter Headlam, excluded by his enemies from the play com-mittee, sat, unaware of these cross-currents, in an unworldly trance, totally absorbed in the music and in the crimson robes which his own researches had shown to be the authentic colour worn by the choroi of Aeschylus. Dilly knew, indeed, that his beloved master had become increasingly vague, insisting, although he seemed in excellent health, that his health was failing and his days were numbered. The work for the second part of his Tripos, Dilly wrote home, had "begun to bore", and he dismissed still more acidly the prospect of the Civil Service. He was determined on a permanent Fellowship at King's, and the chance to be of use to Headlam in his definitive edition of Herodas.

A papyrus of the *Mimiambi* of Herodas (or Herodes, or Herondas, for even his name was, and still is, in doubt) was one of the more striking acquisitions of the British Museum from the excavations at Oxyrhynchus in 1889. These finds had excited the whole world of learning. Even Bishop French, on his last journey, had been given news of them by the Sultan of Muscat, but although a scholar himself, he had commented: "Human sciences are passing; only God's word abides."

The Herodas was a little roll about five inches high, preserved in the dry sands of Egypt, worm-eaten, rubbed, missing in parts, written out, not too carefully, by a copyist in about AD 100. It gave a complete version of some of the mimes, or satiric dialogues, which since ancient times had been known only through allusions or quotations in other Greek authors. Herodas was not a very good writer—not considered as such by the great authorities, who graded Greek and Latin literature as carefully as they did their pupils' work. He was an oversophisticated, sprightly, not very clean-minded Alexandrian, writing in a distinctive metre, "limping iambics". "Malign fate", Dilly thought, had preserved these mimes when so much else was lost. But their value to classical scholars, grammarians, archaeologists and historians was beyond price.

But who was to edit the mimes? Nothing can be attempted with a newly discovered papyrus, closely guarded by a great museum, without the *editio princeps*, that is, a clear text deciphered and transcribed by an expert palaeographer. This was being done, in 1891, by the British Museum's specialist, Dr F. H. Kenyon, while the honour of the first critical edition, after his work was completed, had been entrusted to W. G. Rutherford. But, to the horror of the world of learning, Kenyon suddenly married and went off on his honeymoon, thus selfishly delaying the *editio princeps*. Rutherford had to publish without it, exposing himself to the cruel mockery of German critics. Other editions followed, but none were satisfactory, and the work of scholarship waited for the deeply respected Henry Jackson, Regius Professor of Greek at Cambridge. But Dr Jackson, who seems never to have consulted the papyrus himself, delayed, distracted by "innumerable worries", and distressed by the terrible discovery that one of the mimes took place in a sex-shop.

None of these things were upsetting to Walter Headlam, who knew more than anyone else about Herodas, but refused to stand in the way of Jackson, and treated the many editions as an excuse to put off his own. Brilliant expositions, delivered in an airy aside, were taken down on scraps of paper by Dilly and John Sheppard, and added to the ever-mounting piles. Difficulties, as always, Headlam referred to the whole of the rest of Greek literature. He distrusted archaeology: "so easy to take a spade!" And Herodas must be brought to life, as Aeschylus had been. He and Dr Jackson might act out one of the mimes at Trinity, or they might demonstrate how the Athenians, on festival days, danced on a slippery goatskin until they fell flat. His imagination took wing. When he was thrown out of his horse-and-trap he exclaimed, as he sailed through the air: "Now I shall never edit Herodas!"

But this kind of light-heartedness is possible only for the essentially serious. To present an unknown author to the world, even if he illuminates only an obscure corner of corrupt Alexandria, and to do it in the spirit of true scholarship is, after all, not an unworthy task. And Headlam did care a little about fame, even if he was too unmethodical to set about winning it.

The situation had grown more complex. In 1900, to quote Dr Kenyon's words, "a small box which must have remained in the possession of some native" was sent from Egypt to the British Museum. It was found to contain papyrus fragments, "some of them reduced to mere powder," and those fragments proved to be some of the missing portions of the Herodas papyrus. It would now be necessary to reconstruct what was left of Mime VIII, *The Dream*, and Mime IX, *The Breakfast*, like a jigsaw puzzle. A scrap of papyrus glued into the wrong place would destroy the sense entirely. Six years had passed since the box arrived, and still no agreement had been reached between scholars.

This, then, was what Dilly wanted to do. He did not care that, in spite of winning the Chancellor's Medal for Latin verse, he got only second-class honours in the second part of his Tripos. He did not care whether the Apostles thought him a thing of beauty. Just before he went down, he wrote and produced a little farce, *The Limit*. The play dealt with the tribulations of Delicia Crackle, a college bed-maker, and Dilly bicycled on to the stage as Screachey, the aesthete, complete with long black beard. Then, in 1907, he went down, content to keep body and soul together until he could return as a Fellow.

That Easter, Eddie and Dilly took Ronnie on an expedition to Rome. Like the trip to Germany, it was paid for by the Newtons in the hope of some educational benefit to the boys. The little party, in straw hats and white flannel shirts, were respectably lodged at the Pensione Bethell in the Via del Babuino, at the rather high price of forty-two shillings a week.

Ronnie, who was nineteen, had by now been for a year at Balliol, where he had gone on a first scholarship, but somewhat reluctantly, feeling that in leaving Eton, where for six years he had been a favourite with both the boys and the masters, he had been exiled from an earthly paradise. "I feel curiously schoolsick," he wrote to Winnie. He had gone up to Oxford, however, with a number of brilliant friends from his election and had found his feet at once; only now, in Rome with his brothers, he was reduced once more to the status of the youngest, the Little Grampus. He attended the English Church, kept the coffee hot for the moment when his elders would deign to get up, and went out to try to buy *Punch*, in which Eddie's poems were now appearing regularly. Ronnie was trying to write a short story himself, in the manner of Hugh Benson, the diary of a priest who, attempting to exorcise one of his parishioners, is possessed by a nameless, hideous evil. Meanwhile Eddie and Dilly had got hold of a Baedeker which told them that the top of the Via del Babuino was "a haunt of artist's models, chiefly natives of the

Abruzzi," and they sometimes left Ronnie to his own devices, although Dilly refused to learn any Italian beyond the sentence "These lavatories are dirty," and ordered everything he wanted in Latin. Yet he managed to check the kinds of marble on the walls of a large number of churches, to see whether green malachite was as rare as it was said to be in the *Choliambic Fragments*. This, needless to say, was an errand casually suggested by Headlam.

In the autumn, Dilly went to teach classics and ancient history at St Paul's. The school was then in Hammersmith, and he found lodgings at 37 Talgarth Road. In class, he made no attempt to keep order, but was "loved by all". He used to say that the VIII form at St Paul's were so clever that he had to sit up half the night to keep ahead of them, and that this seriously impeded his social life.

Eddie was also in London. After coming down from Corpus he too had done his share of schoolmastering, a year at North Manchester Preparatory School, which prepared boys for Manchester Grammar. Like Wilfred, but unlike Dilly and Ronnie, he was able to keep order and stood no nonsense. "He comes into the room and smiles at me," he wrote on one boy's report. "It is not enough!"

The years at Corpus were to be the only years of his life during which he did not work hard; but he wanted to write, and suffered, as generations of authors have done, at the stuffy and inky boredom of the classroom. In 1905, after a number of attempts, he had some verses accepted by *Punch*. In 1906 the *Manchester Courier* took a piece on the elections—the Liberal landslide during which, in Manchester as in London, the crowds stood in the cold streets to watch, as red and blue rockets shot up into the sky to give news of a Liberal or a Conservative victory. A few weeks later the journalist James Bone, the "London end" of the *Guardian*, came back to Manchester to do an article on the Old Ship Inn; he promised to help, if Eddie could get down to London. The *Courier* gave him a letter of introduction to Clement Shorter, the editor of the *Sphere*; finally, the Bishop arranged to raise his allowance to £150 a year until he found his feet. Eddie settled an outstanding bill of 16s 9d for cigars, and set off.

Many years afterwards, he used to regret that he had come to London too late; to become a real "character", he said, one must have arrived before the Diamond Jubilee. But the fog-bound London of autumn 1906 was exciting enough, and he felt like a country boy in the capital. His family expected an account of the historical buildings and institutions; Eddie concentrated on the theatres and music halls, the transport, of course—one whistle for a motor-cab, two for a hansom—politics, the life of the streets and the newspapers.

Fleet Street, with the Empire it served, was in its great days, with hardly a warning shadow of the long decline to come. As James Bone described it, it was still the Street of Adventure, short and undistinguished in appearance, with cookshops, cheap tailors, provincial papers crowded into upstairs offices, but above all the din, "that terrific pulse of the news that, once heard by a youth on his first newspaper, is never forgotten till his own pulse runs down." The district was crowded with typesetters and compositors, and "the meanest tea-boy felt that he was part of a great power that could make war, though it could not make peace."

Editors seemed all-powerful, the reporters were heroic bohemians who emerged from the Cheshire Cheese and the Press Club to write copy for a drunken friend, who might make a rapid recovery, so that his editor was faced with two stories at once. There was a quartet—James Bone himself, Philip Gibbs, the essayist Robert Lynd, fragile in his Rhymesters' black cloak, and that fine writer H. M. Tomlinson, whose father had been a foreman in the East India Docks. They were, as Lynd said, "the sort of people our mothers warned us against". All four accepted Eddie as a promising beginner, and helped him.

Though the Street was dominated by the daily press, the 1900s were the heyday of magazines—*The Strand, The Pall Mall Gazette, Tit-Bits, Pearson's*—covering a wide range of interests as well as solid fiction and "astonishing facts" (or "it is not generally knowns"). Although Eddie was later to write: "What is the difference between literature and journalism? None, except that journalism is paid, and literature is not," this was a time of great popular writers, who were happy to contribute to the magazines. Joyce, in Trieste, was struggling with the second version of his *Portrait of the Artist as a Young Man*, T. S. Eliot, at Smith Academy, was feeling "the disillusion only possible at sixteen", but the public had many years yet to become aware of them, and meanwhile they enjoyed, without perceiving any subtleties, the stories of Hardy, Conrad and Kipling. Furthermore, they read poetry. The "pocket anthology" fitted into a Norfolk jacket, and could be taken out on long weekend walks; it had fine thin pages and a piece of ribbon attached as a bookmarker. *The Golden Treasury* (1891 edition) was the right size for this, so too was *A Shropshire Lad*. "Poetry," Eddie wrote, "is presumably to be felt. It is presumably, by feeling, to be understood."

There was also a large public for the art, or craft, of light verse, in which all four brothers excelled. "Every newspaper editor, I think," wrote H. A. Gwynne of the *Standard* in May 1907, "is looking out for a good versifier, and if Mr. Knox is able and clever in this way, I think there will be no doubt of his being able to get his foot on the journalistic ladder." Eddie combined Dilly's ear for metre, and Ronnie's skill in rhyming, with a political sense and a certain dry response to life's unpleasant surprises which was all his own.

"It was very stultifying, having no money," he recalled. The *Courier* had paid £3 7s 6d for five poems, and *Punch* 10s 6d for a contribution. His first lodgings were in Trevor Square, Knightsbridge, then "a very humble place", but the best he could manage. "My landlady had three classes. The highest were 'carriage folk.' Beneath them were what she called 'middle-class people like myself.' And the third was the Poor, in speaking of whom she mingled a certain amount of sympathy with a tinge of contempt. The trouble was that of course I never knew where I belonged; every time I paid my bill I knew very well that I was in the third grade, but I could never find out where she placed me." Soho attracted Eddie, who had a keen appreciation of its cheese and wine shops, but the district was favoured by Dilly's Apostolic friends, in whom he detected an unwelcoming coldness. He decided to try Bayswater; the atmosphere of the Edwardian boarding house is preserved in a letter from a fellow lodger, about a bet on the Derby:

> I am sending you 12/6 and sticking to the other 10/6 for the present, and as I want to pay Frank as soon as possible I owe you now exactly £1—what ho! I am having a monopoly of the beautiful women in this house now you are gone and [the landlady] says every day 'What a small party we are now, you will have to do all the talking for those that are away Mr. Brownfield.' But they haven't got much out of me yet in the conversation line. Miss Battle says she is pining for you and hopes you will soon be back.

But outside the lace curtains was the poverty of the pavements, barefoot children, the terrible bedraggled feathers of the unsuccessful prostitutes. In his notebook Eddie wrote verses which he never published, in which the muddy street-market in women is forced by the light of its own gas-lamps, "as out of steel and stone grow fire," to confess the squalid truth.

A poet at heart, he did not expect to be one by profession. At this point he was sending out twenty contributions a week, of which one might be accepted (though payment was sometimes "overlooked"), three "held for consideration", and the rest rejected.

Like every freelance, he could tell the sound of them as they fell through the letterbox on to the doormat. He was prepared to write on anything. The *Tribune* favoured political issues, the *Observer* wanted epigrams on Women's Rational Dress, "which," J. L. Garvin wrote to him, "is diverting to me." Fiction was always a possibility, and Eddie began a novel:

> 'Edward Smith stood on the top step of his house in Berkeley Square on a late November evening of 189–. He was immaculately dressed. A fine drizzling rain was falling.'
>
>   I never went further than that. There were so many reasons why. What does 'immaculately dressed' mean? Wasn't I merely giving a

hint to the reader that the fine drizzling rain would spoil Edward
Smith's clothes? And if so, Edward Smith ought to have called a cab.
I was sick of him. I hated him.

Eddie tore up his manuscript, forswore fiction, and determined to
lead his life as a truth-teller, as indeed all the four brothers, in their
different ways, were to do.

Not surprisingly his digestion, always a weak point, began to
break down, and he was advised to try the fashionable vegetarian
régime of Eustace Miles. Ronnie, still at Eton, and up in London to
see his writer brother, was somewhat disappointed to be taken to
the Eustace Miles restaurant, where charcoal biscuits, grass and
raisin salads, and "peptonised cocoa" were served; another hazard
was the Sunshine Apostle, dressed (according to Eddie's diary) "as
John the Baptist, or even more sacredly," who commanded the customers to eat fruit and go naked, as in the Garden of Eden. After
Ronnie had been sent safely back to Bishopscourt, Eddie felt im-
pelled to go to the Gaiety, drink too much brandy, and return to
Bayswater at five in the morning.

"*October 7:* Started Eustace Miles diet *in earnest.* Feel like a
cow. . . . Went to call at Miss B.'s flat. No response to the bell. Began
an ode to a bus-horse. Subject promises well. Can find no news in
today's papers. Bored."

Punch accepted the ode. But he needed regular commissions, and
if possible a job, and he began, with his distinctive mixture of modesty and dash, to try his luck at personal interviews.

"When I began to write," he observed dryly in 1952, "it was much
easier to get advice than payment. I do not know whether that is
still so today." Robertson Nichol, the fluent editor of *The Bookman*,
warned him never to exceed three thousand words a day, advice
which Eddie had no difficulty in taking. He was depressed by the
hall of Nichol's house, piled with review copies and leaving only a
narrow tunnel for entrance and exit, which seemed altogether symbolic of the fate of a book reviewer. The most important introduction he had, however, was to Edward Hulton, proprietor of the *Daily*

Despatch. Through the manager of the *Manchester Guardian*, Eddie was told: "You should be prepared to explain fully to Mr. Hulton what you think you could do, and ready also to volunteer a specimen of your own work." Shrinking from the prospect of the specimen, he was ushered into the room:

> To my surprise it was not a very large room. There were two chairs in it, one in which he sat at the desk, and one close beside it. I thought he would ask me to sit in the second chair and talk to me about my life and my art. He did not do this. He left me standing where I was, and pulling the second chair rather closer, placed his own feet upon it. I did not feel that I should do any good work for that paper, and the whole interview was a failure.

Occasionally he had a stroke of luck. A friend asked him to do the theatre notices for the *Standard* while he was away, and in this way Eddie saw the early appearances of the enchanting Irish Stage Society at the Court. In those days the critic had to leave by the end of the second act to get his copy in by midnight—which was why Act Three was often said to be "much inferior to the others"—and was obliged to wear full evening dress with a "gibus", a top hat with springs, which could be folded and sat upon. This was necessary, even for wild Celtic and nationalist drama. A little later, he had an interview with the *Saturday Review*, but they offered only a hundred pounds a year for three articles a week, including the political column, and he would have to learn shorthand typing at once.

Desmond MacCarthy, the most genial of Irish critics, had been at King's, and wanted to help Dilly's brother, as he wanted to help everybody he met. He also knew everybody. Eddie must come with him and ask advice from James Barrie, who was at the height of his fame, though he could sometimes be a little disconcerting, unless the side of him which spoke to adults, and which he called "McConachie", happened to be foremost. Buoyed up by Mac-Carthy's confidence, the two of them called at 133 Gloucester Terrace, where they found the room empty, except for a large dog, with which Barrie used to play hide-and-seek in the Park. While they waited, Eddie in sheer nervousness hit his hand on the marble mantelpiece. It began to bleed profusely. MacCarthy was aghast. Barrie could not bear the sight of blood. They tried to staunch it with handkerchiefs, and with the cuffs of MacCarthy's soft shirt, which became deeply stained. Barrie appeared in the doorway, took one look at them, and withdrew. Kind-hearted though he was, he was obliged to send down a message that he could not see them.

Eddie judged it was time to call upon Owen Seaman, the editor of *Punch*, who now reigned, heavy, scrupulous and autocratic, in the Bouverie Street office. Eddie described to him the *Saturday Review*'s offer. "And what did you say to this indecent proposal?" Seaman asked.

He himself did not pay high rates, but he knew that in this young man he had a writer of light verse whom he could not afford to overlook. He hinted, in a tone as serious as the Bishop's when addressing ordinands, that there might, in time, be a vacancy on the staff. Meanwhile, Eddie succeeded in getting his first job, as sub-editor on *The Pall Mall Magazine*.

The *Pall Mall* first appeared in 1893, running stories by Hardy and Conan Doyle, Kipling's *Barrack-Room Ballads* and illustrations by Aubrey Beardsley; and in 1907 it was still a "quality read". The editor was Sir Douglas Straight, now at the end of a varied and successful career, and passionately interested, for the moment, in bicycling and in exploring the Thames in his steam-launch. Much of the work was left to his assistant. "Two vast hampers stood upon the floor, one of manuscripts coming in, the other for those to be sent back. I had to pass them from one to the other, and there was a danger that on very hot afternoons, when one was sleepy, one would accidentally reverse the process and have all the stories to read again." Most were historical romances, "with rescued heroines and overturned wine-glasses. We were much inhibited in those days." On the other hand, Straight would have moments of great attention to detail; when they printed an illustrated story in which the hangman "quite naturally" happened to live next door to the condemned man, he was worried as to whether a hangman ought to wear gloves.

Eddie was dispatched to find out, and walked up and down all day outside Pentonville, "not liking to go in and ask."

His own contributions, whether signed or not, were all read at Bishopscourt, and he wrote home dutifully; he knew he had justified himself in the eyes of his father. But lodgings in London could be lonely, and in search of sympathetic companionship, Eddie would do much. For the sake of Mary Creighton, who lived with her mother, the widow of the Bishop of London, he endured visits to their terrifying house, where you had to go through the drawing room to get to the lavatory, and where the Bishop's study was kept exactly as it had been on the day he died. Mrs Creighton crushed him, and so did Mary, because he was only a journalist. Very different was Peggy Beech, the spirited actress daughter of the Rector of Great Bealings. Her most successful part, one of few, was Beauty in *Pinkie and the Fairies*. She refused Eddie's proposal of marriage, but then changed her mind. "How awkward it is," Eddie noted in his diary, "when you have led a lady who has rejected you to suppose that you will love her for ever, and then find that you were mistaken—but she fails to realise it." Arriving, entirely self-invited, at Bishopscourt, where the lawns were "infested with missionary garden-parties" and Mrs K. was almost at her wits' end, Peggy threw open her travelling-bag and took out a large Bible. "I know how to behave in a Bishop's household!" she cried. But if she was disappointed in her reception, Peggy Beech was not likely to lose heart. "LIFE interests me vividly," she wrote, "PEOPLE—THE PRESENT—THE FUTURE—for me THE PAST is over and done with—DUSTY AND SAD."

It was Winnie, the most loyal of sisters, who had to entertain the colourful visitor, for Eddie suddenly found himself called away. Wilfred was at student camp that summer. Dilly, lingering at Talgarth Road, had news from Cambridge of Headlam and his imaginary ailments. He was convinced that he was dangerously ill, but his pupils had contrived to steal his medical dictionary, after which he had been perfectly happy again. He had flirted mildly with the young Virginia Stephen, had chalked a young lady's nose in a billiards-room, and had appeared at the college ball to dance the post-horn gallop. In June 1908 Dilly was hoping to meet him in London; he was coming up for a conference.

Headlam reached London without mishap, which in itself was a matter for congratulation, but that night he collapsed in his hotel bedroom, and died. He was forty-two, and he had not yet edited Herodas.

Dilly went up to King's for the rest of the summer vacation, and was given the room directly under Maynard Keynes, now a lecturer in economics. Shortly afterward, Keynes moved into Headlam's old rooms, and the faded crimson curtains were rapidly cleared away, with the familiar muddle of years. George Thompson, another of Headlam's pupils, inherited the notes on Aeschylus; John Sheppard and Dilly set to work on Herodas. Dilly became a Fellow in the following year, 1909.

Ronnie, in an affectionate attempt to please everybody, went to camp (which he hated) with Wilfred, then to Blackpool to help with the Mission, but he was not quite in a settled frame of mind. He was reconciled to Balliol, though he still regretted its great days under Jowett:

> My heart leaps up when I behold
>   A rainbow over Balliol Hall,
> As though the Cosmos were controlled
>   By Dr Jowett, after all . . .

His academic career, however, had met with a slight but noticeable setback. He had got only a second class in Honour Mods, not because, like Dilly, he had lost interest, but because he had been so confident of his knowledge that he had not bothered to re-read his texts. No one doubted that he was an exceptional scholar, but the second class distressed him. He would have preferred, like Newman, to fail altogether.

His faith was undisturbed—it was necessary for him, he said, to believe either everything or nothing—but he had come to feel the need not only for ritual but for private confession and absolution.

He had told his father, who had not forbidden it—but how long would it be before the situation at home grew unendurably painful?

In other ways he must, at twenty years old, come to terms with his emotions. At school he had felt, like most sensitive boys, intense affections. On this subject A. C. Benson wrote: "I do not fail to ask the younger boys, especially those that are likely to be exposed to temptation and who make friendships easily and widely, two or three times in a half whether they are on the right path." But he need not have been disturbed about Ronnie, to whom these innocent obsessions had been part of "youth all round you and within you, and the river flowing through it all to remind you of transcience and eternity." Now at Oxford he still made friends "easily and widely", and his mantelpiece was invisible beneath his many invitation cards to conferences, lectures and debates. He did not see Wilfred as much as before—as he put it to Mrs K., "there have been less meetings of the Oxford branch," partly because they no longer believed the same things, partly because Wilfred looked with some reservations on the "carriage folk"—the golden generation, charming and spirited, but undisputably "other", who were Ronnie's closest circle. Julian Grenfell and Charles Lister, Lord Ribblesdale's second son, had been at Eton with him and had come up to Balliol in the same year; though Ronnie certainly did not cultivate these people—they loved him unreservedly and wanted him for a friend—it was still true that he romanticized them, just a little.

What was he to do with his life? He had to work for his Finals, but already there were suggestions of a Fellowship at Balliol or Trinity, and both Balfour and F. E. Smith had conveyed hints that he would be acceptable as a private secretary. That would mean a glittering future in the world outside Oxford, and outside the Church. The idea of the priesthood, in fact, had scarcely occurred to him as yet.

"I have had a romance," he wrote to Mrs K., in June 1908; he had been bicycling with an Oxford friend, Guy Field, and had had a puncture:

We coasted into the next village, called Oakley, and asked a cart if there was a pub about. The cart said that there were five. When it had gone a little way, two people out of it came back and said 'Wouldn't we like to mend the puncture at the Vicarage?' They were the Vicar's two daughters. We said 'Delighted'. So I mended the puncture very efficiently, while they held lanterns and conversed with us.

True, an impartial critic could not call either of them extremely beautiful. True, also, that we left without any exchange of addresses. True, that a young man helped me remove the mud-guard, whom Guy Field takes to be a fiancé of one. But who shall say it was not a romance, because the threads were broken?

Such things, of course, had to be treated light-heartedly, in the style of the fragrant Edwardian tales of summer which Eddie was still putting into his hamper of rejected manuscripts. But it shows Ronnie delicately poised, in spite of all his achievements, between this way and that. God speaks to us through the intellect, and through the intellect we should direct our lives. But if we are creatures of reason, what are we to do with our hearts?

IV

1907–1914

Knoxes and Brother

IT WAS SUGGESTED MORE THAN ONCE that the sons of Bishop Knox, like the sons of Bishop Benson, ought to form some kind of firm or co-operative with their intelligence as capital; in that case, Wilfred said, it would have to be called Knoxes and Brother. He was acknowledging the tendency to think of him as the most reliable, quietest, but least brilliant, and so forth. This was a misconception, but certainly, in the decade before the First World War, Dilly and Wilfred seemed as far apart in their spheres of life as it was possible for the family temperament to be.

Dilly was very happy at King's, where Monty James was now the genial Provost (the Lodge door was never locked, and whisky, cards and tobacco were always ready in the hall). True, James was said to be disturbed by intellectualism and to rap sharply on the table with his pipe: "No thinking, gentlemen, please!" and Dilly blamed him for the intrusion of ghosts, mysterious footfalls and general peering into the Beyond which was to disturb the college in future years. But the atmosphere, even without the irrecoverable charm of Headlam, was lively. Maynard Keynes, now in impetuous pursuit of reform, pressed for a higher dividend for the Fellows, reorganization of the catering, enquiry into the working conditions of the staff and the resignation of the Bursar. Dilly was one of the "Young Turks" in support of Keynes against what was said to be the leading principle of King's—never to do anything for the first time. Although he found it almost impossible to be in time for the Councils of War, held before the college meetings, he attacked the Bursar through the columns of *Basileon*. In successive numbers he appealed to the Bursar to inspect the rats in the Fellows' bedrooms, then to come to the rescue of the rats because the rooms were now so damp that they were being driven out by water rats, lastly to provide better care for the water rats whose "nasty cough" kept the younger Fellows awake at night. At the same time he felt a deep, though cautious, admiration for Keynes's insistence that money, including the college funds, was there to be spent. Keynes had succeeded in pushing up the Fellows' dividend from £110 to £150, ensuring, as Moore would have recommended, an increased distribution of what is intrinsically good.

Cambridge was still, as a contemporary put it, suffused with the golden glow of homosexuality in its most creative aspect, a source of emotion and art, and a relief from hard thinking. The amiable abstracted figure of Dilly, among many shifting intrigues, impressed Lytton Strachey, with his highly developed sense of comic structure. He had not objected to Dilly's presentation of him as Screachey in *The Limit*; he had been certain, in 1906, that Walter Lamb, Henry's brother, was in love with the "divine ambiguous Knox". "Knox very graciously asked me to lunch on Sunday," he wrote to Duncan Grant. "Lamb and Keynes were there too. I was of course too timid to say much, and Keynes and I soon departed, leaving the lovers, or quasi-lovers, nose to nose upon a green velvet divan. I hoped for at least a declaration; but alas! they merely talked (as I learnt afterwards from Walter) about the *Cambridge Review*." The following January Dilly appeared "wonderfully décolleté" (which probably meant that, as occasionally happened, he had forgotten his tie) at one of the evening "salons" held by the amiable classicist John Sheppard, who later became Provost. "Sheppard remained a block. Good God Almighty!" But Dilly, as his letters show, had only come to discuss the gross errors in the Crusius edition of Herodas.

By February, Strachey himself had fallen in love with Dilly. "You must forgive me, please," he wrote, "if I can talk of nothing but Knox. I came back from Cambridge having only seen him once—but the impression was so wonderful! Oh dear! You needn't be jealous! I'm as far away from him as from you!" Walter Lamb had tried to dissuade him by swearing that "Knox liked everyone equally", but what enraged Strachey was that he would never have a chance to find out; and meanwhile he was routed by the arctic cold and—though he does not mention rats—the pervasive damp of King's. In February, however, he was offered a room at Trinity, and knew that he must put his fortunes, and the "Knox question", to the test. He stayed several weeks, and had begun to regard Dilly (or Dolfus, or Adolphe, as he preferred to call him) as an Endless Possibility. But in March 1907 he tore himself away "with infinite tears".

> My beloved Adolphe, too, it was sad to part with, though I quite failed to find more in him that I had always found before. Did I tell you that he had a wonderful veil of ugliness that he is able to lower at any minute over his face? His method is, you see, to lure you on with his beauty, until at last, just as you step forward to seize a kiss, or whatever else you may want to seize, he lets down a veil, and you simply fall back disgusted. Isn't it a horrid trick? And then, of course, when you've decided that the whole thing's absurd, and begin to wonder what you could have found in him, he removes the veil, and says he must go back to King's.

The veil may have been partly composed of pipe smoke, since Dilly told Eddie that Lytton, although exceedingly jolly, needed "fumigating" at times. Strachey was perplexed, too, by the elusive quality of Dilly's mind, approaching every problem by indirections. In May, however, came a much worse shock. "Did I tell you the dreadful news about Knox?" he asked Grant. "He's taken to nippers! Yes, permanently—and that dreadful kind without rims!"

It was true that Dilly's eyesight was strained, and although he soon exchanged the nippers for horn-rimmed spectacles, without the slightest idea of the effect produced in either case, Strachey could not bear to go and see him on his next visit to King's, in June. The episode ended for him in London, as he sat in St James's Park with his friend Swithinbank.

> How nice to sit with Swithin in the sunshine! I talked to him about Knox, and told him about the nippers, and how appalling it was for me, because I'd had a passion for him. He said, 'I have a passion for him too, sometimes.' I replied, 'Well, you'll never have one again! You'll never get over the eye-glasses.' He said, calmly, 'Oh, I should take them off.' Rather wonderful? Can you imagine us talking about Knox on our penny seats, and forgetting all about the Colonial office?

"I want to write a moral story on the subject," Strachey added, "but I suppose I shall be too lazy—called 'The Spectacles.' " It would certainly have given an example of the imperviousness which carried Dilly through the pressures of life as though over charmed ground. He became, however, a good friend of Strachey's, at one with him over the matter of "the deluded individual J.C.", and continuing to hope against hope that Strachey might one day finish his projected *Life of Jesus*.

In 1910–11 two newcomers to Cambridge had a considerable influence on Dilly. One was an undergraduate of King's, Frank Birch (Francis Lyall Birch). Birch was a many-sided human being—a rather dull historian, an acceptable drinking companion, a mysterious private personality, a brilliant talker and a born actor. In his impersonations, as in those of all great comedians, there was a frightening element. He excelled in "doing" one of his classical tutors, J. E. Nixon, who had only one eye and one hand, and was reputed to be taken to bits altogether at night, so that nothing could be seen in the room at all. Birch liberated in Dilly the vein of wild fantasy which Wilfred had showed in his letters from Rugby, and Eddie in his contributions to *Punch*.

The other arrival in Cambridge was A. E. Housman, who took up the Kennedy Professorship in 1911, and from whom Dilly counted himself lucky to receive a glacial few words, now and then, at the Classical Club. Housman's poetry was important to all the brothers, but particularly so to Dilly, who revelled in its sombre advice. On the flyleaf of a copy of Manilius which he had given to Headlam, Housman had counselled him to confine himself to the things of this earth; with this Dilly sympathized and still more with the tension of *A Shropshire Lad* arising from the balance between reason and unhealed emotion:

> And fire and ice within me fight
> Beneath the suffocating night.

Housman, too, could be allowed to understand English metre. The three-stress rhythm of *Is my team ploughing* affected Dilly so much that he bit right through the amber mouthpiece of his pipe, which was heard by those in the rooms below him to crash to the ground.

This was Dilly between 1907 and 1914—expanding cautiously in the Apostolic friendship, encouraged by Birch to appear as, for instance, Cecily in *The Importance of Being Earnest*, carried away by poetry and motor-bicycles, and beginning his career in pure scholarship. His Fellowship dissertation had been on the prose rhythms of Thucydides; his argument was said to be unacceptable, but so clever that nobody could contradict it. Then he returned to Greek poetry. Mr Ian Cunningham, a recent editor of Herodas, writes:

> He discovered, more or less simultaneously with one of the greatest, if not the greatest, modern classical scholars, U. von Wilamowitz-Moellendorff, what is now known as the Wilamowitz-Knoxian bridge. This is a highly technical point of Greek metre. A bridge is a point in the verse where word-end is forbidden. This one relates to the iambic trimeter of the early period—Archilochus, Solon, Semonides, Hipponax.

To be remembered by a few because of a rule about a word that doesn't end in lines of poetry that scarcely anyone reads—if Dilly ever desired immortality, it would be of this kind. In Housman's words, all exact knowledge "pushes back the frontiers of the dark," and consoles mankind for his discovery that "he does not come from the high lineage he fancied, nor will inherit the vast estate he looked for."

The "vast estate"—the belief in life after death—Dilly, ever since his second year at Cambridge, had decisively resigned. In the Lent term of 1906 Dean Inge, who had himself been a Fellow of King's and was the most intelligent preacher that the Church could put into the field, had been asked to speak in chapel on the errors of intellectualism. The Dean appealed for a working faith, "in fact, if not in name, Christian"; evidently he was prepared to settle for this, but he failed to move the rationalists of King's. He told them that the intelligence should not be insulted by the apparent contradictions of faith—the mathematical concept of infinity itself involved contradictions. But the mathematicians remained firm. Georg Cantor had shown them that it didn't.

"I do not know myself where dear Dilly is in these matters," the Bishop wrote to Ronnie, "and he gives me no encouragement in trying to help him." More comforting was the knowledge that Wilfred's time of blank disbelief was over. After three years without faith in anyone or anything in particular, Wilfred was drawing to the end which Ronnie had set for himself ever since they had been small boys together at Edmundthorpe: the priesthood.

This does not mean that, at this stage in their life, either of these young men was an ascetic. On going down from Trinity, with a first-class degree, Wilfred had in mind a career in the Civil Service, and took a post as junior Examiner at the Board of Education. Hard though it is for anyone who knew him in later life to credit it, he was known in those years as "the dandy of the Board". Ronald and he went to buy silk ties together in the Burlington Arcade, under the guidance of Eddie, who knew about these things. Ronnie, moreover, although he had friends of all kinds and was so popular that he hardly ever took a meal by himself, was, as has been said, warmly accepted into the Coterie, that is, the children of the Souls. The fathers of the Coterie fished and shot tirelessly, administered the country, and, like Chesterton's Man Who Knew Too Much, "were born knowing the Prime Minister," while their dominating wives, with an air of authority, almost of divinity, diffused an atmosphere of spiritual refinement and joy, uninhibited gossip and an over-whelming interest in each other. The difficulty of growing up in these circumstances was great, and the Coterie felt it; it could be seen in Julian Grenfell's noble savagery and his determination to dominate wild nature by shooting and killing, and in Charles Lister's erratic socialism. Ronnie, to them, was "golden" because of his wit and sympathy; they asked no more, but a visit to one of their great country houses could be formidable. There was, for example, the question of practical jokes, a constant threat to the weekend guests of Edwardian society. Ronnie recollected one sumptuously formal dinner party, at which he took his seat after grace, only to realize that a "plate-lifter" had been hidden under the stiff damask table-cloth to upset his soup plate; but, warned by years of rough-and-tumble at Bishopscourt, he was able to cut surreptitiously through the rubber tube which connected it, while his host was left at the head of the table, operating it in vain.

It was the ease with which Ronnie did everything, the shy and almost apologetic way in which his witticisms appeared, the sudden bursts of high spirits and improvisation which seemed to come from nowhere, which made him a legend in his own generation. His lim-ericks seemed to materialize out of thin air, and no one could re-member when he first said them. Frances Cornford, in a letter of 1910 to Miss Jourdain, recorded that there was "a man called R. A. Knox" at Oxford, who had written

> There was a young man who said: 'Damn!
> I have suddenly found that I am
>   A creature that moves
>   On predestinate grooves,
> Not a bus, as one hoped, but a tram.'

(Ronald used to say later that he supposed he must have written this, but regretted the implied betrayal of the Birmingham tram sys-tem.) Lytton Strachey, coming to Oxford straight from Cambridge and Dilly, had called Ronnie "a Christian and a prig", but unless he simply equated the two things, it is hard to see where his impression came from. Ronnie spoke everywhere, debated everywhere, on both sides of the question if necessary, canoed through every lock and reach (he was not strong enough to row, as Wilfred did, but made use of his uncanny sense of balance), bicycled everywhere, was welcome everywhere, but he did not talk, except to those few who would understand it, about his spiritual life. Here the current was set. Both he and Wilfred, though from quite different points of approach, were becoming "Romanizers"—that is, convinced Anglo-Catholics. If they offered themselves for ordination as priests, they would be undertaking something totally different from what was understood as ordination at Edmundthorpe, or by their father in Manchester.

The Anglo-Catholic movement (Wilfred objected to this term, and preferred "English Catholics" to show that we were still divided from the rest of Europe, but shouldn't be)—the Anglo-Catholics felt, and feel themselves to be, not outside but inside the Catholic Church. The Reformation, in their view, made no decisive break, nor did the establishment of the Church of England under Elizabeth. The Pope had declared that the ordinations of Anglican priests were invalid and that they were not truly priests, but the Pope was wrong, and could be shown historically to be wrong. The tradition had not been broken; indeed, man could not break it. The English Church retains its ancient authority to guide and rule, and its religion must be, as it has always been, sacramental. The priest renews the crucifixion of Christ every time he blesses the bread and wine. In the sacrament of penance he conveys the power of God to forgive sin and heal the soul.

Sacramentalism had never been totally extinguished in England. Again and again people had rediscovered it. As T. S. Eliot was to put it: "I made this; I had forgotten." The Anglo-Catholics looked back, in particular, to the royalist priestly Church of Charles I. The family community of Little Gidding, whose chapel was desecrated and destroyed in 1647, was a sad memorial of this time. Then, in the early nineteenth century, the Tractarians had asserted the authority of the Church against any worldly power (this was the subject of Tract 1) and proclaimed a Church of England which would not be half-asleep, but "the living representative of God on earth." Then Newman offered the vision of the *via media*, a Church with Catholic doctrine and a Protestant freedom to inquire and choose. But the Oxford Movement could never have made its electric impact on Victorian England through doctrine and historical knowledge alone. It impressed through the personalities of its leaders, and by the beauty of holiness, which, once recognized, can never be forgotten.

The English are said to be the least theological nation on earth, and it was only as a means to an end, and a clearer method of explanation, that the Tractarians turned to Ritualism. Eucharistic vestments, holy water, candles, bells, incense and so forth were simply a way of showing truth through symbols which anyone could grasp. Unfortunately Ritualism shaded into the aesthetic movements of the late nineteenth century, and the desire for beauty, or at any rate some sensation, to break the tedium of everyday life. The Ritualists had expected to be misunderstood, and were not surprised at violent opposition. They were accused of mumbo jumbo, of fancy dress, or betraying the country to Rome, whereas they had tried to show that England had always been European and Catholic. They knew that they were risking prosecution in celebrating the English mass. There was considerable support for legal action against them by the Bishops of their dioceses.

The Anglo-Catholics of the early twentieth century felt that they were fighting a "soldier's battle" with the Church and State on one hand, and on the other with Rome, who rejected them unless they would agree to submit to reordination. The object of the struggle was always to draw English Christians closer to European Catholicism, so that we could stand together against a materialist Western world. It was here that the real confrontation lay. "The Catholic religion is a life," Wilfred wrote, "and its rules are a way to secure that life."

Authority in an industrial society can be claimed only by those who understand its effects. After the secession of Newman, the movement had ceased to be academic; it turned to the ordinary parishes, and above all to missions to industrial cities. This concern for the bottom of the heap was one of the true signs of life in Anglo-Catholicism.

It can be seen how Evangelicalism, of Bishop Knox's sturdy old-fashioned sort, was shocked and wounded by every one of these developments. To the Evangelical the reservation of the sacraments was deeply objectionable, because to him the whole of life, not only the bread and wine, was sacramental, and God was equally present everywhere. The emphasis on penance and absolution, with the priest as intermediary, did away, it seemed, with the old direct relationship of the Christian and his God, with the words of the Bible to guide him. Newman, whom the Bishop regarded as a misguided weakling, had certainly been a man of holy life, but then, he had been brought up as a child in a good pious Low Church vicarage. European Catholicism was hatefully un-English; so, of course, was Ritualism; plainness—the Bishop had hesitated even about wearing a surplice at the beginning of his ministry—was also a way of showing truth. As for the social mission, concern for the poor had found, for more than a century, its champions among the Quakers and Evangelicals.

He deplored all Wilfred's doctrines, but could not disapprove of what he was doing. During his Oxford vacations, and even after he went to the Board of Education, Wilfred lived at the Trinity Mission, in what is now Oxford Road, Stratford E5. In these surroundings he immediately felt at home.

The University Missions were then at the height of their activity, and—except for King's Mission, which was agitating to get rid of religion altogether—they were based on a chaplaincy with meeting rooms and boys' clubs. Trinity Mission was in the charge of a very large Old Etonian, the Rev. "Pombo" Legge, not at all spiritually inclined. He told Eddie, who came down to see how things stood with his younger brother, that he considered religion a matter of hygiene; services, like cold baths, were necessary, but should be over as quickly as possible. The rest of the day could be spent in re-laxation, for Pombo's powers of doing nothing were quite excep-tional. He was happy to leave everything to Wilfred.

Stratford, West Ham, is not in the dock area itself but on the "back rivers", supposed to have been made by King Alfred to drain the Thames and leave the Danish fleet high and dry. In the 1900s these streams were used for particularly noisome small businesses—fat melting, creosote boiling, tanning and the manufacture of sausage skins and sulphuric acid. The whole area rested on what George Lansbury called "rather shaky marsh land". Drainage was bad, and the sewage ventilators discharged gas, rather than letting air into the sewers; the incidence of infectious illness, particularly diphtheria, was high, and in many of the little houses a stretcher could not be turned round, so that hospital cases simply had to be carried out by porters. In spite of the 1906 Education Act, school-ing was uncertain, and although there was the "Truancy" for ha-bitual absentees, most of the children were part-time attenders, working a twenty-hour week for about eightpence. Philanthropists objected to this more than did the children themselves. Crimes were mostly what the police called "family cases"—wife-beating, attacks with fishmongers' knives and dockers' hooks, cruelty to donkeys, children drunk in the streets on Saturday nights. A recurrent prob-lem was the cheap "low-flash" American oil at fivepence halfpenny a gallon, which warmed the house effectively, but tended to ex-plode; after an accident women and children looked "like a heap of burnt rags" on the floor.

Wilfred was struck by the East Enders' sense of life as a spectacle. They knew it would be a struggle, and had the measure of it. When a woman told him that she didn't so much mind being knocked down with a flatiron, but "drew the line" at a wooden leg, she showed the West Ham instinct for comic drama. As to missions, everyone was used to them. The Salvation Army took their stand on the corner, the secularists attacked all religion from the Cromwell Club. The very name "settlement" suggested dwellers in an alien land, and "mission" was worse, implying that the mission-ers had been sent from a better place, and would return there. Wilfred objected, too, to the notion that they were "doing good". Doing good, like saving one's soul, ought to be the by-product of activity, not the reason for it.

Eddie recalled that what the Stratford boys really wanted to know was what brought anyone down there at all. "You're not doing this for nothing. What are you getting out of it? Are you writing a book about it?" They respected only those who could keep order. The Rev. Pombo Legge, who had done a bit of heavyweight boxing, sometimes bestirred himself to knock their heads together. Wilfred was too slightly built for this. He remembered that, to quieten the unruly Sunday school at Aston, his father had employed a curate who was "something of a mesmerist", but he did not believe the East End boys could be mesmerized. At football matches, he said, he made it a principle to send somebody off in the first five minutes, to assert authority. But the survival test was to go swimming with them in "The Bricks", a murky pool on Wanstead Flats which they much preferred to the new Municipal Baths. This was rough, but no rougher than his first term at Rugby, and much less so than a seaside holiday with Eddie and Dilly.

To his father, he tried to explain in what way he had become a convinced supporter of Labour. At Oxford, Ronnie and he and Charles Lister had founded the Orthodox Club, which pretended to be socialist and printed its invitations on red cards, but it was time now to put away childish things. West Ham was one of the classic training grounds of the Labour movement, and the corner of Beckton Road was one of its first schools of oratory. Wilfred believed that Christianity could work with it and through it. In 1910, when the unions were restrained from contributing to the party funds, he invited his father to give something to the expenses of George Lansbury, who was standing for Bow and Bromley. The Bishop replied that by socialism he understood the exaltation of "society" at the expense of the individual, both body and soul. Had Wilfred considered this?

In 1911 and 1912 the shipbuilding company at Canning Town

closed down, and there was unemployment all over the East End; the National Insurance Bill seemed to come only just in time. Ronnie felt that "The Bill is the best we can do, but we can't expect to like it." Eddie was prepared to rejoice with Wilfred, but added: "How are we going to pay the salaries of all the officials?"

Wilfred's moral guides at this time were Billy Temple, now President of the Workers' Educational Association, and Lansbury. Temple's fearless idealism has been described as comic, but church history should be judged, not by whether it is successful, but by whether it is right or wrong. George Lansbury was an Anglo-Catholic, whose attitude in 1909 was defined in his *The End of Pauperism*: "Kneeling with others at the altar of the sacraments will and can bring no real peace unless those who so kneel spend their lives as brothers and sisters, and this is quite impossible within a system of life which depends on the ability of the children of God to dispute, quarrel and fight for their daily bread." Both Temple and Lansbury saw that society must be unified before it could be healed, or, in Lansbury's frighteningly simple words, "a poor man or woman must be held of equal social value with a rich man or woman." Both dreaded, however, the idea of the state as a vast soup kitchen, believing, as Wilfred most consistently did, that the only valuable help is what we give each other. But to preserve the ethos of the old Friendly Societies and coal clubs in large-scale politics would, as he foresaw, require a miracle.

If the concept of wholeness drew Wilfred towards the sacramental church, for Ronnie it was the ideal of authority. All four brothers had brought impatience to a fine art. Ronnie felt something like despair at the English genius for irreligion—the comfortable feeling that there is a good deal of truth in all religions, but not enough to affect practical conduct. This seemed to him the legacy of Protestantism. "If you have a sloppy religion you get a sloppy atheism." If truth existed, then there must be one truth and one only, handed down in an unbroken line, a truth about which "theorising is forbidden and speculation unnecessary". It was as a champion of authority that Ronnie prepared for the priesthood.

He was indulged—or so, at any rate, his brothers thought—in not being required to enter a theological college or to do a year's parish work as a deacon. He had been offered the chaplaincy of Trinity, and he was to tutor in logic, divinity and classics while he prepared himself for ordination by meditation and study, in his own way.

Even as a schoolboy, long before his vocation was clear, he had seen that close human relationships might be an impediment to his service of God. Deeply attached to his friends, and "conscious for the first time how much my nature craved for human sympathy and support, I thought it my obvious duty to deny myself that tenderest sympathy and support which a happy marriage would bring." His intimation was justified in 1912, when, as an English Catholic priest, he took a vow of celibacy.

The feeling among Anglo-Catholics was one of ferment and hope, a determination to defy the Establishment and press their cause. The campaign had its advance guard of young curates, committed—with a public still keenly interested in church affairs—to set their world on fire. Certain churches, at strategic points throughout England, were felt to be advance posts, which must be held at all costs. One of them was St Mary's in Graham Street (now Graham Terrace). Ronnie had no connections there, but the Vicar, J. C. Howell, was an understanding friend, and it was here that he said his first mass, in September 1912.

His father, of course, could not possibly lend countenance to such a ceremony by attending it. He had prayed since Ronnie's nursery days that this favourite youngest son, this naturally religious young soul, should one day enter the Church, but Ronnie's ordination, when it came, was the culmination of years of bitter argument. At home in Manchester Winnie tried to take the brunt of it, to help the hard-pressed Mrs K. By now she had taken a degree in history and was beginning, in the intervals of parish work, to write her own books. But she worked on her *Life of St. Louis* with her ear open for disputes, ready to fly down from her room to act as peacemaker, and dreading Sundays, which Dilly, if he was there, persisted in treating exactly like any other day, while Wilfred and Ronnie bicycled round Manchester to find a church which observed the Seven Points of Ritual. At first the Bishop showed open bewilderment. "Between ourselves, Winnie, I cannot understand what it is that the dear boys see in the Blessed Virgin Mary." He conceded point after point. He said nothing about Ronnie's rosary, which could be heard clicking in the intervals of the daily family prayers. Alice and Richmond exchanged glances; Eddie's terrier, which was accustomed to wake up only at the familiar intonation of "And now to God the Father", growled ominously. As a deacon, Ronnie wore, even at home, a version of the priests' dress which he had seen on holiday visits to Oberammergau and Bruges. "Someone said," he told Winnie, "I can't remember who, that there are only three cities in the world, Paris (I think, or maybe Rome), Oxford and Bruges." He had acquired a cassock, knee breeches, black silk stockings and buckled shoes. The Bishop, who had to wear silk stockings himself on public occasions, could not imagine why anyone should want to. Ronnie's clothes were looked after by Winnie, who dared not entrust them to the outspoken Richmond. At a much deeper level, the Bishop never forbade his sons to go to confession, which was not forbidden in the Prayer Book. He desired to leave every possible way open by which Ronnie might come back to him.

Certainly, Ronnie never concealed anything. All his new "Romanizing" friends were asked to Bishopscourt, and, in spite of everything, his heart was high. "It was almost a part of 'rags' and shocking the elders," Winnie thought, "coming back in soutanes and buckles after huge meetings of the Christian Students' Union to uproarious meetings in the Bishopscourt smoking-room. I was very flattered that Ronnie insisted that I must be at home to make things go! And Wilfred talking about equal distribution of means of production and profits." They drank cocoa (which Wilfred recalled as the great conspiratorial drink of the early twentieth century; trade union meetings in West Ham were usually held at cocoa-rooms). Over the cocoa Ronnie and his circle planned "outrages"—looking back at his younger self, he called it "snapping at all the gaiters in a

cloud of dust." In his study the Bishop heard the laughter, and marvelled at it.

It would have mattered less if they had loved each other less, or,
indeed, if they had had less ability to love. Both of them would have
given anything earthly—anything their consciences would allow
them to give—to make the other happy. To the end of his life
Ronnie tenderly gave credit, whenever he could, to his father's
work, and in particular to his gallant fight for the independence of
the Church schools. Nevertheless, they were destined to lose each
other.

Oxford was Ronnie's chosen ground, and, like Newman before
him, he expected that it always would be. In his rooms in Trinity,
always open to anyone who called in for "teas" or "wines", he had
begun to take up his characteristic position, sitting on the fender,
the "warmest place" which his elder brothers had never allowed him
at St Philip's. Now he talked, smoked, listened and advised from
this point of vantage. Some of his circle might take a more extreme
course. His old and true friend Vernon Johnson, always seen before
in a correct bowler, suddenly appeared "in an unbecoming brown
habit, with a stiff hood looking like an extinguisher, his hair cropped
quite close, wearing rough boots like a workman's." He had joined
an Anglican community under strict Franciscan rule. This was not
Ronnie's way. He was the sparkling preacher of the hour, the irre-
sistible apologist of the English Catholics.

His high spirits seemed to overflow, so that his daily life, even his
life of prayer, seemed not enough to contain them. The Oxford
Union has probably never had such a brilliant speaker as this fragile, seemingly insignificant figure, trembling from head to foot with
sheer love of controversy, supporting himself casually against the
table and speaking, as all the brothers did, apparently without moving his lips. The whole House listened and listened, spellbound by
the power of mind. Ronnie read his speeches, but allowed himself
sometimes to mime. Memorable, to give one example, was a passage
on the disadvantages of clerical dress—beggars single you out, waiters know that you cannot lose your temper and serve you last, peo-

ple try not to sit in your carriage in the train, except spinsters—and each situation was given simply by a slight change of expression. The things he wrote at this time give the delightful impression simply of being young. Some of these were papers and addresses to University clubs. In 1911 he expanded the letter with the dried orange pips, which the four brothers had sent to Conan Doyle, into his *Studies in the Literature of Sherlock Holmes*. This was intended as a satire, not so much, as has been suggested, upon the Higher Criticism of the Bible, but upon all higher scholarship—including the work which Dilly was now embarking on, the recension of Headlam's Herodas. Dilly was engaged in correspondence with Professors Bilabel and Greeneboom; Ronnie invented, as his opponents, Professors Ratzegger and Sauwosch. He set out to show, strictly from internal evidence, that the *Return* stories are clumsy inventions by Watson, who had taken to drink. This would account, for instance, for his neglect of his practice, and the ludicrous errors he makes in the colour of Holmes's dressing gown.

Conan Doyle, to the brothers' disappointment, had not answered the letter with the five orange pips, but he did write to Ronnie when the *Studies* were published in 1912:

> I cannot help writing to you to tell you of the amusement—and also the amazement—with which I read your article on Sherlock Holmes. That anyone should spend such pains on such material was what surprised me. Certainly you know a great deal more about it than I do, for the stories have been written in a disconnected (and careless) way, without referring back to what had gone before. I am only pleased that you have not found more discrepancies, especially as to dates. Of course, as you seem to have observed, Holmes changed entirely as the stories went on. In the first one, the 'Study in Scarlet', he was a mere calculating machine, but I had to make him more of an educated human being as I went on with him. He never shows heart save in the play—which one of your learned commentators condemned truly as a false note.
>
> One point which has not been remarked by the learned Sauwosch . . . is that in a considerable proportion of the stories—I daresay a quarter—no legal crime has been committed at all. Another point

—one of the few in which I feel satisfaction but which I have never seen mentioned—is that Watson never for one instant as chorus and chronicler transcends his own limitations. Never once does a flash of wit or wisdom come from him. All is remorselessly eliminated so that he may be Watson.

Conan Doyle also explained the vexed point about the impressions of the bicycle tracks. Holmes was "too indolent" to explain that one can only tell which way a bicycle is going if marks are left on a steep uphill or downhill track. And this, he felt, "with many thanks and renewed amazement," was quite enough on the subject of Sherlock Holmes.

With the same deceptively easy-looking agile brilliance, Ronnie entered the field of theological controversy. In 1912 he had been asked to join a group of eight Oxford Fellows who met in each other's rooms each Friday. The object was to work out a minimum doctrine which would be acceptable to all Christians. Ronnie was there to represent the extreme young High Church position. There was an idea of preparation against the future, when Christianity would have to struggle for a hearing in a world where most would regard it not as untrue or even as unthinkable, but simply irrelevant. Was it possible to arrive at the "foundations"—the minimum of doctrine with which those who could not accept miracles, or the Resurrection of the body, could still feel themselves Christians? Surely it was neither weakness nor compromise to try to reach this kind of unity, with millions of the half-persuaded and the scientifically minded not far from the brink of belief? The moving spirit of the group was Billy Temple.

This open frame of mind was known in the early twentieth century as modernism, and it soon became clear that Ronnie was quite out of place on the committee. Modernism was explained to him, he said, by a member of the group while they were walking along the track of the new electric railway from Rossall to Blackpool, and he felt an actual sense of physical revulsion. To him it sounded like treachery. All compromise in religion was treachery. Faith was a gift, but also a force, which must be exercised by difficulties, the more the better. The committee were like a crazy, leaky vessel, throwing out Authority with trembling hands to lighten ship, while they should be plugging the leaks and throwing out the bilge. When their joint book, *Foundations*, by Seven Oxford Men, was due for publication, Ronnie went joyously to the attack with a verse satire in the manner of Dryden, "Absolute and Abitofhell". He himself felt proudly absolute; the modernists were timidly retreating towards a bit of doctrine and a bit of faith.

> When on his throne at Lambeth Solomon
> Uneasy murmur'd *Something must be done*;
> When suave politeness, temp'ring bigot Zeal,
> Corrected *I believe* to *One does feel*. . . .

Published in the *Oxford Magazine* for October 1913, which sold out in consequence in one day, "Absolute and Abitofhell" became immediately a collector's item. "I went to the author's rooms," wrote Eric Hamilton, later Dean of Windsor, "in case he had a spare copy to give me. Instead he handed me his own corrected proof, which I have ever since treasured. For all his brilliance, Ronnie was never overwhelming." It was reprinted, in the correct seventeenth-century format, by the Anglo-Catholic Society of St Peter and St Paul, who had begun as a small church-furnishing shop, part of the Medici Society, and now had an elegant private press and offices of their own.

Billy Temple did not resent the pamphlet, he was the last person in the world to do so. Nevertheless, Ronnie was aware of suggestions that he was frivolous, or did not dare to put his views seriously. In 1913, therefore, he wrote *Some Loose Stones*—loose stones, that is, that would bring down the *Foundations*.

Some Loose Stones is perhaps the best book he ever wrote—it is so fresh, so earnest, so full of light and shadow, each dependent on the other. He has, he tells us, the utmost sympathy with those who have no belief, "because I can give no clear explanation of how I came by it myself." But he cannot think that the Church's main concern should be, "How much can Jones swallow?" Unbelievers want an-

swers: "Why does God allow cancer?" They want definition, not ac-
commodation. "The modern church is like a cosy doctor saying:
'Tell us what you want to believe, and we will see about it.' " How
half-hearted, how useless, to concede that the miracles of Jesus are
exceptions to the laws of nature! "You only mean by that that things
do work by a law, but you haven't found the law." *Foundations* had
said that where a natural explanation of an event can be suggested
"there must be very special reasons for falling back on explanations
of a supernatural character." Ronnie calls this a disastrous piece of
bad logic. "Miracles cannot be probable or improbable. They can
only be possible or impossible."

To be a Christian does not mean that one thinks that things are
getting better. "Surely," he adds, in a most characteristic phrase,
"there is room for pessimism." But if the Church holds to its duty to
tell people what is true, he hopes, by the far distant time he is sixty,
to see the tradition restored.

Some Loose Stones was his first serious book, and his first appearance before a wider public, at a time of furious interest in church affairs and in religious controversy. Wilfred, although he was more
interested in reunion and communication than in doctrine, congratulated his brother warmly. Dilly thought the book touching but
ridiculous, and wrote "Some Floating Pebbles", designed to wash
the whole question out of existence. He showed this only to his
friends at King's.

Dilly was travelling to and from Cambridge to work on the Herodas
papyri in the British Museum. His eyesight was affected already;
he ate in small cafés in Soho—Henry Lamb had moved back to
Fitzroy Street—and took the first steps towards the total ruin of his
digestion.

By this time his collaborator, John Sheppard, had so many commitments that he was obliged to leave Dilly to complete the edition
by himself. Dilly had, of course, the expert help of the Museum staff
and of scholars at home and abroad, with whom he sometimes corresponded in that inferior but international language, Latin, and

sometimes in his stiff German. But for weeks and months on end he was alone with the seedy and oversophisticated little mimes—the pander who sues for assault because a girl has been stolen from the brothel; the mother with a delinquent son; the woman whose slave has proved an unsatisfactory lover, and wants him whipped, but doesn't want anyone else to see him naked; the women who complain about servants, visit the temple, can't wait to see the expert leatherworker in the sex-shop—heavens, what a crew! Dilly never became reconciled to Herodas as a writer, but he respected him as a familiar foe. The mimes provided an intensely difficult game in which nearly all the rules were missing, but Dilly intended to win.

Beyond the sorting out of Headlam's papers, crossed and recrossed by the dead master's exquisite Greek and English script, he had six main tasks. First he had, since this was still an accepted convention of classical scholarship, to conduct an attack on all previous editors of Herodas. Dilly was, in fact, rather less violent than most when he wrote of the "stream of editions" based on "illiterate" texts, "Bücheler, more sober, and with an extensive knowledge of obscene literature, but mostly Latin and therefore irrelevant," the "quite inconsistent" efforts of Dr Nairn, and so forth. Next, having cleared the field, he had to arrive as nearly as possible to the correct text. The strips of papyrus had been knocked about a good deal before reaching the Museum, but had been carefully mended. The *Mimiambi* was a copy which had been corrected, at least twice, in a smaller handwriting in the second century AD. The correctors were not grammarians, and not much good at metre either, as they overlooked a number of "false verses". The original copy (P) was made by a slave, probably of average inattentiveness. (Anyone who has taught a class—most scholars have, and Dilly had—can guess how inattentive.) The problem was (and still is) to deduce, from his errors in copying, what the original (P1) in front of him was like, eighteen centuries ago. What kind of handwriting was it, and which words might be written alike, so that the not very intelligent (P) might have confused them? And what missing words—taking into consideration the whole of ancient Greek literature—must have been written in the holes and rubbings and missing portions of (P)? Thirdly, after a painstaking recension of the first seven mimes, Dilly had to make clear who was responsible for the emendations. Headlam's (collected from scattered publications, or found on the floor, or remembered from conversation) Dilly decided to mark [ ], while his own would be [[ ]], and [[[ ]]] represented a mixture of both. To Dilly this system appeared beyond any possibility of confusion; *he* never confused them, after all.

Next, the speeches, since the text ran on without a break, must be correctly assigned to their speakers. Headlam had called this "the most baffling problem in Herodas". Did the gaps in the text indicate hesitations or a change of speaker? And might it not be useful, Headlam had added, warming to his subject, to read the novels of "Gyp", a French lady who wrote salon romances, almost entirely in dialogue? Without trying Gyp, Dilly allocated and reallocated the speeches into what is now accepted as the best arrangement we can get.

Then there were Headlam's notes, which again had to be recovered. They were far too long, but none of them ought to be lost. Dilly added a few on his own account, which could only have been written by him; for example: "To the Greek humorists appropriate misfortune was an enthralling joke. The Greek book of jests called *Philogelus* says: 'A drunkard who had bought a vineyard died before vintage.' We are not amused. Or rather we use different forms . . . 'Have you heard about poor old X?' . . . "

Every generation gets the version of Greece and Rome which it deserves, and so does every scholar. Dilly's judgment of the ancient Greeks was apparently dispassionate, as though they had been his own family. He by no means saw Greece, as some did, as a long golden Cambridge afternoon without Puritan inhibitions. He was somewhat depressed by E. M. Forster's early short stories in which Pan, or a naked faun, tends to put to confusion the stuffy and tiresome English. Dilly was surprised that Forster should have been a pupil of Wedd.

The last major problem of Herodas was the assembling of the

fragments. These Headlam had never had time to study, but a complete text would be impossible until they were fitted into their proper places. Most of the damage was at the edge of the rolls, and the larger pieces, which still kept their original shape, could be treated much like a jigsaw puzzle. The real trouble arose with the badly worn portions. Lamacraft, the Museum's papyrus expert, had no great knowledge of Greek letters; Sir Frederick Kenyon knew everything about Greek and palaeography, but little about papyrus or jigsaw puzzles. In working on the first two mimes, Dilly had noticed something wrong about the strips which Kenyon had already mounted. They had been put close together, whereas there should have been a gap of one letter between them—you could just see the beginnings of the "shadow letter" on the edges—and they had stretched unevenly, so that strip B was a whole line wrong at the top, and a third of a letter too low at the bottom. After some persuasion, the courteous Kenyon agreed to realign the precious crumbling strips. Mimes VIII and IX, however, consisted of fragments only, and in Dilly's view they were, as they had been arranged, a complete hash, but they were so brittle that the Museum would not consider remounting. The last two mimes, therefore, became a crisis area, and years of work, perhaps a lifetime, stretched ahead. Papyri were still coming in from Oxyrhynchus. He must examine everything of roughly the right date and familiarize himself with every possible variety of scribe's handwriting. Even then, he might need an inspired guess.

Sometimes Dilly relaxed. In the summer of 1912 Maynard Keynes reserved the whole of the Crown Hotel at Everleigh, in the middle of Salisbury Plain, for six weeks. Some of his guests behaved badly and with such reckless disregard of his landlady's feelings that Keynes had to pay forty pounds extra, but the mid-July party, with Dilly, John Sheppard and Duncan Grant—no women—was one of uninterrupted happiness.

Eddie thought that Dilly ought to get married, perhaps to Henry Lamb's unconventional sister Dorothy. But nothing came of this, and casual meetings, in the London of 1907, were difficult. Eddie described, in *A Little Romance*, his introduction, in a crowded room, to a charming Miss Robinson—"The weather is dreadful, is it not?"—and how he had to wait for several weeks, and another introduction, before he could reply—"What else is to be expected of an English summer?" Dilly, in company, was always gravely charming, but stammered and became "Erm", and he never seemed to be alone with a young lady for any length of time. In Eddie's opinion, if ever this should happen, Dilly would be defenceless.

Eddie felt that marriage must be the best solution for his brother for the very human reason that he wanted to get married himself. In his letters to Mrs K. from Balliol, in 1908, Ronnie mentions more than once that Eddie had appeared in Oxford, but could not stay long; he had to find a chaperon; he had to find a straw hat; he had to take out Christina in a punt.

Christina Hicks had come up to Somerville to read English in 1904, with a scholarship, five pounds a year for clothes and books, and a letter from the college reminding her that she must change her dress for dinner, but "must bring no fal-lals, as they only collect dust." She was a gentle, spirited, scholarly, hazel-eyed girl, a lover of poetry and music, and a determined, though not a militant, suffragette. She was also particularly ready to laugh at herself. When the Holbein *Christina of Denmark* arrived at the National Gallery in 1907, her friends noticed the resemblance, not in the face, but in the tranquillity of the hands.

Like Eddie, Christina was one of a large vicarage family. Her father, Canon Edward Hicks, was a rector in Salford, one of the poorest parishes in the Manchester area.

Thomas French himself was not more unworldly than Edward Hicks. Son of a small Oxford tradesman who got into difficulties, he had struggled for years to get the family out of debt. He entered Magdalen Choir School knowing practically nothing, for he had been taught nothing, and within a few years was a Fellow of Corpus and a leading expert on Greek inscriptions. In fact, he had helped Kenyon to assemble the Aristotle and Herodas papyri for the Museum.

At Corpus he became deeply attached to Ruskin, who had a set of rooms in the Fellows' Buildings. Though he found it needful to check some of Ruskin's extravagances (the Professor had wanted to go out and harangue the Oxford farmers into planting "the lovely red clover" instead of the pale variety) he reverenced the great teacher who "showed him a pathway through life." In 1872 Ruskin gave him a number of *Fors Clavigera* in which he had marked a passage contrasting the peasant with the scholarly recluse, "the peasant being always content to feed the recluse, on condition of his becoming venerable." "I am not ashamed to confess," Hicks wrote, "that this piece of irony has haunted me through life."

He turned his back on a college living and went first to the exceedingly rural parish of Fenny Compton, then, after thirteen years' hard parish work, to industrial Salford. The Greek inscriptions had to be fitted into what spare time he had. Perhaps his greatest sacrifice was in 1906, when he was asked once again to work on the papyri, and to collaborate on a dictionary of Hellenistic Greek which would show, for the first time, what many of the words in the New Testament really meant. But he did not feel justified in leaving Salford.

Hicks and his wife, Agnes, for the first thirty years of their married life, were as poor as church mice. "I never heard my father say he regretted the life of scholarship," Christina wrote, "or make great reference to it." The rule was "plain but good". Music the children taught themselves, and they were never short of that. Occasionally they would write down a list of all the things they wanted but couldn't afford, and then burn the piece of paper. This is a device which is always worth trying.

Poverty affected the Hicks children, however, in different ways. Neither Christina nor her elder sister ever felt it as a hardship, although they found it impossible, to the end of their lives, to take a cab or a taxi without feeling guilty. "Cabby" was their word for "expensive". Edwin and Bede, on the other hand, the two elder sons, were sent out to Rangoon as clerks in a shipping firm, and it was their intention to make as much money as they could, and enjoy themselves as returning Nabobs. Ned, the youngest, was cheerful and musical, happy, as a small boy, to carry their music and their shoebags round to parish concerts. A scholar of Magdalen Choir School, he made friends with another young tenor, Ivor Novello. Ivor was a holiday visitor at Salford, where he followed Christina round like a faithful pet dog, begging her to marry him.

Ned was now at Oxford, and was thought to be, like so many other young men, under Ronnie's influence. To the Hicks family, whose religion was "the beauty of holiness, quiet worship and the steady discharge of common duties", Ronnie seemed nothing but a wild extremist, who might, they feared, be "getting at" their youngest.

Edward Hicks was not made a bishop until he was sixty-seven. He was regarded, because of his Ruskinian socialism and his opposition to the Boer War, as a dangerous man, but by 1910 his wisdom and scholarship could hardly be put on one side any longer, and he was appointed Bishop of Lincoln. There was satisfaction both in the world of scholarship and at Fenny Compton, where the villagers said: "Hicks is *our* bishop; we broke him in."

By this time, Eddie had admitted to Christina that he had once felt strongly about Peggy Beech, but could not now imagine why, because it was impossible for him to think of marrying anyone but herself. They loved each other; but Eddie's only regular job was still with *The Pall Mall Magazine*, and he did not think he could look after her on his salary of two hundred pounds a year.

Eddie was, however, placing more verse and prose in *Punch*, and improving his acquaintanceship with Owen Seaman.

I was determined to do the thing in style [he wrote of an early visit to the old offices at 10 Bouverie Street], and I chartered a hansom cab for the occasion. 'Many and many a time', said the driver, 'I have driven the great artist, Mr Phil May, to this address.' When I told Seaman of this strange coincidence he said, 'The Cabmen always tell one that. They all have the notion that Phil May went to sleep in their cab after the *Punch* dinner, and spent the night in the mews.'

It was the old office in Bouverie Street, with small rooms, except for the dining-room, and narrow and rather perilous stairs. The machines were on the premises, so that the jokes, however long they had been in arriving, did not have very far to travel.

Knowing the Editor only as a brilliant satirist who had been a schoolmaster, I was still more impressed by the stag's head which was almost the only ornament in his sanctum. I told him that I was writing verses for Garvin, the omnipotent editor of the *Observer*, and I told him why. Garvin had explained that a few verses here and there would help the look of the page and form a good break in the editorial columns.

This shocked Owen, who controlled the politics of England entirely in verse. He had, indeed, a strong sense of vocation, and I remember his saying sadly about somebody or other, 'he is the kind of man who doesn't take his humour seriously'.

Eddie, grateful for the encouragement, went up to Fleet Street to find another of Phil May's cabs. Evidently, Seaman had formed his life on a solemn, indeed heroic, vision of what a *Punch* editor should be. At one time, he told Eddie, he had been a member of the Samurai, a society who had vowed themselves, through meditation and clean living, to evolve a "higher human type". No one must know that his family had been "in trade"—a ladies' haberdashers, Stagg & Mantle; this was one of Owen's endearing weaknesses. *Punch*, under his guidance, forgot its early rollicking days, and became a supporter of the Constitution. Owen took his correspondence away at weekends, like a cabinet minister, and answered it from country houses. Here he was a valued inmate of the bachelors' wing; indeed he apparently ousted Max Beerbohm as a favourite guest, driving him into exile in Italy; this episode was described by Beerbohm in *Maltby and Braxton*. By now, Seaman was nearly sixty, and apparently installed in the editorship forever. It was clear that *Punch* was no country for young men, but Eddie was prepared to serve his apprenticeship, hoping in time to join the staff and to work with Seaman's assistants, the bland E. V. Lucas and the young and radical A. A. Milne.

Eddie's early contributions to *Punch* were often imitative of Calverley, of Barry Pain's *Eliza*, even of Seaman himself. Later on he considered that imitation was not a bad thing for a young writer—"it increases the word-hoard". But his own distinctive style emerged. He had an ear for rhyme superior even to Ronnie's, so ingenious, so delicate—indeed, Ronnie and he claimed that there was no word, in English, Greek or Latin, to which they could not find a rhyme. In the fogs of the London winter, Eddie made "nimbus" rhyme with "knocked down by a dim bus". When the birds sang, "soloist" rhymed with "blow lowest". When he watched a young lady "crimping" her red hair at a neighbour's window, he wrote

> Phyllis, farewell, if that's the name
>> By which your parents had you christened,
> Long ere your beauty flashed to fame—
>> Or even if it isn't.

The skill in rhyming Owen Seaman appreciated, though he usually made a number of schoolmasterly alterations. He was more doubtful about a kind of lunatic fantasy to which Eddie was inspired by quite ordinary domestic incidents, perhaps the words on the side of a bus, or on a packet of something. Then his thoughts took wing, like swifts in late summer, and made a kind of crazy sweep, skimming back in the end to their starting point. At one of the large Kensington stores, for example, there was a Great White Sale; Eddie imagined this Great White Sale travelling through glittering seas, ever onward, fleeing from the harpoons of a thousand lady shoppers.

Pseudonyms were much used in Edwardian Fleet Street, and were part of the powerful mystery of the Press. Eddie took the pen name "Evoe", partly to distinguish himself from E. V. Lucas, partly because, according to the dictionary, "Evoe" was "a cry of rejoicing uttered by the followers of the wine-god." The word was pronounced "E. V.", but as most of his public read it as "Ev-oey," or "Eave-oh" (a variant of "Heave-ho!" he thought), the little joke fell flat, a good training for a professional humorist.

Bishopscourt was sympathetic to the idea of marriage. After a formal tea party, the Bishop pressed Christina's hand and said: "Well, my dear, I believe your influence is good; God moves in mysterious ways." Christina, though a little dashed at being called a mysterious way, was not at all vain, and remained firm even when Mrs K. added: "I have always heard it said that your elder sister is handsomer, but I tell them the younger has more spirit."

The engagement seemed long. In the June of 1912 Mrs Hicks wrote from Lincoln to Mrs K.:

> My husband and I are beginning to think that it is too long to put off the wedding to next May! They are both getting worried, I think. Eddie is coming here on Sat: next and we think it will be as well to settle something by then. He can't get anything more certain in the way of working at present but after all they have enough to begin with (if it only continues!) and perhaps if the furnishing can be arranged it would be best to let them start. Xtina is not aware of this letter nor (of course) is Edmund and you won't mention it. Xtina says 'it *does* seem a long time till May'. She is anxious because he is lonely. They might begin in a flat she thought.

A small Hampstead house was found, No. 55 Haverstock Hill. Hampstead was not too "cabby" in 1912, and both families contributed odds and ends of furniture. Mrs Hicks sent the second-best forks from Lincoln, and had electric light installed. Eddie brought with him all the bills and papers in two hat boxes. When he was obliged to answer a business letter he emptied the hat boxes onto the floor, and began: "Sir, On consulting my files . . . "

The wedding, on 20 September, aroused "extraordinary interest" in the *Lincoln Chronicle*, who were able to use the headline BISHOP'S SON WEDS BISHOP'S DAUGHTER. The bells of the cathedral were "fired"—that is, the whole peal rung at once—and, almost equally remarkable, Dilly was induced to enter St Hugh's Chapel, and to act as best man. The young couple departed to "an awfully jolly farmhouse on the moor" near Porlock. It poured with rain, and they were extremely happy.

Winnie, too, was thinking of marriage. The strain of the endless discussions between Ronald, Wilfred and the Bishop was beginning to tell. "I began to think," she recalled, "that it would be a relief not

to have theological discussions at every meal." Out of her admirers
she had almost decided on a small, quiet, reliable, clever and hon-
ourable Scotsman. James Peck's father had been a ruined ship-
builder, who at one time had taken refuge in drink, but the son had
emerged all the stronger from his misfortunes. "I do feel that one
would be absolutely *safe* with him. Every time I see him it seems
more possible in a queer sort of way," Winnie wrote to her father.
James Peck had a sound old-fashioned Scottish appreciation of literature, and hoped to share, through poetry, the emotions which he
found it hard to express. Winnie and he corresponded by postcard,
giving the page and line number in *The Golden Treasury*. This was
too much of a temptation for her brothers, who made trifling alterations to the postcards as they lay in the hall, so that Shelley's

> No song but sad dirges,
> Like the wind through a ruin'd cell,

was answered by Wordsworth's

> For still, the more he works, the more
> Do his weak ankles swell.

In the end, Winnie was glad to get away from them all, but only
for the time being, then her affection poured out again. She was
married to James in the autumn of 1912, at Manchester Cathedral.
Eddie, who was one of the ushers, found that the crowd of well-wish-
ers was so great that he had to go back to Bishopscourt, in his hired
frock coat, by tram. Scotland seemed far away. They all, but Ronnie
in particular, missed her. To his studies of Bradshaw he now added a
minute knowledge of all the railway connections to Edinburgh.

Ronnie, it may be remembered, had taken stock, while he was
still at Eton, of his own temperament, which "craved for human
sympathy and support". While his elder brother and sister were finding happiness in marriage, his tender nature ("He was the *kindest*
person I ever met," Winnie said) searched his environment for a response.

His new friendships, though in no way sensual, were deeply emotional, and although physical presence was in no way part of them,

he believed that they would survive death. "The love of friends," he wrote, "which in this world depends so much on a trivial communication like the curl of a lip, or the lighting up of an eye, will somehow be a thing more immediate and more intimate when we are true selves." "I am a personal person," he wrote to another friend, "whatever I haven't got, I think I have sympathy."

There was a circle of undergraduates who came up to Oxford in 1911–12, whom Ronnie loved and influenced, and who came to love and influence him. "It is hard to give a definition or even a description of them," he wrote in 1917, "except perhaps to say that in a rather varied experience I have never met conversation so brilliant—with the brilliance of humour, not of wit. The circle is broken now by distance and by death . . . At the time of which I am speaking two of them had already adopted what I heard (and shuddered to hear) described as 'Ronnie's religion.' " These two were Harold Macmillan and Guy Lawrence.

The friendship with Harold Macmillan had begun with a disaster, wounding to Ronnie, and the first real check in his career. Macmillan left Eton in 1910, and that autumn his family wanted a private tutor to coach him at home for a Balliol scholarship. At first Dilly, who was a friend of the elder brother, Daniel, came for a few weeks. This was a failure, Dilly was found austere and uncongenial. Then Ronnie came. There was an immediate sympathy between teacher and pupil, and Ronnie, feeling that the seventeen-year-old boy was in need of spiritual guidance as well as coaching in the classics, begin to explain the hopes and the beliefs of Anglo-Catholics. Then, at the boy's request, he took him to an Anglo-Catholic mass.

"Could you rather pray for me?" he wrote to Winnie at the end of October. "I've a most heart-rending and nerve-racking dispute going on with Mrs Macmillan, not about money this time, but about things 7000 times more important. Don't tell anyone." In reply to Winnie's anxious inquiry he explained that the family had asked him to give his word never to mention religion to Harold again. This Ronnie could not do, so he had had to leave, and "by now I'm extremely (and not unreturnedly) fond of the boy, and it's been a horrid wrench to go without saying a word to him of what I wanted to say." But when, two years later, Harold Macmillan came up to Balliol the friendship between them returned, unbroken.

> My dear, of course don't stop coming to Mass [Ronnie wrote in January 1914 to another of the group, Dick Rawstorne], I think it will get more familiar as you go on—Harold will be serving me, I expect, every Saturday next term at a quarter to nine. Only don't expect to understand all about it until you are part of it all . . . I can't allow, with any patience, your idea that the way I worship God is good for me, but not for other people. I know you think I'm prepared to make fun of everybody and everything, but I mean what I do, and I am quite deliberately staking my soul on the result. Do come and talk to me sometimes next term. I shall be at home every Wednesday, and always lonely for you.

This letter, and many others like it, conveyed Ronnie's hopeful affection and enthusiasm as he gathered round him his company of souls.

Of all this company the one that Ronnie loved best was Guy Lawrence, who came up to Trinity as senior classical scholar in 1912. Guy Francis Lawrence was a brilliant, brave and athletic, but also a nervous and delicate, young man. He was the son of a Chancery lawyer and a grandson of George Lawrence, the romantic historical novelist. He was very fair, very handsome and highly strung. At Winchester he had been made to take the female parts in Shakespeare productions, but he hastened, with relief, to discard these as soon as he joined O.U.D.S. His temperament was deeply religious, and by the time he left school he was thinking of taking orders.

During his second term at Trinity, Guy broke down, and had to be sent to San Remo to recuperate. "I think it is disgraceful of Ronnie to absent himself from Manchester for Christmas," Eddie wrote to the Bishop, but Ronnie was at the Hôtel de Londres in San Remo, where Guy was gradually recovering the strength to return to University. The hotel was a kind of genteel rest home, the management requesting priests not to appear there too often for fear the guests should think somebody was dying. While Guy rested, Ronnie wrote a short story, once again in the style of Hugh Benson. A young man accompanies his friend, who is suffering from a nervous breakdown, to the Côte d'Azur. On a tour of the hill villages he visits a ruined church, haunted by the spirits of dead peasants who were attending mass there when an earthquake swept them away. Trapped in the church, alone in the darkness, he struggles to control his fear.

> He tried hard not to think of his friends, but it was no use; one by one they came and took his brain by storm. In an agony of loneliness he stretched out his arms as if to fling them round some warm protecting body, and when they closed upon air he shook with sobbing. His whole body shook with the unquenchable thirst for human contact . . . Yet when his brain cleared, it cleared completely.

To Guy, Ronnie was his spiritual director, but, from an earthly point of view, it was with a certain wistfulness that Ronnie wrote, "I have a theory that everybody in the world really wants to run errands for him, and it's only the people whom he doesn't deign to fag who come to dislike him." As always, he dreaded the undue interference of emotion, yet now he allowed himself to trust it, and it did not betray him. A prayer which he sent that year to Rawstorne begins:

> Oh God, I submit my affections to Thee, beseeching Thee to take from me all particular objects of my desire, all friendships and acquaintance, however harmless in themselves, which Thou seest to be a distraction to my soul, or to interfere with my love for Thee . . . I desire to love even my enemies for Thee, and my friends only to Thee.

As 1913 turned into 1914, the character patterns of the four brothers had taken shape for their lifetime. Eddie could never forget that he was the eldest, Dilly that he was the second, Wilfred that he was the cheerfully and necessarily philosophic third, Ronnie that he was the baby. Eddie looked for responsibility, Dilly for independence, Wilfred for reunion, Ronnie for authority. All needed love, Wilfred and Ronnie because they had had so much in childhood, Eddie and Dilly because they had had rather too little.

Wilfred, down at the Stratford Mission, had taken the first steps towards ordination. His bishop directed him to study theology at St Anselm's in Cambridge. Here, entirely on his own decision, he took a vow not only of celibacy, but of poverty. Celibacy, he once suggested at a conference, was only an aspect of that difficult frame of mind, humility—an attitude to created things, including friendship and love, which made it possible to renounce them. This did not mean he underestimated the strength of what he called "the temptations of the flesh incidental to youth and liable to return with equal severity in middle life; we simply have to recognize them for what they are, and take appropriate means to cope with them." Wilfred, at this time of his life, resembled Dilly in hardly ever speaking to a woman at all, except for Winnie, Mrs K., his aunts at Edmundthorpe and Christina, who won him over without difficulty.

By poverty he meant something specific. Whatever he earned, he would never keep more than a hundred pounds a year (this was in 1912; he had to put it up later), except for a small sum to guard against being a burden to others in old age. With this vow went the duty not to indulge in regrets on the subject, not to become stingy— "the danger," he called it, "of clinging unduly to what remains"— and, hardest of all, not to mind being regarded as a delightful eccentric who, like the birds of the air, neither knows nor cares what comfort is. This idea was particularly irritating. Wilfred was the young man who had chosen his ties in the Burlington Arcade, and he loved good wine, good tea and the best tobacco. But renunciation must never be seen in terms of loss.

What did the brothers expect from the next five years? Wilfred would be a deacon in 1914, a priest in 1915, and his dearest hope was to work side by side with Ronnie in the Anglo-Catholic movement. This did not mean that he saw eye to eye with his brother in everything. Ronnie was mistaken when he told Evelyn Waugh that Wilfred was "like me, only more so". Wilfred had grave doubts about the Society of St Peter and St Paul—for example, about one of its publisher's announcements for 1912:

> In this twentieth century the Society of St Peter and St Paul would seek to rouse Catholics from their sad worship of material things,

from the strife of strikes and haunting Insurance Acts, to some degree of merriness, by printing for them the *Hours of Blessed Mary* in the vernacular. How sad Caxton would be if he were to come again to visit this merrye England and find all merriness gone from us!

This reference to the dock and rail strikes of 1911 caused Wilfred to use two favourite words, "bilge" and "tripe". Yet he believed, without sentimentality, that he and Ronnie could work together, as brothers and priests, on their own lines, and remain as close as they had been in Uncle Lindsey's garden. The failure of this hope was the greatest blow of Wilfred's life.

Eddie, the journalist, saw more clearly into the future. He had already felt a premonitory gloom in 1907, when Straight had commissioned for *The Pall Mall Magazine* a feature article on a visit to the German Navy:

My friend the Kapitän-sur-Zee delivered his soul with a fiery eye, and an inexpressible emphasis, in that little white-painted cabin set with photographs of British naval officers.

'The German Navy,' he said to me, 'is strictly for defence. These people who write for the newspapers—yes, on both sides—they lie. The Emperor himself told me, walking on this quarterdeck, that his intention was peace . . . We are a serious people.' The captain called a midshipman. 'Show this gentleman all—everything—*alles!*' he cried.

Eddie had been very much more impressed by H. G. Wells's *War in the Air*, which he persuaded his editor, with difficulty, to print as a serial in the following year. In 1912 he wrote to his father that he could only hope that the cousins (George V and Kaiser Wilhelm) would decide to be polite to each other; otherwise he would be obliged to join the Territorials, the last thing he wanted to do. His job hardly seemed to cover his Tube fares into London, and Christina was expecting a baby.

Wilfred was what was then called a "Lansburyite"—a total pacifist—but, somewhat inconsistently, he went to Territorial camp every summer with the East Enders. Early in 1914 he and Ronnie were both at Bishopscourt "holding the fort"—not very efficiently, one would have thought—while Mrs K. went up to Edinburgh; Winnie, too, was expecting her first baby. This was a chance to talk at length, but, whatever they discussed, it seems not to have been the possibilities of war. Ronnie had expectations of a peaceful summer term, with only three lectures a week, and six pupils, and he had devised a method of teaching logic by card games, which he copied out onto rather perishable slips of cardboard. In the Long Vacation, the August, that is, of 1914, there was to be a reading party at More Hall, a country house retreat in Gloucestershire. Guy Lawrence was coming with some of his closest friends, Harold Macmillan perhaps, although his family were likely to disapprove. Ronnie was to choose the wine, and the housework would be done by resident lay-brothers. All was set fair.

> I never read the papers at this time [Ronnie wrote in *A Spiritual Aeneid*], and it was only in casual conversation I learned that all was not well with Europe. Then the bugles went round to call up the Naval Reserves, a big German cargo ship sulkily submitted to be towed across the Sound to its long resting-place and as I travelled north to stay with [Guy] in the Midlands, I read the Foreign Secretary's speech.

As for Dilly, one never knew what he would think or say. Cambridge, as 1914 approached, was in a delicious turmoil over the rumour that the Master of Trinity had gone mad, and was shooting at the Fellows as they came through the Great Gate. "Ah, there is dear Dr Jackson! Bang!" King's was convulsed by new appointments as Bursar and junior Dean, and by the disappearance of the porter's cat. When darker clouds gathered, Dilly surprised his family by declaring that he thought "the whole of Cambridge" should join the Territorials, including Lytton Strachey. But Erm did not really believe that his future would be interrupted. By 1916 he confidently expected to have finished editing Herodas.

V

1914–1918

Brothers at War

WAR WAS DECLARED ON 4 AUGUST 1914, at eleven p.m. On the following evening, Eddie saw people dancing in their enthusiasm on the tables of the Café Royal. He came home by the Tube train, hung up his bowler hat, and whistled for the terrier, Caesar. He was thirty-four, an age when it is awkward to interrupt a promising career, and he had hoped to take Christina and his year-old baby son for a holiday to Whitby.

Neither of them doubted that the cause was a just one, or that the Germans must be made to restore Belgium. It was something, in any case, that we had undertaken, as a nation, to do. "I knew, and he knew, that he would have to go," Christina wrote in her diary. "Going", at that moment, meant joining the first quarter-million auxiliaries who were enlisted in 1914 to reinforce Kitchener's Army and the Territorials. It was assumed that since the war would be fought at sea by Britain, and on land by the French, the quarter-million would be quite enough to fulfil our obligations.

The war might not last long. Belloc, who had emerged, as editor of *Land and Water*, as the continental expert, declared in October that the Germans had already thrown in their last reserves. Not very

much appeared to be ready for the reserves at home. Eddie drilled
all weekend; there were no uniforms; he learned to slope arms with
his umbrella. "It seems that we are to have 400 rifles shortly," he
wrote to his father in November, "of a somewhat antiquated pattern, and also, they say, a machine-gun, so that we shall be extremely
deadly—probably about the time the next European war takes place.
It is now possible to sleep in camp permanently if one wishes it. I—
strange to say—don't." Kitchener at this time was hesitating between two or four machine-guns for each regiment.

By Christmas Eddie was a temporary second lieutenant in the
Lincolns, and wrote to his Fleet Street editors to say that after the
emergency he hoped to be working for them again. Owen Seaman
wrote:

> I am very glad for your sake (not for my own, except as a matter of
> *Punch*-family pride) that you have got a commission. I hope the Muse
> may recover under canvas. Let me know your address and books shall
> be sent to you . . . If you don't get sent to the Front we may meet
> somewhere in an anti-raiders ditch! . . . Good luck.

Seaman also gave Eddie to understand that he himself was a
marked man; the German Intelligence had special orders to keep
him under observation, because of some dispute in a hotel in Baden-
Baden.

The proprietors had feared that *Punch* must close down, but were
glad to be proved wrong; humour proved to be a necessity, even
though an agonizing division soon appeared between the jokes at
the front and the jokes at home. After the first battle of Ypres in
November 1914 the British armies, at the cost of 32,000 casualties,
held on to the Channel ports, and both sides dug into positions
which were never altered by more than about thirty miles during
the next few years. After this the main task of an infantry regiment
was to be shot at or shelled.

Eddie had joined the Lincolns, instead of the Artists' Rifles, because it made him feel closer to Christina. Her elder brother, Edwin,
had returned from Rangoon to join the regiment; her younger

brother, Ned, had already done so. The 4th Battalion had its head-quarters in the Drill Hall in Lincoln, and Christina, with baby Rawle and a stout nursemaid of fifteen, was to spend the time of separation in what Eddie hoped would be the tranquillity of her father's home.

However, as soon as war was declared, Bishop Hicks (whose comment had been "England does not want this war and I hate it") turned over the episcopal palace to anyone who needed shelter. The first-comers were the Belgian refugees, who began to arrive in October.

> They fled from Antwerp to Ostend [the Bishop wrote to Christina], then in Ostend they had to hurry away in a steamer for fear of the Germans, leaving all their goods behind them in *les malles* in the station. So beyond a little bag, they had nothing but what they stood up in. This was a real sorrow to them, for it made them, they thought, look contemptible: dear souls! They like, at present, to live in 'Tina's room' and the rooms adjoining, upstairs. There they have their meals, after the continental manner.

All over England the refugee problem followed a familiar pattern, early generous welcome giving way to friction. Ronnie, waiting at the station in his long soutane, was asked doubtfully by a lady, "*Êtes vous Belgique?*" and did not like to answer "*Non, je suis Angleterre.*" At Lincoln every cooking pot and pan was soon ruined; but to the Bishop his guests were always "dear souls".

Ned, removed, at least for the time being, from the dangerous influence of Ronnie Knox, was sent to Gallipoli. Eddie was lucky enough to miss this. The 2/4th Lincolns began their duties in Ireland, in County Kerry, which was supposed to be dangerously Republican; but they found themselves peacekeeping in a peaceable area. Eddie unfortunately had time enough to draw caricatures, an art he gave up altogether in later life, and one of his drawings caused him to fall foul of the Adjutant. He was also very nearly killed in the regimental horse races. Being light and agile, he was put up on the favourite, but had to wear two cartridge belts to bring his weight up to the handicap; the belts came loose and almost battered him to death. Afterwards he was asked why he had not pulled up, but this had simply not occurred to him.

For Eddie, horses were one of the redeeming features of the opening months of the war. He loved to watch them, particularly if they were cantering freely in the open, moving, as they always do, in a half-circle. He had an idea that it is because we always require them to move in a straight line that we have never quite tamed them.

By 1916 the battalion began to be impatient to be "out there". It was the year of Verdun, where the French casualties were so heavy that for the time being the fighting on the Western Front had to be largely left to the British Army. Haig had tried a mass breakthrough on the Somme, with losses of about 65,000 men, and it was said that the Higher Command were disappointed with the new drafts from the Midlands and East Anglia, because they were too stupid to do anything more than advance straight forward towards the enemy in daylight, and be killed. Disenchantment had set in, conscription was introduced for the first time, and still the Lincolns wanted to join their other battalions in Flanders.

In December, Christina gave birth to her second child in somewhat cramped conditions in the Bishop's Palace. Eddie did not get compassionate leave, perhaps because of his difference of opinion with the Adjutant. The 2/4th had been brought back to England to bring up their equipment to scale, preparatory to embarkation for France.

Winnie had never seen Wilfred so distressed as on the day when his beloved Territorials were recruited into a general service battalion. There was not much chance, after his ordination, of his joining them as a chaplain. The Chaplains' Department of the War Office was firmly opposed to Anglo-Catholicism; they felt, for example, that it was not the business of a priest of the Church of England to administer the last sacraments to the dying on the battlefield. In that case, Wilfred asked, could he be a stretcher bearer, or train as a medical orderly? The Bishop of London told Wilfred—who was still only a deacon—that he could not.

Ronnie was inclined to agree with this decision. He had returned, in the Michaelmas term of 1914, to an almost empty University. "Oxford is quite indescribable," he wrote to his father. "A cloud of depression hangs over it which it would take several Zeppelin bombs to pierce." None of his friends had been able to come to the house party at More Hall; his advice to them to stay and take their degrees, instead of rushing into uniform, fell on deaf ears. They would not listen to reason, or even to affection disguised as reason. His influence seemed suddenly to count for nothing.

In truth, his friends were in another world of experience. Julian Grenfell, a natural soldier, had already joined the army. Harold Macmillan and Charles Lister, among so many others, were training for commissions. Guy Lawrence was at Belton Camp with the 7th Battalion of the South Staffordshire Regiment. "Yes, I think Gi is happy," Ronnie wrote to Dick Rawstorne. "With fifty people to run errands for him he's happy, and they're happy, so what's the odds? But oh, my dear, the thought of his going to the front."

Finding the deserted colleges intolerable, he went to teach classics, without pay, at Shrewsbury. Here he thankfully re-entered for a time the world of childhood, devising ingenious games for the boys, or challenging them to translate "motor-car" (= "a smoking vehicle") and "Zeppelin" into Latin. In the casualty lists he began to read the names of his friends, the first ones to be killed in action. Others were standing by to go out, and "the nearer it gets to the time," Ronnie wrote, "the gloomier life is. I can't think, you know, how women stand it at all." Then, in the spring of 1915, the foundations of his belief in the Church, which had been so secure, without loose stones, began to tremble.

Both Guy and Harold Macmillan expected to be sent overseas before long. They turned to him for spiritual direction. Having reached a point of extreme Anglo-Catholicism, could they be content with it? If they had to die, they wanted to die in absolute certainty. Should they "pope" now? The fashionable word revealed the depths of embarrassment and trouble. And Ronnie, as a priest, found that he did not know what to say. If they came back alive in a year's time, he was not sure that he would still be an Anglican himself. What kind of an answer was that?

His first unmistakable intimation, Ronnie tells us in *A Spiritual Aeneid*, was in May 1915, when Wilfred, now an ordained priest, said his first mass at St Mary's, Graham Street. Ronnie travelled up from Shrewsbury to be there:

> We had been brought up together, known one another at Oxford as brothers seldom do. It should have been an occasion of the most complete happiness to see him now . . . in the same church, at the same altar, where I had stood three years before in his presence. And then, suddenly, I saw the other side of the picture.
>
> If this doubt, the shadow of a scruple which had grown in my mind, were justifiable—only suppose it were justifiable, then neither he nor I was a priest . . . the accessories to the service—the bright vestments, the fresh flowers, the mysterious candlelight—were all settings to a sham jewel; we had been trapped, deceived, betrayed, into thinking it was all worth while.

Ronnie said nothing as yet to anyone about his doubts. Wilfred wrote to his father to tell him that there were fifty-five communicants in the church and the collection taken up was one pound and one shilling, but both of them knew, neither of them needed to say, what it meant to Bishop Knox to have a second son ordained, even though once again he did not feel able to attend an Anglo-Catholic mass. Wilfred began life as an assistant curate, with his vicar, J. C. Howell, as his confessor and friend. He got permission to go on living at the Trinity Mission—in what Ronnie called "almost habitable lodgings" in Caroline Street; St Mary's was in a smartish district where Wilfred felt somewhat out of place, except in the rows of slum cottages which were then still standing behind Ebury Street. "He is still remembered in the parish," writes the present vicar, John Gilling. "People in the cottages used to darn his socks for him while he waited barefoot."

Ronnie was in a state of shock. The chapter of *A Spiritual Aeneid*
which described this period is called "Seeing a Ghost". Two days
after Wilfred's first mass, Guy Lawrence wrote that he had been received into the Catholic Church by the Jesuits at Farm Street. "My
mind was made up for me," he wrote. "God made it clear to me, and
I went straight to Farm Street . . . I know I am happy and I only long
for you to be happy with me. Come and be happy. Harold will, I
think, follow very soon . . . You've been and are my best friend, Ron;
there is no shadow between you and me."

In the event, Macmillan put off his decision until after the war,
"if I'm still alive." If so, he meant to get away from home, from
Ronnie, from every outside influence, and relearn his belief for himself. Neither he nor Guy loved Ronnie any the less, but they did not
need him as they once had done.

> At present [Ronnie wrote to Rawstorne], I'm like a top that's got out-
> side its grooves and is spinning about all over the place, and you can't
> tell whether it'll get side-tracked into the groove again or go clean
> off the board. But I'm afraid I shall never be broad-minded, Dick—
> unless I pope, perhaps: I think I might turn into rather a broad-
> minded Roman Catholic . . . But oh, Dick, I do hate it all, and I do
> hope you'll hate it less than I do. Do for heaven's sake not get a fever,
> there's dangers enough without that. God bless you, my dear, you've
> been very good to me.

Dick Rawstorne was due to sail for Gallipoli. The Dardanelles
landings began in February 1915. Charles Lister went out with the
Naval Division, was wounded three times, and died in August. Guy's
battalion had relieved the Naval Division, and Guy himself came
through unhurt, but the losses were terrible; as he put it, "an almost
full parade of the regiment is now in paradise." His nerves were
wearing thin. He was invalided home, and "I think Gi isn't quite so
well," Ronnie wrote to Dick, "because I was to have gone there for
the weekend, but he's put me off." The shadow had fallen. Then
Dick himself was taken prisoner by the Turks.

While the slaughter continued on every front, Ronnie fought his own battle with himself. He made a list of reasons—not the most important ones, but still important—for and against his conversion to Rome.

You'll be more popular in the long run.	But you'll first lose all the popularity you've got.
You'll get rid of the prayer-book.	You'll miss the Authorised Version.
You'll be able to get an altar when you want it, even abroad.	But you won't say mass in old Parish churches, like All Saints, York.
Your fellow priests won't be married.	But they'll be much more vulgar.
It will distress Guy and Harold if you don't.	It will distress your father if you do, and many who have been kind to you.

It will be seen that nobody could be more cruelly hard on Ronnie than he was on himself. He began to consider the idea of entering a monastery, and devoting his life to the memory of his dead friends. To outside observers his will power seemed to be "slipping away like a piece of soap down the drain". "Don't break all our hearts," said Howell, at St Mary's. He spoke for Wilfred, who could not bring himself to say anything.

In August 1916 Ronnie went to Hickleton to consult Lord Halifax, the great supporter of Anglo-Catholicism and Church re-union. At the house party he met a most singular person, the Jesuit priest Father Martindale. Martindale, in the nursery language of the Knoxes, was Ronnie's "haunt". Their lives crossed at many points, Martindale, quite without intention, acting as something between a warning and a reproach.

Charlie Martindale—he was christened Charlie—was nine years older than Ronnie. His biographer, Father Caraman, tells us that he was sickly from birth—"I cried; I didn't like the world; nor do I." Like Ronnie he had been brought up by elderly relatives, promised brilliantly and won every conceivable academic prize, but his reaction against middle-class life was early and violent. Before his reception into the Church he had gone to work as a hospital porter; after ordination he became a Jesuit, because he had heard that the Oratorians and Benedictines "were all gentlemen"; he was expected, because of his wretched health, to confine himself to a life of scholarship (he did, in fact, write nearly five hundred books, and was asked by the Vatican to collate their manuscript of Ausonius) but he broke away, appeared in unexpected places, conducted missions to seamen, dockers and incurables, all of whom loved him. He never stayed long in the houses of the great, and was only at Hickleton to collect some details for a biography of Hugh Benson. Ronnie, who was eagerly looking forward to consulting Martindale, felt that this would make a bond between them; he did not know that Martindale, who had had to struggle with his own temptations to homosexuality and undue sentiment, disliked Benson's work and hated the idea of writing the *Life*, which he had undertaken only after pressure from the Benson family.

Ronnie described the meeting more than once, always telling the story against himself. In a conference at Oxford in 1936 he recalled how he must have looked, in his smart buckled shoes and consciously "Roman" cassock, while Martindale hurried in, thin and shabby, "with a face like an extremely animated skull, not dressed in a cassock at all, but in a rather seedy frock-coat which didn't fit him too well and I think I knew in that moment that this was the real thing . . . Anyway, I went and talked to him that evening while he was packing up to go somewhere else. Father Martindale was always packing to go somewhere else." As the priest flung his shoes into a suitcase, Ronnie told him, in agony of mind, that he was coming to believe the Church of England "hadn't got a leg to stand on". Ought he not to take the plunge and become a Catholic at once? The answer was completely unexpected: "Of course you couldn't be received like that!" Ronnie felt the sensation, familiar since childhood, of being hit suddenly in the wind.

Father Martindale had not intended a rebuff, simply a call to positive thinking. The effect on Ronnie was decisive, but for a while he drifted without moorings. His only certain conviction was that he must leave Shrewsbury. His last address in the chapel of the school which he had loved so much had none of his usual humour. He took Newman's subject, "The Parting of Friends", and the boys, he thought, had a suppressed air of wanting their money back.

Wilfred bore as best he could with these apparently endless hesitations. The idea of a separation was terrible to him, but he tried to concentrate only on Ronnie's unhappiness. The best thing for his brother, he thought, might be a hard spell of work in a parish.

In spite of everything, there were moments when they could laugh together. Sometimes they laughed so much that, as in former days, they felt like rolling about the pavement. This was the case when they were walking up Whitehall and saw Erm coming out of the Admiralty, all dressed up, as Wilfred put it, like Lord Nelson. Both were too overcome to ask him what he had done with his telescope. They exaggerated a little. Dilly was in the uniform of a sublieutenant, R.N.V.R.

Bloomsbury and Cambridge attitudes to the war varied. Of those closest to Dilly, Henry Lamb, who had medical training, served with the R.A.M.C., Frank Birch joined the Navy as an ordinary seaman and amazed the lower-deck concert parties with impersonations of Wedd, Nixon and Monty James; Maynard Keynes was needed at the Treasury. Of the cast of Dilly's play, *The Limit*, four were to die at Gallipoli.

Dilly, determined that his motor-bicycle should be of use, made strenuous attempts to enlist as a military dispatch rider. "It seems it's mostly night-riding," Ronnie had anxiously written home, "so there's not much chance of Erm, with his sight, being accepted." Dilly's contention was that in the darkness there was no difference between good and bad sight, but a demonstration of his riding led the selection board to reject him decisively. His future, however, had been decided for him elsewhere.

At the beginning of 1915 he was asked to join I.D.25, the depart-

ment of Naval Intelligence which became better known as Room
40. He was to become a cryptographer, that is, an expert in the art
of reading secret writing, a system which in wartime ranged from
the crucial signals of Higher Command down to a junior officer in
the trenches, struggling by candlelight with his muddy codebook.
"Who would appreciate an obituary such as: He died like a hero, his
last words being XB.35.06.7K2?" asked *Punch* in 1917. The answer
might well have been: the regulars of Room 40.

By the time Dilly joined Room 40 it had come a long way from
its amateurish beginnings. When war was declared the Admiralty
had no cryptographic room at all. Alfred Ewing, who had been a
professor of mechanics, had been asked to see what he could do
about getting up a department. He found himself, as he says in his
own account of those years, "in the thick of special work quite outside my ordinary lines," and reduced to looking through the dusty
codes at Lloyd's and the Post Office to learn even the rudiments of
the business. He was a good organizer, however, and he had three
pieces of luck; he got on well with the terrifying Admiral Fisher; he
was given the current cipher and signal book of the German Navy,
picked up by the Russians from the body of a drowned seaman; and
he knew that the Germans could not send messages by their under-
water cables—the British Navy had cut these on the first day of the
war. All German signals, then, must pass either through Allied or
neutral cables, or by radio. Calls from their shore stations or between their ships at sea could all be intercepted by our directional
radio stations, which rapidly learned to identify the sources and the
call signals. Our operators covered positions across the vast face of
the waters extending from the Arctic Circle down to the Cape
Verde Islands.

For I.D.25 itself Ewing recruited naval officers, and as the work
grew heavier he was allocated Room 40 (which is still used as an office) in the Old Buildings of the Admiralty. At first the possession
of the codebook made solutions fairly easy, and Ewing himself took
the signals, in their bright red envelopes, to Fisher and Winston
Churchill in the war room.

It may be wondered, and Ewing did wonder, why the German

Navy did not suspect, even at this early stage, that their code was compromised. Ewing came to the conclusion that it was because of the English reputation for stupidity; Ewing, however, was a Scotsman.

But early success (in particular the forewarning which led to the Dogger Bank action) earned for Room 40 the fate of all departments that do well. It was taken over, in this case by the Director of Naval Intelligence, Captain Reginald Hall. Under his hypnotic blue gaze and furious energy the work was reorganized and redivided, and the modest fifty personnel, keeping two-man watches round the clock, were greatly increased. Hall foresaw the complications that were to come, and imperiously told the Treasury that he must have more money for more codebreakers. Why "Blinker" Hall made up his mind to recruit university dons for Room 40 is uncertain. Having gone to sea at the age of fourteen, he cannot have met many of them before. Dons are clever, but how did he know that they would be clever in the right way? International business would seem a more promising field, and there were in fact brilliant cryptographers in the department from the City. The French and the Germans re-cruited serving officers. But Hall wanted dons.

It was no easy matter to "sell" them to the Treasury and the Navy. Gilbert Waterhouse, W. H. Bruford and Leonard Willoughby were lecturers in German, and seemed admissible, but John Beazley was an expert on ancient sculpture and pottery; Frank Adcock, the Dean of King's, was a classical historian; Frank Birch, drafted back from active service, was also a historian; and Dilly came straight from the papyri. It was much to Hall's credit that he managed to turn this awkward squad, who muddled up six bells and six o'clock and failed to salute admirals in the street, into a more or less naval department. Once in, however, they settled down well enough. Senior Common Rooms had prepared them for this much stranger room, cut off from the ordinary world. And for accuracy, discretion and secrecy they could be absolutely relied on.

You reached I.D.25 through two arches in the Old Buildings. The basement acted as a kind of telegraph office. Intercepted messages coming in by land-line were printed out and sent up by pneumatic tube in shuttles of the kind that can still be seen in some old-fashioned shops. In the enormous Room 40 itself, the shuttles rattled into wire baskets at the rate of two thousand a day, with a sound like a Maxim gun. "Tubists" sorted them into their time-groups and put aside those beginning SD (*sehr dringend,* very urgent). The signals were still in the familiar code, but this was super-enciphered by rearranging the letters in vertical columns under a keyword. The key, which in 1914 had been changed once every three months, now changed every twenty-four hours. At midnight the watch on duty set to work frantically to find the new key. It was alleged that if they solved it they fell asleep again immediately; if not, they hung their heads in shame as the new watch came on.

But Room 40 was only the central cell of the hive-like organization. It was surrounded by rooms which were all marked "NO AD-MITTANCE. RING BELL"; but there were no bells. In the rooms were specialized units: directional, diplomatic (Desmond MacCarthy worked in this), Baltic Traffic (set up by Frank Birch), the Card Index, on which every signal was registered, and so forth. There was also an administrative staff, though much smaller than in most de-partments, but no tea ladies, and no cleaners. Room 40 was never dusted until the war was won.

Dilly, once his capabilities were established, was asked to work on problems very much more difficult than the day-to-day decipher-ment of Room 40. He was assigned Room 53, at the end of a dark cul-de-sac, and described by Frank Birch as "no bigger than a bathing-machine". The table in the middle was so large that you could only just squeeze between it and the wall, and Dilly himself conspicuously failed to look naval; long thin wrists stretched out from the cuffs of a uniform that hung on him like a sack. His work was presented, as it had been in his Eton days, in inky scribbles on sheets of dirty paper, frequently mislaid. It was supposed that he kept his spectacles in his tobacco pouch to remind himself that he had taken the tobacco out of the spectacle case, substituting a piece of stale bread to remind himself that he was always hungry. Room 53,

however, had one great distinction, the only bath in I.D.25, in constant use by the night watch. Dilly himself, working on amid soap
and steam, could not have done without it. Hot water speeded up
his perception of analogies. He had solved many *cruces* in the text
of Herodas in his bath.

He was looking for "ways in" or "cribs", the essential clues to an
unknown cipher. Even a few phrases in clear might provide these.
In the 1914–18 war, the cryptographer looked for groups represent-
ing place names, which were likely to recur, and repeated messages,
which he could assume were preceded by the words *besser geben* or
bitte wiederholen (send more clearly, please repeat). Sometimes, too,
the signal might be sent on by an outlying German station in a simpler code, or one that he knew already. The idiosyncrasies of radio
operators came to be recognized like those of old friends, or like
the copyists of the papyri. Any of these indications, however, could
be confused by meaningless *blinde signale* or nulls, of which the
Germans grew increasingly fond as time went on. Above all there
was a certain art, a certain flair with which Dilly was born, for the
shadow patterns of groups of letters, no matter in what language,
revealing themselves, like a secret dance, only to the patient
watcher.

I.D.25 had its *splendeurs et misères*. In 1917 it almost faced disaster. In the early days of the war, Jellicoe had been accustomed to
walk in and ask with confidence, "Can I count on a quiet night, gentlemen?" But in February 1917, through a misunderstanding rather
than an error, he was given a misdirection which led, he considered,
to the disappointing outcome of the Battle of Jutland. A number of
people at the Admiralty were not displeased. They had always distrusted Intelligence anyway. When, shortly afterwards, the Germans
introduced a new codebook, Admiral Sir Thomas Jackson exclaimed, "Thank God I shan't have any more of that damned stuff!"
Room 40 began to suspect that many of their deciphered signals
were being filed unread, and were deeply resentful. Hall shrewdly
chose this moment to reorganize the department once again, this
time under a delightful, breezy and efficient sailor, William James,

who did not pretend to understand cryptography—"around me were
a number of civilians and R.N.V.R. officers, all talking a strange language and doing strange things," he wrote—but who gave everyone
new courage. "It was an astonishing sight," he added, after a tour of
the cramped rooms and their scholarly inhabitants. And these were
serving with the Navy!

After Frank Birch had joined the department he shared a house,
No. 14 Edith Grove, in Chelsea, with Dilly and another friend.
Birch gave musical parties every week, inviting Madame Suggia, the
great cellist, who lived nearby. Dilly chose these occasions to work
all night at Room 40, so that the guests were spared his observations
on music; Birch had probably counted on this. Dilly used to have
breakfast at the Ship, a public house in Whitehall, before "dodder-
ing", "wandering" or "prancing" (all Frank Birch's words) home to
Chelsea.

He had not forgotten his family. In the summer of 1916, knowing
that Ronnie had left Shrewsbury and was at a wretchedly loose end,
he suggested that he might just as well come and work in the department. To Dilly, all the long-drawn-out suffering over his
youngest brother was a matter of unrealities; we pray, no one an-
swers, the Churches dispute to the death over how to go on speaking to someone who is not there. But he gladly made room for
Ronnie between the end of the table and the bath, and so another
unlikely figure, "in clerical garb", as Admiral James put it, joined
the already unlikely Room 40.

Ronnie mentioned once, quite mildly, that Dilly had never explained to him exactly what he was meant to be doing. In any event,
a transfer was soon arranged for him to a small branch of the War
Office which specialized in reading the newspapers of neutral countries. It was M.I.D.7—"not 70," Ronnie wrote to Mrs K., "the poor
tax-payer isn't expected to support 70 military intelligence departments"—and the pay was six pounds a week. Among the quota of
old men and bored disabled officers, the "captain person", as Ronnie
called him, could hardly believe his luck in getting such an intelligent clerk, still more so when, in the autumn of 1916, Wilfred began

to come in on half-time duty. Wilfred's motives for doing this were mixed. He, too, had lost many friends in Gallipoli and Flanders, and he wanted to be nearer to his brother before he lost him also. Distressed at the failure of the Anglo-Catholic movement to protest at the continuance of the war, he wanted to work harder himself. He had resolved to take no holidays at all until a peace was signed. He and Ronnie toiled away on different floors of the building. There was a Zeppelin scare, "and Wilfred didn't see anything," Ronnie wrote, "but then, he didn't bother to go to the window and look out."

All through 1917 his father wrote to Ronnie with increasing urgency, as if by words he could be held back from the brink of a gulf. He begged him, if he could get leave, to come up to Manchester. "I'm afraid you must look forward to seeing me with some pain, considering the direction my mind is now set in," Ronnie answered, "but you will believe, Paw, that if I could help it—well, there isn't any need to finish the sentence." Winnie, for once, was powerless to help. Deep in the anxious business of rearing babies and of not giving offence to the genteel society of Edinburgh, she could not join them; they must fight it out for themselves. The Bishop, in letters that are pathetic in the truest sense, tried to enter into further controversy with this favourite son, so evidently favoured by God and man.

> I could have wept almost at the thought of what might have been [he wrote, and again, reaching the central point in his argument], it is quite true that if there is a God He must have revealed Himself, but is there any reason to suppose that it is necessary that His revelations of Himself are such that there must be one and only one true interpretation of them all? . . .
>
> I am amazed at my own boldness in entering into the lists in which you are a far more skilled and practised contestant. I remember so well the kind of pity with which I used to regard my dear Mother's, and even my Father's arguments with me. The fact that I now see I was often in the wrong in spite of my Greats, &c. is not likely to make much impression on you. But what can I do? . . . I can

but make my poor attempt—which for its very length will bore you long before you have read it, if ever you do read it. At least say to yourself—Well, Father must love me or he would not worry so much about me. If I return to the fray you will have to forgive me—Ever your loving father, E. A. Manchester.

It was from their father, as well as their mother, that the Knoxes inherited their tender hearts.

In reply Ronnie tried to explain his need for an absolute spiritual authority, comparing the Church of Rome to a shop window in which there was no need to examine the goods, because over the door was a sign THIS IS THE TRUE DEPOT ORDAINED BY CHRIST HIM- SELF. "I should not have used the metaphor," the Bishop answered, yet he strove to understand. Among the heavy extra duties of wartime, he felt bowed down. Not for many weeks did he add to his reasoned arguments a direct personal appeal. He was suffering; Ronnie pleaded in return to be allowed "to follow what I feel is God's will, wherever it leads me, quietly and without fuss." Whatever happened, he promised never to preach in the Manchester diocese while his father was still there.

Ronnie not unnaturally believed that, in the third year of the war, his "going over" would be of interest only to his family. "I've twice been asked 'How's Ronnie?' by people who mistook me for Wilfred." He resigned from Trinity, and, at the suggestion of the Abbot, went in September to make a retreat at Farnborough. The weight of indecision—which, as he knew, can become a habit—fell from him. "I came to my conclusion yesterday," he told Winnie, "you'll realise what it is." On 22 September he was received into the Catholic Church.

He did not feel any special illumination, but he was so happy that he wanted to laugh out loud all through dinner in the refectory. He had found authority. "Ultimately the Catholic Church challenges one with the question: 'Look in my eyes. Can you trust me?' And the rest is all quibbling."

Ronnie was mistaken in thinking that his conversion would go unnoticed. The press commented freely; the *Westminster Gazette* called him an utter reactionary, who perhaps wished to restore the Stuarts, the *Guardian* said that Rome "had landed the biggest fish since Newman"—another metaphor which the Bishop would not have used. To his friends it was, as Harold Macmillan put it, "a parting of the ways." From his family there were no reproaches—certainly none from Wilfred, although he was told that his brother's conversion had lost him his own chance of the chaplaincy at Merton.

> Of course it won't make any difference; why should it? After all our views are far closer than they were when we were at Oxford, when I never believed in anything, and it never made any difference there . . . I can't say how sorry I am, but it certainly won't make any difference as far as I'm concerned.
>
> I doubt if there was any real point now in your waiting till after the war . . . unless there was any chance of your finding out after all that you were sorry you'd been received, it's so much better for you to recover your effectiveness as soon as you can, to say nothing of your happiness. If I ever felt anything else, it can only have been part of the selfishness for which I am so justly famous.

But it did make a difference. The love remained, but so did the lifelong disappointment and regret. For the Bishop the fires had died down, and he could send only his resignation to the will of God, and a little news from home.

> The rest are all well. Mother is out digging in the garden, after having done the work of 10 women from morn to sunset. The other day she dug by moonlight. With overflowing love, dearest boy, and ever your most loving father, E. A. Manchester.

Surely one would think it must have been as clear then as it is now that if human love could rise above the doctrines that divide the Church, then these doctrines must have singularly little to do with the love of God. But in 1917 it still appeared to them all that Ronnie was "lost", and that whatever merciful words were said he was divided from his family by an invisible door of iron.

Guy Lawrence was not given to overstatement, but the news

brought him intense relief. "Ron, dear, I *am* glad you're back with me again. It makes a lot of difference to me." Guy had recovered, and was with a Training Reserve Battalion—the 102nd, so great had the wastage and the replacements become. Ronnie, he said, must "be quick and become a priest". On his return from France, when the war was over, he hoped to become a postulant at the Oratory. The family understood that in the event Ronnie also would become an Oratorian.

The glimpse, in the Bishop's letter, of Mrs K. digging the vegetable garden by moonlight gives the feeling of the darkest and hungriest of the war years. Britain very nearly starved in 1917. In the spring of that year three hundred U-boats ranged the deep seas, and one in four of our merchant ships failed to return to port. American shipping losses were also high. The two great necessities were to find a way to protect the convoys, and a way to bring the United States into the war. Room 40 made a significant contribution to both, by breaking two codes.

Breaking a code is more difficult than breaking a cipher, or at least any cipher that was in use in the First World War. A high-grade codebook transposes every word, and sometimes every syllable, into a random group of figures or letters. The codebook is in two parts, one alphabetically arranged for encoding, one numerically for reading back:

032	ab	000	England
461	Amerika	001	heute
168	an	002	angriff
211	auf	003	zurück

To get even higher security, any words which are likely to recur frequently may be encoded in, say, five or six different ways, so that *heute* (today) may appear as 001, 563, 287 and so forth. Groups of letters are sometimes used instead of numbers. To relate the two lists, many hundreds of thousands of words long, is exceedingly difficult without an effective "way in". Stops, if they can be identified, will help if the language is German, because they are likely to have a verb, with its characteristic ending, in front of them. The code-breaker writes any probable solutions into his list in pencil; it makes the long columns of blanks look somewhat more human. Ink is for certainties. But even with great skill and patience, and an adequate amount of material to work on, his task may take years. He prays for a miracle.

In February 1917 the diplomatic section of Room 40 produced the solution to the Zimmermann telegram. This was a signal from the German Foreign Minister, offering the Mexican government active support in their claims to Arizona and Texas as a price for coming into the war and launching an attack on the United States. The exposure of these German proposals was crucial, and it was said that nothing else would have reconciled Texas and the Middle West to a European war. The "way in" for the codebreakers, in this case, was the lucky purchase, or theft, by a British agent in Mexico City, of a copy of a second telegram from the post office. This Western Union telegram repeated the first one in a simpler code which had been in use since 1907, and which Room 40 could read without difficulty.

For the Zimmermann solution Dilly felt professional admiration, but also some professional jealousy. "Can't we buy something from the post office?" became his plaintive murmur in all kinds of situations, even quite inappropriate ones, as for instance when things were left behind at a picnic. He had no such good fortune, in 1917, with his own assignment. He had been detailed to work exclusively on the special flag-code, that is, the code used by the German Commander-in-Chief. All the energies of the German admirals, with their High Sea Fleet still confined to port, were concentrated on unrestricted submarine warfare. Breaking the flag-code would mean intercepting the operational orders of the U-boat campaign at the highest possible level, and discovering at the earliest stage what information the enemy had about our sailings. The U-boats, which could not communicate at all in deep water, chatted to each other freely in low-grade cipher when they surfaced, but this was a routine matter for Room 40. The flag-code was quite unknown and did not correspond with any system the Room had met. The only certainty was that it consisted of three-letter groups, some corresponding to words and names, and some to syllables.

James remembered, as one of the "astonishing sights" of his department, the little room where Dilly sat "labouring" over the apparently insoluble. But "nothing is impossible". No worksheets, of course, were ever kept, and of the steps he took towards the solution there is a record of only one, but it is very characteristic both of Room 40 and of himself.

One afternoon Dilly (who by now ignored the correct watches and was living in the office) sorted through a heap of signals which had just come up the tube. They were a practice session by a German naval radio operator, sending in the flag-code. Some of the three-letter groups he was pretty sure he could recognize. They were the equivalents of en, the commonest bigram in the German language. But even so, it struck him that there was an unusually high proportion of *ens* for a short message:

```
--  --  --  --  en  --  --  en  --  --  en
--  --  --  --  en  --  --  --  --  --  en
```

As Dilly looked at the lines, they took on the appearance of poetry, or at least of metre, since metre, as he strangely declared, is "the raw material of poetry". What metre? He suspected dactyls, and if both lines ended in *en*, there was probably also a rhyme. The kind of radio operator who would choose a lyric for his practice signals must be sentimental, a sentimental German, and the poetry might be romantic. Could one of the *en* words be *Rosen*? The German experts, who were also professors of literature, were housed in a drafty room along the passage; they identified the poem, and the roses, almost at once; they were two lines of Schiller's:

> *Ehret die Frauen; sie flechten und weben*
> *Himmliche Rosen im erdliche Leben.*

> [Give reverence to women; they plait and weave
> Heavenly roses in this earthly life.]

This gave Dilly nine or ten new groups, including the useful *leb-* and *erd-*, and even such tiny beginnings can constitute a "way in". The rest was hard work, perhaps inspiration in the bath, and the help of his three clerical staff; there were now four people in the tiny room, referred to as "one for each letter and one for the pot". The three-letter flag-code was broken in the summer of 1917, and so many convoys were saved that in October James was made a captain.

Room 40 had recovered totally from its disgrace after Jutland. "Blinker" Hall, who had piloted the department through with such success, had great ambitions for it, particularly on the diplomatic side. As a result, there was another expansion (the staff numbered a hundred by the end of the war), and this had far-reaching effects on the life of Dilly. More stenographers were needed, their discretion must be absolute, and it was thought best to turn to ladies of county and service families. At the end of 1917 Dilly was allocated a new secretary. She was Miss Olive Roddam, the daughter of Lieutenant-Colonel Roddam, of the ancient and distinguished Northumberland family the Roddams of Roddam.

The first embarrassment was the bath. Miss Roddam worked office hours, not the naval watches, so that it was a matter of finishing one's bath and getting dressed correctly in uniform before she arrived. This was a serious alteration of routine. Then there was the problem of working at such close quarters with a young lady in a room as cramped as No. 53. Eddie had always said that in spite of Dilly's intellect, and in spite of, or because of, his uncertain contact with daily life, he would be quite powerless if he was thrown together for any length of time with a normal, pretty young woman. Eddie was right. *Himmliche Rosen im erdliche Leben!* Dilly did become powerless, and before many weeks had passed he fell in love with Miss Roddam.

At the end of February 1917 the 2/4th Lincolnshires were stationed at Havant, ready to go. Eddie had at least been spared the miserable Christmas of 1916 at Bishopscourt, when Ronnie and his father had scarcely been on speaking terms, and had been reduced to leaving notes for each other on the hall table. Christina came down from Lincoln to Havant to say good-bye. Afterwards Eddie wrote to her, in the words of hundreds of thousands of young officers, that it was a pity that she hadn't come to the station because they hadn't entrained until 1:53 after all, and they could have had another hour and a half together. The battalion was pretty well supplied with everything, including a pierrot troupe which had unfortunately tried to imitate Pelissier's Follies. "I'm afraid most of it is rather above the men's heads." He expected to go with the advance party, and she was the dearest wife a man ever had. When he got back, he would draw some more pictures for his four-year-old son.

The Lincolns were brigaded with the Leicesters to go out as the 177th Brigade in the 59th Division. In the first week of March they went up the line to positions south of the Amiens-Villers-Carbonnel road. Amiens was a staging post; the brigade was a routine draft, already almost unidentifiable in the mud, of another vast offensive which was to end the war, as before, in a few weeks. "The trenches are in very bad condition," reads the Regimental Diary. "It has been necessary to dig men out." The first casualties were from trench fever, and among them was Christina's elder brother Edwin. Bishop Hicks, who was at Lincoln, in the grip of his last illness, asked that nothing about "victory" should be put on the grave of his dead son.

Ludendorff had withdrawn to the prepared forts of the Hindenburg Line, and what was termed the Allied advance was, as the old sweats hastened to point out, nothing but a trudge forward over a few miles the Germans hadn't wanted. The Lincolns crossed the river Somme at Brie, and in April made their first set-piece attack on the Hindenburg Line "on a position reported to be evacuated, which turned out to be very much not so." There were heavy losses. "Teddie writes that he hopes they're going in the right direction; they all look the same," Mrs K. wrote to Winnie. His only request had been for candles, and if possible a few onions. The battalion settled down to trench warfare for the summer of 1917.

During the immobile three months, Eddie became expert at shooting rats with a revolver as they came over the top of the dugout, and he got to know the men very well. The Lincolnshires had a curious double reputation, on which they prided themselves. On the one hand, they were considered ludicrously rustic; they were said to clean their teeth with soot, and to be permanently sleepy from eating the poppies in the flower-growing districts. On the other hand, they were known as preternaturally "fly". Guy Lawrence had written back from Gallipoli that the Lincolns had delayed just long enough at the embarkation point to get the deck cabins. And they had no rivals in getting themselves dug in comfortably.

Eddie was a poet in the front line, yet he did not feel able to do what Owen Seaman had asked him, and contribute to *Punch* from the trenches. He knew that Seaman expected something light, and as he explained many years later: "I found that humour in the camp and at the front was so much more technical and so much less refined than it seemed to be in the papers, that I contributed nothing during most of those four years. But to their great credit the artists at home produced a continuous spectacle of surrendering Germans and happy good-humoured British riflemen."

The inhibiting factor was not resentment, but affection.

English humour is distinguished by cheerful endurance [he said]. I saw that in the trenches; I don't mean behaviour in action or under heavy fire, when, whatever you say about it, people are not amused, but ordinary behaviour under terrible conditions. I mean the men who sang doleful marching songs saying that they didn't want to fight and wished they could go home, which other nations would have sung if they were about to mutiny or run away, or songs about Tipperary, where they had never been and didn't want to go.

Why did we join the army, boys,
Why did we join the army?
Why did we come to France to fight—
We must have been bloody well barmy.

It did not seem to Eddie that the feeling of 1917 could be put better than that. But his failure to write anything was not intended as a criticism of Seaman's *Punch*, which came punctually up the line, once a week, with the mail.

In August his week's leave came up. He arrived in Lincoln to find that the Bishop had given up the Palace completely, turning it over to a Red Cross hospital, while he and Mrs Hicks, Christina and the babies were managing in the lodge. Rationing was very strict. What was margarine? *Punch* had given the answer to this: "I take thee, dearest margarine, for butter or for worse." Christina said that she did not trust it, and would prefer to bring up the children on dripping.

On the way back to the front, with a single evening to spend in London, he managed to assemble his three brothers for a dinner at Gatti's. It was the first time they had all been together since his marriage. Dilly, towering over them in the glasses and improbable uniform, was, at first, abstracted, Wilfred and Ronald miserable. Eddie relied on champagne—the price did not matter that evening—to work its magical effect, and for a few hours, among the flashing gilt and the long mirrors of Gatti's, they were back at St Philip's Rectory, accusing each other of every possible crime and incompetence. Then they were happy. The next day Eddie found the 59th Division preparing to move from the Somme to the Ypres sector, in time for the battle of Passchendaele.

The brigade was on the north side of the salient, ready to advance in yet another of the "waves", which, this time, were to break through to the U-boat bases on the coast. The weather was fine, which was as well, since all the ditching and drainage system in the area had been destroyed in the preliminary barrage. The ruined land sank under mud and water which had been carefully held back for centuries.

On 26 September the division were to attack from the Menin Road and push eastward to consolidate the old enemy positions. It was taken for granted that there would be no opposition. Indeed the official account was "successful advance with little resistance". But the reality failed to live up to the report. The Germans counter-attacked and shelled heavily, and the 2/4th Lincolns held on, for two days, with great difficulty. On the first day, a sniper, left behind in a farmhouse to pick off the British officers, shot Eddie through the back. The bullet lodged somewhere in the left shoulder, and ended his usefulness in the Third Battle of Ypres.

Bishop Knox had determined not to communicate with Ronnie again for at least a year, but when the news came that Eddie was a casualty, he sent it on at once to all the family. Eddie had first been reported missing, then been picked up out of a pool of blood in a shell-hole and shipped back to England. "You will be glad to be out of the fray for a while," Aunt Fanny wrote from Edmundthorpe.

In a series of hospitals, he experienced a black nostalgia for his own men, still bogged down at Passchendaele, and the usual longing to get back to the only place where the disillusionment and loyalty of war could be understood. "This time last year the frost broke in the trenches," he entered in his notebook:

> I knew what fear was and I lived with fear
>> Now there are only comfortable things,
> Oh, God, to be again where I was then
>> This time last year.

The hospitals, in fact, scarcely qualified as comfortable things, and, as a patient, his satirical spirit returned. His shoulder had to be re-broken twice. In the morning there were remedial exercises, and in the afternoon he was supposed to take a walk with his left arm in a splint, "a cross between a strait waistcoat and a portion of the dentist's chair where the glass of hot water ought to be." The streets were full of soldiers and once he had to salute two hundred and fifty times on one walk. Why not, he asked the doctors, let him salute with the left arm to give it exercise, and put the right arm in a sling "to gain sympathy"? His superiors called a special committee to decide whether a wounded officer might be permitted to salute with his left hand, but they decided against it.

Ronnie's hours at M.I.D. ended at three-thirty; he was living with friends in Kensington, and he went home every afternoon to write the history of his conversion, *A Spiritual Aeneid*. As soon as possible, he took the first steps towards his new priesthood. Once again, in his brothers' view, he was somewhat indulged. He did not have to go to a seminary, and in the words of Father Corbishley, S.J. (in *Ronald Knox the Priest*), "few outside the ranks of the clergy will appreciate the remarkable liberality of such an arrangement." Cardinal Bourne recommended him to live at the Oratory, "as a mixture of paying guest and theological student," he told Winnie. He had his own quiet room, overlooking the carriages and treetops of the Brompton Road, where he could study and put his thoughts in order, and wait, under God, for the return of Guy Lawrence.

The end of the war brought the changed light of day into the seclusion of Room 40. The U-boats were handed over at Harwich, the German fleet surrendered at Schillig Reede and the professors of German literature went as interpreters. The Foreign Office was negotiating with the Admiralty to take over the whole department. To many, looking back on it, the strange world of decipherment seemed like a dream. During the past four years they had read over fifteen thousand enemy signals; all waste paper now. The dark linen curtains which had been fixed across the windows during the Zeppelin raids were taken down at last. A ball was given at the Savoy; some of the ladies of Room 40 had their hair cut, and some "shingled"; Miss Roddam was shingled; Dilly, like some great wading bird, attempted the fox-trot. That morning, all of them had received a form to fill up, stating whether they wished to stay in Intelligence after the conclusion of hostilities. Dilly had no two thoughts about it. He was eager to get back to King's, and the still unfinished Herodas. He was also beginning to wonder in his turn whether, on what he could earn, it would be possible to propose marriage.

On Armistice Day itself everyone working in Whitehall turned out into the street. The crowds were at first quite silent, then a subaltern going by on an open-topped bus gave a solitary cheer, and suddenly there was a riot of noise from Westminster to Trafalgar Square. Then people went off to get drunk.

The "last push", which the young officer on the bus had survived, took only three months from the first breakthrough, but the losses during those three months were surely the hardest of all to bear. On 28 August, during the final advance near Arras, and only a little way short of the Hindenburg Line, Guy Lawrence was killed. He was twenty-five.

Ronnie wrote to an old friend, Francis Urquhart of Balliol:

> There was a time when I used to dread your handwriting, because it might mean fresh bad news. Well, you've got to have it from me this time, if you haven't heard already—yes, the very worst news . . . This is only just to tell you. I'm too numbed still to think, far less to write about it.

The numbness lasted long enough for him to feel, after it wore off, that he had a scar, rather than a wound—that is, a profound sense of what he had lost, rather than the loss itself. But what had been the total effect on the Western world of so many million mourners of so many million dead? "What kind of state of mind are we in?" he wrote to Winnie, after a friend of his, a Magdalen don, had just shot himself dead in his rooms; "What has the war done to us?" Certainly this brilliant and indulged youngest brother, who was now thirty years old, could never again be thought of as spoiled. "One has to grow up some time," he wrote, at the end of his *Spiritual Aeneid.*

In his letter to Urquhart, Ronnie did not even mention Guy's name; he could not bring himself to do so for another two weeks. He had not even heard the news directly, because he had given up reading the casualty lists, and had never been in touch with Guy's family in Worcestershire. A handful of faded letters are the only record, after half a century, of his dark hour, and they show nothing except how he brought himself to bear it.

Faith maintained him—not a greater faith than Wilfred's when he had to face the separation from Ronnie, or the Bishop of Lincoln's when his son died in the trenches, or Christina's when she got a telegram to say that Eddie was missing—not greater, but the same. Meanwhile there remained for Ronnie only one certainty in his waste land, the knowledge that he was called to be a priest.

He was ordained at St Edmund's Old Hall on 5 October 1919, taking the anti-modernist oath "against all Liberal interpretations whether of scripture or history". Looking back on the scene, he felt that "it was something of a disappointment that the Vicar-General was not there to witness the fervour I put into it. He had gone out to tea." On this ordinary enough occasion, Ronnie had taken a step, and received a privilege, greater than he could hope to describe. He had been warned at Farnborough that "one does not become a Catholic in order to be happy"; still less does a man become a priest to forget suffering. But "if happiness means to be fighting under colours of whose ultimate success you are assured, whose temporary reverses provide, nevertheless, the authentic thrill of battle; if, in a word, happiness is to be where you are meant to be—why, yes, I am happy."

"Well, they have him now, and they will make no sparing use of him," Bishop Knox wrote gloomily to Winnie. Rome had taken from him his dearest pledge. In the closing chapters of his memoirs, he tried to sum up the loss and gain.

> I have not succeeded, as my father succeeded, in bringing my children up entirely in their father's faith, and for this I take no small share of the blame, so far as it is blame, to myself . . .
>
> When Ronald was quite a small boy at school one of his masters challenged the class with the words: '*Ἡμεῖς μὲν πατέρων*—can any of you finish that line?' Ronald instantly replied: '—*μέγ' ἀμείνονες εὐχόμεθ' εἶναι*—It is our boast that we are far ahead of our parents.'
>
> These words seem to me to embody, at once, the effects of a Public School education, the spirit and temper of the age in which my children grew up, and the exceptional vivacity of their character. They were determined to be better than their parents had been, and to do better than their parents had done, and to live in the spirit of the restless first decades of the twentieth century. Who shall say that this ambition was in itself wrong or unnatural? That it led some of them

in directions often very costly to those whom they loved and who loved them, cannot be denied, and here I find the saddest of the experiences and remembrances of my life, records of the most humiliating of my failures. Against these I set the treasure of the full and over-flowing measure of my children's love, surpassing all that I deserve.

Eddie was not demobilized until April 1919. Even that was relatively early, since the date of demobilization depended on the length of war service and the number of wounds. He was signed off with his gratuity at the Crystal Palace, the last military command which he received being "Mind the step". Meanwhile he had acquired the lease, or so he thought, of another little Hampstead house, this time in East Heath Road; but it turned out to be mysteriously inhabited by John Middleton Murry and Katherine Mansfield, whose comment was: "Portland Villas! It sounds like one of those houses where a few guests are taken, mental not objected to." Meanwhile, Eddie and Christina, with the two infants, were homeless in an over-crowded London. It might, he thought, be easier to live, with their few possessions, in a furniture van, with horses and auxiliary steam, and pull up outside any likely property until it fell vacant.

He had begun to contribute again to *Punch* in 1918, but a regular job was absolutely necessary. It was simply to support his family that he worked for eighteen months at the Ministry of Labour, where, he said:

We were supposed to be discovering appointments for ex-officers, but were chiefly, I think, trying to find appointments for ourselves . . . The first duty of a civil servant, I gathered, was to decide at what date he would take his holidays, the second to decide at what time he would have his tea . . . I also, rather hastily, asked for a doughnut at teatime, but soon got tired of them. But at the same time I felt, perhaps owing to my army training, an overwhelming inability to alter any regulation once made, and I think the man who was employed to bring them felt the same. So I put the doughnuts in a drawer. When I left the Ministry, I had a whole drawerful of doughnuts, and I have often wondered what the officer who succeeded me did with them.

What were the other possibilities? Little else was discussed by his old Army friends. One of them, who had bought a small grocery in Nottingham, wrote:

> You had better start something like this, it pays and is alright when one gets over the shop part, but I am lucky in that I supply all the 'knuts' of the city, and know most of them as an ex-officer. I must say it strikes me as Comic sometimes, when I am at one of their Houses and suddenly think that I gave my hostess a pound of Marg at 1s 2d in the morning wrapped up in a paper bag.

Eddie, he said, would be most welcome as a partner if he would care to become a "Practical Dairy Farmer". But the prospect seemed daunting, though less so than the Civil Service. Eddie was now in and out of the *Punch* offices, helping with unimportant routine jobs, and hoping, in time, for an assistant editorship. In a reckless moment, he handed in his notice to the Ministry. Meanwhile the family could not continue in lodgings. Christina thought they might try living in the country.

VI

1919–1929

The Twenties

AT THE END OF THE GREAT WAR, Eddie was thirty-seven, Dilly thirty-five, Wilfred thirty-two and Ronnie thirty. The new decade, the 1920s, accepted them as a natural phenomenon. In 1922, in the Michaelmas term, the Cambridge Union organized a debate, at which all four brothers were to speak. The motion proposed was "That This House Believes That the Whole World Over, There's No Place Like Home." Eddie and Wilfred were to speak in favour, Dilly and Ronnie against. "Ronnie was usually the best speaker," Winnie considered. "Dillwyn was hesitant, Wilfred was more appealing than Ronnie, who laid down the law too much, Eddie was an awful speaker, so brilliant, but hated it and was too nervous to be heard." But the upshot of the debate will never be known. On the appointed afternoon a thick yellow fog descended over London and made it impossible for any of them to get to the station.

After the Great War, the money left by the Bishop's first wife (Ellen French) was divided between the children; it was apparently a provision of the will that the youngest child should have turned thirty. The history of this legacy was as follows. Wealthy old Mr

Ronnie and his mother

Bishop Knox

Two of the Knox boys, Wilfred and Ronnie

Eddie and Christina

Dilly,
by Gilbert Spencer, R.A.

Dilly

Wilfred on his motor-bike with his fishing tackle

Clockwise from left:
Eddie ("Evoe")
The niece
Ronnie with the Waugh family

Jansen, Ellen's grandfather, had adopted two nieces and had two daughters of his own; to each of them he left £160,000. In the French family (Bishop French, of course, did not touch a penny of it) it was divided between eight children, and after that between six Knoxes, who received about £3,000 each, mostly in railway shares— "an excellent example," Winnie said, "of how to get rid of inherited money without spending it."

Bishop Knox retired in 1921, handing over his see to William Temple. The diocese, in gratitude for his many years of devoted work, had already presented him with a majestic Daimler "whose machinery seldom failed to work," and with his portrait, to be painted by the Academician of his choice. In any artistic matters the Bishop was quite at a loss; he tramped wearily round the Academy until rescued by one of Mrs K.'s sisters; she chose the artist A. T. Nowell, who produced a delightful portrait, in which the Bishop is apparently about to rise from his seat and knock somebody down with a Bible. Finally the diocese subscribed to buy him a house for his retirement, and Mrs K. supervised their last move, to 18 Beckenham Grove, Shortlands, in Kent.

The house needed repair, but very soon acquired the true deep leathery fragrance of a Victorian rectory. Huge roses and cabbages appeared in the garden; all the strange heavy old implements were back in the kitchen, things for ironing clerical collars, opening oysters, sharpening steel knives; Alice and Richmond, whose ages nobody liked to ask any more, still presided there, grumbling tenaciously; Ethel was installed in her room with her typewriter and her work for the Christian Missionary Society, all the letters she had ever received, all the old toys, all the old books; when the four sons came to visit, they became, as soon as they passed through the stained-glass front door, the "dear boys" once again. Indeed, the two priests, Wilfred and Ronald, became Iffie and Whooks.

It must not be thought, by the way, that Ethel, who had now become Aunt Ethel to three nephews and a niece, was at all discontented with her lot. Her Victorianism was not of the kind that appeared in twentieth-century novels. She did not like the outside world, and was proud to stay at home. Her bits of jewellery were put away for "the Miss Knox of the next generation". When her niece married, she put them away with a sigh, because now there would be no Miss Knox.

The Bishop settled down immediately to write a further refutation of the Tractarians, and to prepare the opposition to the threatened changes in the Prayer Book. "It is an anxious time," he told Winnie, "the Press are concentrating on the wrong points. I even wrote a letter to the *Scotsman* to try to head them off, but it was not printed—perhaps they did not recognise E. A. Knox, Bishop, any more than Dobie & Co [the grocers], who send in my accounts addressed to K. Bishop Esq." But, even in retirement, he was formidable. "Peg away," he wrote, putting all his scholarship at the disposal of the Parliamentary opposition. In 1928, when the Commons rejected the Prayer Book, he was warmly congratulated: "The generalship of the octogenarian has resulted in a great victory. To you, more than to any man, this decision is due."

In appearance, the Bishop had grown increasingly stout, and his wheezing presence in the study was perhaps more alarming than he knew. Mrs K., however, now silver-haired, was as elegant as ever. Still exceedingly busy, and always with Ethel to care for, she never seemed in the least hurry. At teatime she presided with a small kettle boiling over a spirit lamp, so that a little hot water could be poured to warm each cup before the tea was put in. At her elbow there was a "curate's friend", that is, a bamboo framework holding four plates so that the curate need not go round the drawing room offering each cake separately; on a table there was always a book of French poetry or memoirs, with an ivory knife to cut the pages.

At the end of the 1920s Mrs K. was persuaded to write an article for the *Daily Chronicle* in a series entitled "Mothering Famous Men". In this she recalled the Birmingham schoolroom days, but at once a discrepancy appeared; while Eddie, as Evoe, and Ronnie had become more and more well known, Dilly and Wilfred were less and less so, particularly Dilly, behind the closed doors of Room 40. The features editor printed pictures only of Mrs K. herself and of Ronnie ("a most accommodating friendly child") and Eddie ("a sensitive nature behind a coating of reserve"), both guileless in their Eton collars. Dilly had to be described simply as "a classical scholar", and Wilfred as "an Anglo-Catholic priest".

Wilfred had been expected to "go over" when Ronnie went, but there was never any question of his doing so. In 1917 his vicar at Graham Street, who was also his confessor, J. C. Howell, died after an operation; then in the following autumn, after the loss of so many friends on the Western front, came the spiritual loss of Ronnie. Wilfred, always independent, had been driven into himself. As soon as the war was over, he staked all his hopes for his Church on one pamphlet, printed in 1918 by the Society of St Peter and St Paul: *At a Great Price Obtained I This Freedom.*

They were the words of the garrison commander in Jerusalem to St Paul, who had claimed consideration as a Roman citizen. Paul's reply was, "But I was free born." How could the Church earn the right to be called free-born again? And what had gone wrong with the Church of England anyway? Wilfred's answer was painfully direct. "The poor object to the church, because it is rich. There is a general feeling that the church is a church of the rich, governed by the rich for the rich. The feeling is largely inarticulate, but it is widely and deeply felt." All Anglo-Catholics should lead the way by demanding an absolute separation of Church and State, and they should be prepared to pay the price, that is, to give up all the money and patronage derived from the State. Priests must live on what they earn. A hundred a year would, he thought, be a fair living wage for a priest. A priest shouldn't want a living wage, which meant "bringing up a family in the style customary among the upper middle classes. I cannot find among Our Lord's charges to his disciples that they should live in the style customary to the upper middle classes." Bishops, perhaps, might have five hundred pounds a year. "Their palaces could go, or be used as diocesan seminaries, a far better use than the present one." Church buildings, or some of them, could stay, because they would be genuinely needed if the clergy were poor and gave up all idea of social status, "an absolutely unmixed advantage, since it will teach England to respect a priest as the representative of God, not as a gentleman from Oxford. Then we can follow the carpenter of Nazareth, and rid ourselves of the unholy alliance of the Church with middle-class respectability that has led to the deadness of English religion."

If Wilfred could have had Ronnie still standing by him, what might they not have done? As things turned out, the question of corporate reunion with Rome was obsessive, and occupied nearly all the time of the successive Anglo-Catholic conferences. Although Wilfred himself became a leading Anglo-Catholic apologist and historian, he was intensely disappointed by the failure to respond to *At a Great Price*. He had written it with the urgency, not of inexperience, but of something that had been long held back and desperately needed saying. Christ was concerned with the condition of human beings as He found them on this earth, and took every kind of risk to show this. Couldn't the Church of England take the one risky step, the first one, of ceasing to be respectable? Whatever support Wilfred expected, it did not come.

But his loneliness found its own relief. Ronald was at heart family-loving and domestic, Wilfred community-loving and sociable. In 1920 he was introduced to a community, the only one, perhaps, in which he could ever have felt truly at home. It had the odd distinction that the same thing could be said of nearly all its members.

The Oratory of the Good Shepherd was not, and is not, in fact a community at all, nor is it a guild, nor an order, nor could it have been in origin anything but English. The vagueness of its definition, and the absolute certainty of its members as to what they are, makes it one of the many unseen and unknown currents that quietly deepen the life surrounding it.

It is a religious brotherhood of unmarried priests and laymen which gives its members the help (not the compulsion) of a close fellowship and a common rule. This help extends to both daily work and the spiritual life, or, perhaps, makes them the same thing. There is a Superior and a Chapter General which meets every year, but some members live in communities, some are scattered from end to end of the world. For these, meetings are rare, and letters must keep them in touch. At the fixed hours of prayer, wherever they may be, they know and feel themselves together. For prayer, stillness is necessary, and this is difficult, because busy activity seems more rewarding. Stillness, however, does not mean inactivity, but peace.

The Oratory "grew", or "originated", like any natural form of life, in Cambridge just before the Great War, but it was very characteristic that two of the founding members, Father Waggett and H. L. Pass, a layman from St John's, were such individualists that they could not get on and worked from houses at opposite ends of the town. After the war, when the O.G.S. expanded, they expressed their ideal somewhat more formally. They recognized that they were in a world "hostile to Christianity and sick of old watchwords," which had nevertheless shown the apparently boundless extent of human courage and self-sacrifice, even when all confidence in the Higher Command had gone. Sacrifice, in the name of Christ, has remained the keynote of the Oratory, whose duty is unselfish action, loyalty and love. "They shall be absolutely forbidden to speak ill of other bodies of Christians." There were to be none of the "quick or harsh judgements that harden differences" on anything or anybody, and this charity would be hard to put into practice, because other people are not only infuriating, but boring. The O.G.S. faced this from the beginning. "It is fortunate for us that loving and liking are not the same thing. We are not called upon to like our neighbour, but to love him." This comment, by one of the Superiors, George Tibbatts, shows how practical unworldliness can be.

Self-sacrifice is a matter of organized will. If possible, those living in a group should share their earnings. Certainly, every member is called upon to make sure, at the end of every month, that he has spent as little as possible on himself, and, furthermore, that he is not pleased with himself for having done so. Each Brother may ask for six weeks a year free board and lodging with any other. Before any decision, from accepting a new appointment to buying a new typewriter, one should (but does not have to) consult the other members as to the right course to take; one should (but does not have to) accept their advice. The Oratory gives up, in a sense, less than the other orders, but each individual has the entire responsibility of self-discipline, "and being quite unknown we have not the judgement of the world outside to control us." But they have the great comfort of belonging to an understanding community.

A distinctive duty of the O.G.S. is the "labour of the mind", a special duty of thought and study, to meet the questions of the twentieth century. Every Brother has his own private rule of writing and reading and of not sinking back into a doze or "glancing" at the newspapers. The "labour" takes many different forms; Eric Milner-White, for instance, one of the earliest members, was a fine musician who arranged for King's College Chapel the much-loved Festival of Nine Carols and Lessons. But each member must be sure that no question put to him by an unbeliever is too difficult for him to try to answer it, and he must do this, too, without "embarrassing holiness".

In scholarship, the Oratory is to avoid jealousy of those who are quicker, impatience with those who are slower; in doctrine, to remember that intolerance usually turns out to be the worship of ourselves; in worship, to avoid above all things "the impression of the Conservative Party at prayer." The recognizable note of the Oratory is joy, not to be confused with heartiness. Joy is simply evidence of the love of God. "And after all, what else is there in the world that matters? To love and be loved—it is all contained in this."

The membership of the O.G.S., always small, is growing yearly and has spread to Africa, India, Australasia and the United States; its centre is no longer a University; like Keynesian economics, like the assumptions of Bloomsbury, like the atomic research programme, it radiated outward from Cambridge, and left it behind. Those who wish to become members have a probationary period of from one to three years; as always, they are free to leave whenever they like. It is a community that is rarely talked about, and never talks about itself.

It would be absurd to suggest that there were no difficulties at the Oratory, or that it completely reproduced the spirit of the household of Little Gidding, which had partly inspired it. The majority of the Brothers were brilliant and eccentric, and eccentricity, by definition, leads to divergency. There were differences, though these, in the spirit of the place, were charitably settled; each of the members modestly considered himself very ordinary, while the others, when you came to think about it, were odd.

Wilfred himself, even as early as the 1920s, was certainly unusual in manner. His transparent honesty could give offence. If he was busy, and was asked if it was convenient for him to spare a moment, he simply answered "no." If he forgot an engagement, the best he could do by way of apology was to say, "I didn't come to dinner with you yesterday." Some of those who were attracted or interested by the O.G.S., without necessarily intending to join it, found him, at first encounter, puzzling. Malcolm Muggeridge recalls that he was greeted with an almost unintelligible remark out of the side of the mouth, followed by a number of disjointed sentences. Could they connect? Well, that was the fascination. There was just a chance that if you stayed long enough, they might. Canon Jack Bagley, who did become a member, first arrived when Wilfred was gardening and had a hoe and a spade flung at him, with a command to "Get on with it." Others, falling over a wheelbarrow, were sternly disregarded, or were suddenly left alone at ten o'clock, the retiring hour, without explanation.

In 1920 the O.G.S. had acquired a building in Lady Margaret Road which became Oratory House; the members, Wilfred included, sold out their shares to meet the freehold price. It was an unbeautiful, inconvenient, poorly lit red-brick building, with very cold passages and a tangled garden. Here Wilfred came to live when his novitiate was completed, in the summer of 1921, with the Warden and six undergraduates. One of them, Fred Brittain of Jesus, has left a description of the routine. There was a married couple to do the cooking, but the residents cleaned their own rooms and waited at table; most men in those days had very little idea how to do this, and still less how to manage the cooks; one couple was found dead drunk in the pantry. Breakfast was taken in complete silence, which seemed irritating at first, afterwards helpful; the centre of the whole day was the time of meditation and prayer.

Another early lay member was Joseph Needham, later Master of Caius and the great historian of Chinese science. The openminded discussions at the Oratory, he has said, showed him "the great need for a re-thinking of Christian doctrine and practice in the light of scientific knowledge, for example, in the attitude to sexual questions, race relations and social justice." He noticed neither the cold nor the irregular cooking. Wilfred Knox "was one of the people from whom I learned most in my youth from personal experience and contact; a demonstration of how to combine a deep attachment to devotional and liturgical traditions with a totally liberated and fearless search for truth."

Wilfred was most certainly deeply attached to the liturgy, without, however, being able to sing one note of music correctly. For tone-deafness there was not much to choose between him and Ronnie; on the eve of his ordination as deacon Ronnie had gone down to the bottom of the drive at St Edmund's to practise singing the *Ite, missa est*; "I did think I could cause no annoyance to anybody there, but every rook in Hertfordshire rose shrieking in protest." At the Oratory, Fred Brittain acted as Wilfred's Vicar Choral, and describes him as joining in the carefully arranged service "like a bull-frog". Brittain still regarded him with qualified amazement.

> Wilfred Knox was not a handsome man, and his complete indifference to his outward appearance did not help him to look any more so. He was shy with strangers . . . and his extremely nervous laugh, accompanied by a hysterical intake of the breath, was the reverse of attractive. He generally wore a pair of stained grey flannel trousers, very baggy at the knees because they were never pressed . . . Out of doors he wore a somewhat greasy and battered black trilby hat, and if the weather was wet a cheap raincoat. All his clothing indeed was cheap, as it was apparently part of his rule of life not to spend an unnecessary penny on clothes. He used to go into outfitters' shops asking for 'the sort of shirt a workman wears'.

That "apparently" shows the very private nature of the self-discipline at the Oratory. Raggedness was not supposed to evoke pity. Wilfred registered mild annoyance when gifts of underclothing and wine appeared in his bicycle basket after a service at the parish church. These windfalls were, as far as possible, shared. And, dismayed though Brittain was by the grey flannel trousers—soon to become part of the archaeology of Cambridge—he characterizes Wilfred as "witty, humble, shrewd in his judgement of men and affairs, charitable, compassionate and saintly." Certainly at the Oratory Wilfred's loneliness was healed, and he allowed himself the heresy, if it was one, that there will be a place for such small communities, still together, still understanding one another, in the life to come.

The garden, where Jack Bagley had had to dodge the spade and hoe, was Wilfred's daily resource between two and four in the afternoon. Gardening was simply gardening, therefore the best of recreations. "I always start pruning my roses on Lady Day, not out of devotion to the Rosa Mistica, but because it is an easy fixed date to remember." Smith, the cook's husband, who did the vegetables but never exceeded his sphere, claimed to have brought Father Knox to gardening, but Wilfred had always known how to do it. Ronnie recalled that at Edmundthorpe they had each been given a patch of earth, but only Wilfred's had flourished. Ronnie, however, really liked the temporary sense of power in a garden, popping fuchsia buds and blowing tobacco smoke into white flowers to make them turn yellow. Wilfred would not have stood for this at Lady Margaret Road. On the subject of plants, only Mrs K. and Christina were permitted to offer him advice.

Part of the summer was spent with the Cambridge Mission to fruit-pickers, at Hickman's, a grim-looking field close to the main road. Most of the fruit-pickers came down from the East End, and it was a privilege for him to meet them again. In June, he and Eddie went fishing.

Out of the many parishes in England where they had been on holiday with the Bishop, the brothers settled, for their fishing, on

Kington in Herefordshire. It is a little hill town, a sheep and pony market, on the debatable Welsh borderland. The stream they fished was the Arrow, which rises in the Marches, runs through the main street of Kington, and falls into the Lug at Leominster. "Arrow" in Welsh means "rough water", and, though beautiful, it was not an easy stream. It was, as Eddie wrote, "rather too full of herons and otters and kingfishers and cows", and densely over-grown with bushes on both banks. Sometimes Eddie suspected that the cows might be eating the trout, so few were to be seen.

But the rule of the local club was "no wading"—laid down, apparently, after Henry Tudor crossed the Arrow on his way to the battle of Bosworth. And on the principle of "doing the most difficult thing" the brothers remained devoted to this lovely water for more than twenty years. They knew every kingfisher's nest in the bankholes and every gradation of the light during the evening rise, when the trout come up to the surface like dancers. Set them down in the darkness by the Arrow or the Lug, and they could tell you in a moment by what reach or what deep pool they stood. Their meeting point every year was a shop in Leominster, kept by a Miss Blomer, who knew nothing at all about fishing, but could tie any fly that was described to her; each of them kept a record of catches, and at the end of the day they exchanged books, and accused each other of being fanciful.

During these years of restored happiness Wilfred found writing moderately easy. On holiday he read only detective stories; back at the Oratory, working direct onto his frightful typewriter, he wrote apologetics and historical theology, and began his great study of the background of St Paul; but he also published a small, modest book, which has become a great favourite, *Meditation and Mental Prayer*. He made no claims for it; it was only a summary, he said, in convenient form. It takes the reader, in the most disarming way, past all the real difficulties. All prayer, Wilfred tells us, is answered. As for those who feel that the whole idea is beyond them, "a person who is not clever enough to practise mental prayer is not clever enough to be entrusted with the ordinary affairs of daily life, and ought to be shut up in an asylum or a private home." Wilfred could be very astringent at times.

When Eddie went back from holiday he was still a countryman, or, rather, a commuter. Christina and he had decided to try somewhere within easy reach of London, where they could keep hens and grow vegetables and put up a swing for the children, and everything would be cheap. In this expectation they found a homely mock-Tudor house with a lawn and a cherry tree, in Balcombe, near Haywards Heath in Sussex.

Balcombe, to quote the title of the book Eddie wrote about it, was An Hour from Victoria; Sussex, favoured by writers since the turn of the century, was now the centre of the second wave of the Georgian movement. The bookshops, Eddie found, were stacked with volumes of poetry in which "innumerable writers stated their firm conviction that Sussex not only contained Downs, but that these Downs were adjacent to the Sea." These were the pale followers of Belloc and Kipling; meanwhile the simple fellows with smocks and clay pipes in the bar parlours turned out to be regional novelists, on the lookout for Sussex hinds. But even these were outnumbered by the weekenders. On Saturdays the lanes smoked with the adventurous traffic of the 1920s.

The village itself was a different matter, and the young Knoxes were discreetly welcomed. The rector suggested that as he believed Eddie was a writer, he might try a history of the local Ancient Ironworks, and act as secretary of the debating club, which met in a room hired from the Village Institute. Here—or so he insisted—Eddie proposed debates on: "The League of Nations"; "That Mr. G. B. Shaw is the most promising young dramatist since Shakespeare, and his future may be looked forward to with confidence"; "That this Club strongly opposes the Einstein Theory of Relativity, and considers it injurious to health and morals". But no one came, until he proposed: "That the butcher's prices have increased, are increasing, and ought to be diminished". There was only one butcher in Balcombe.

The presiding genius of Sussex, as has been said, was Hilaire Belloc. Kipling, who was living at Batemans, received guests, but went out very little. Belloc, though much broken down by his wife's death, still strode across the downs with the energy of an old Gaul, and kept up the true customs of Merrie England at King's Land. Ronnie, as the coming Catholic writer, had been to stay with him for the Christmas of 1921, and, perhaps as a sequel to this, Belloc suddenly appeared at Balcombe one Sunday in the following June and said he had come to luncheon. In spite of the high concentration of poets in the area he was very conspicuous, solid, almost cubical in shape, heavily dressed in black in the summer heat. Eddie recalled that Belloc had once, when standing as Liberal candidate for Salford, come to Bishopscourt and suffered terribly from the sour claret; when asked how he slept, he replied that he hadn't, and had had to sit up all night reading. At Balcombe, however, there were one or two bottles of good hock, but before they could be fetched, Belloc, marching in, produced from under his black garments a flagon of his own wine, apparently bottled by himself. After this doubtful compliment lunch began well enough, until Belloc uttered a cry, more like the horn of Roland echoing over waste places: "Bread! But we eat like the English, without bread!" In those days the baker brought "two small browns", or whatever was ordered, every morning in the pony-trap; in the afternoon there was no more to be had. Belloc could not accept a small brown as bread, and was, perhaps, doomed to another sleepless night.

A few years afterwards, Belloc showed his weary and sympathetic side when he wrote to Eddie about his satire, *Belinda:* "It is the only book I have written with care since *The Path to Rome* and I hope I shall never write a book with any care again, for care is a great burden." Eddie, who was making a list of things he could and couldn't do in case of emergencies ("I can't milk or do the things that work electrical things; I can saw wood and if the two cuts don't meet, bang it about until the piece comes off; I can't bake; I can work a lift and black boots and polish brown ones and do bacon and eggs— learned in lodgings"), added privately that, though he admired him very much, he could not entertain Hilaire Belloc.

As Evoe of *Punch*, his correspondence grew. To take only two items from the "files", now the drawers of a desk, rather than a hat box: a letter from a Polish reader, addressed from Warsaw to "The Very Renown Evoe of *Punch*, care of the *Daily News*"; from America, an invitation to give humorous evenings for the International Chautauqua Association, "Brings Entertainment to Your Door, Every Kind for Every Occasion". But Eddie, like Ronnie, never felt quite confident enough to make a personal appearance in the United States.

During the Twenties he was particularly well known as a parodist. Parody, an art which has declined with the disappearance of a recognizable literary style, depends on the finer shades of exaggeration. Eddie was gentle—much gentler, for instance, than Max Beerbohm—but wonderfully accurate. Walter de la Mare was a favourite subject, perhaps because Eddie loved his poetry, perhaps because it was so difficult to render delicate uncanniness by delicate absurdity. In Eddie's "The Lost Bus" the driver has a moustache green with moss, the destination boards trail with weeds, and, entangled in its own magic syllables, "topples the bus and heels". The idea appealed to de la Mare himself. Indeed, with a few exceptions, the authors were enthusiastic; Edgar Rice Burroughs, for instance, the author of *Tarzan*, wrote rather unexpectedly from Tarzana Ranch, Reseda, California, that "you have saved me from oblivion".

Owen Seaman raised his remuneration to twelve guineas for a poem. It was time to branch out a little and to buy a motor-car. A gleaming new Citroën arrived, about which Eddie found it difficult to make any comment, except "to sneer because the speedometer had to be wound up by hand". With the car came the lady driving teacher, Miss Gompertz, in leather gauntlets, the very spirit of the 1920s. "I don't want speed to brace my nerves; I want it for its own sake." Nevertheless, every time the Citroën passed a breakdown or a puncture, Miss Gompertz gave instructions to pull up, with the quiet words: "Let us not forget the chivalry of the road."

The car had to be kept in a kind of byre or hen-roost—what Eddie called a "wild garage". On one occasion, stopping abruptly to avoid a goat, he turned the car over onto its side, without the least damage. The villagers, he thought, were disappointed; Miss Gompertz had not given instructions on how to address people through the windscreen of a car turned over on its side. But Eddie was far too impatient ever to be a good driver. That had to be left to Christina.

Balcombe, before very long, proved to be too far from the heart of things. In September 1920 Eddie had been invited to the Table— the weekly meeting of the *Punch* editorial staff. "You will not find us a formidable body," wrote Philip Agnew, the managing director, "(please remember that we do not even dress for dinner) and we shall gladly welcome our new man." In 1921 he joined the regular staff. After work there were the clubs, then an important part of the professional literary career. Eddie had been elected to the Savile in 1920, although Christina and he both felt the ten-guinea subscription was going to be hard to manage, and the Garrick in 1925; in 1921 he had been a guest at E.V. Lucas's famous Garrick dinner for Charlie Chaplin, when Barrie had asked Chaplin to play Peter Pan. In fact, unassertive as he was, Eddie's wit made him much in demand as a guest; he was a host, however, by temperament. All this was difficult if one lived an hour from Victoria.

The hens, the lawnmower and the rabbit hutches were sold; they would have to return to London. But, once again, they were hopeful of finding something in Hampstead, where they had always been happy, and the air was quite fresh.

Dilly, also, had moved to the country, but with considerably more reluctance, and, in his case, for a lifetime.

He married Olive Roddam in July 1920, at Ingram Parish Church in Northumberland. It is no criticism of the Roddams, an hon-ourable line of squires and soldiers whose lands were first granted by King Athelstan, to say that they were somewhat uncertain how to get on with the gaunt and hesitant bridegroom, about whose "war work" so little could be said, who was known to be very clever, and, although a bishop's son, rather different from the kind of man they had expected Olive to marry. She had formerly been engaged to the son of a neighbouring landowner, a young man called Christopher; they had agreed that if he did not come back from the Front, and Olive married, she would call her first son after him. Christopher was killed in 1914 and Olive's brother in 1915; it was partly to recover from the shock that she had gone to London to work in the Admiralty; she had come back with Dilly.

Dilly was somewhat on his own at the wedding. One of his Cambridge friends was best man. Bishop Knox could not come; he was in the thick of the Lambeth Conference, battling over the Prayer Book. The brothers would have liked to come, but in his nervous agitation Dilly forgot to ask them. He was most anxious to please, but worried, even by the kindly hospitality of the Roddams. The gifts—the old lace, the piano music, the enormous quantities of silver and china—where could they be accommodated? What kind of life could he offer to Olive? He felt himself in alien territory. The *Alnwick Gazette*, which reported the wedding, noted in its editorial that day that "it shows a right grip of the affairs of life that in all our sports we have well nigh thrown off the depression of war, still, however, missing the jolly fellows now in happier hunting grounds. Full cry ahead lie the meetings of the Percy Hunt (with festivities to be generously provided). Yoick! Yoick!" Dilly, with all his anxious affection, could not Yoick. Would he be able to make her even passably happy?

On their return from a honeymoon in Scotland, he took her back to Chelsea. Frank Birch had also married (Maynard Keynes having organized a generous gift from King's for both young couples), and it seemed at first to Dilly that they could all set up housekeeping together in Edith Grove. With this in mind he enthusiastically bought a two-shilling cookery book, and opened an account with the

Kensington Unique Laundry. But the arrangement did not work
out well.

Dilly was still at the Admiralty, though Room 40 was in process
of being transferred to the Foreign Office under the euphemistic
title of the Government Code and Cypher School. Shrunk to a
small department, still under the supervision of A. G. Denniston,
one of the first Naval officers selected by Ewing, its future importance was undecided. Dilly was waiting eagerly for his release.
During the war he had been appointed Librarian of King's, although
he had never managed to get there; and back to King's, with the
Herodas to finish, he firmly intended to go. Meanwhile, it was clear
that Olive would never see eye to eye with the Birches. She was
not flourishing in Chelsea. She was really only at home with the life
of a landed proprietor. In October 1921 he sold out most of his
Great Western Railway shares and bought, for £1,900, a house surrounded by forty acres of sodden woodland on a ridge of the
Chilterns. It was called Courn's Wood House, and was a few miles
from High Wycombe.

The usual troubles of vacant possession followed. Dilly approached every problem laterally. The agents wrote to ask why he
had sent down two people to deal with the valuation who knew absolutely nothing about it—one a lecturer in classics, the other an
electrical outfitter. Fortunately Dilly had as his solicitor the celebrated E. S. P. Haynes. Haynes had believed, until 1914, that a just
world would prevail; since the loss of Grenfell, Lister, Guy Lawrence
and their generation, he no longer thought so; he resigned himself
to good living and to knowing everyone and everything, reminding
his friends that "to eat and drink with the wrong person is like in-
tercourse with an inefficient prostitute." Haynes appealed to Dilly a
good deal more than he did to Olive, but he was an excellent nego-
tiator; he never came much to Courn's Wood, however, after the
conveyance was completed, because he said it was too cold there,
and so it was; a heavy, chalky, insidious chill from the miles of damp
woodland laid its finger on every room, above all the dining room,
where the table stood like an island exposed to draughts from every

quarter, and was only dispelled in Dilly's study by a large wood fire. Victorian concepts remained in the households of the Twenties, and very often it was only in the study and the airing cupboard that one could feel warm.

Two sons were born to Dilly and Olive at Courn's Wood. The first, in accordance with her promise, was called Christopher; his second name was Maynard, after Keynes, who stood godfather. In spite of this dedication, so to speak, to King's, the sweet-tempered little boy grew up to be quite unacademic, while the second, named Oliver after his mother, proved to be a brilliant Greek scholar; if this was an irony of the Fates, it did not wound, for Dilly was extravagantly affectionate to them both when they were young. To push them through the deep leaf mould, he devised and constructed his own vehicle, which Oliver remembered as "a wooden scaffolding erected on a single large wheel". Here the little boys could be secured at a level with their father's nose, and conversation could continue. Dilly also threw himself, with not very well-directed energy, into planting, sawing and building log cabins, all on an improved but unintelligible system. But, do what he could, he never looked, as he tramped up the overgrown paths, in the least like a landed proprietor.

The Headlam-Knox *Herodas* finally appeared in 1922. Much of it, as Dilly warned the academic world through the pages of *Philologus*, had been done on trains going up and down to London. His eyes had been troublesome, and the Cambridge Press had distributed some of the type during the war, so that it was now impossible to make the alterations he wanted. Still, it was a handsome and definitive volume. There was criticism, of course, of Headlam's glorious irrelevancies and too numerous parallels, but, in the words of Professor Arnott, "the imperfections pale beside the glowing achievement not merely for the text of Herodas but for the Greek language and literature in general." Dilly's own work was compared to the restoration of a damaged old master. In particular, in spite of the Museum's unwillingness to remount the wrongly aligned scraps of papyrus, he had arranged and made sense out of the fragments of

Mimes IX and X (*The Breakfast* and *The Factory Girls*), and the almost complete Mime VIII, *The Dream*. In this "purely personal and
even sentimental fantasy", as Dilly called it, Herodas is rusticating
on his pig farm, and wakes his slaves in the early morning to tell
them about his dream, a meeting with the god Dionysus at a
drunken winter festival, which ends with the hope that his poems
will be immortal. This hope had at last been fulfilled. The Headlam-
Knox *Herodas* was worthy of both the master and pupil, and more
than worthy of the salacious old Alexandrian poet.

It was an achievement that was not of much interest, however, in
the High Wycombe and Naphill district, largely inhabited by retired officers and stockbrokers. Dilly went to the local tennis parties
(he played tennis, as he did all ball games, with an unreturnable
spin). He was known as an absent-minded dear. As a relief, he wrote
verses in a notebook; these give an alarming panorama of the neighbours. Many are said to be lucky to escape hanging, and a visit from
the High Wycombe doctors means death within the month. Motor-
cars and even light aircraft have been bought by husbands to get
away from their wives, although the prevalence of adultery is sur-
prising when all the wives look so much like each other. Eric Gill,
the sculptor, who at that time lived on Pigot's Hill, grinds his teeth
with rancorous hatred at the sight of anything as natural as a daf-
fodil. (Gill, in reply, asked Dilly why he did not eat Health Foods;
but in Dilly's view nothing was so unnatural as health.) Meanwhile,
the boredom of the conversation in Naphill and the length of the
stories told by their neighbour, a retired Admiral, added a new terror
to the concept of infinity.

In 1923 Dilly made another contribution to Greek scholarship,
an elegant dissertation on Cercidas, identifying 150 lines on papyrus
as the dedication to an anthology. In consequence, he was offered
the Professorship of Greek at Leeds University. Nothing came of it,
but the letter was one of the very few papers he kept. It was worth
remembering that he might have been a professor.

As soon as the *Herodas* was finished and he no longer had to work
on photographs of papyrus in the train, Dilly bought a motor-bike

to go up and down to London. It meant liberation from the stock-brokers on the High Wycombe platform. Olive was uneasy. She knew that he was in even greater danger than Wilfred, because Wilfred understood nothing whatever about his machine, whereas Dilly *did* understand, but expected far too much of it. And he had not ridden one since he was rejected as a dispatch rider in 1914.

Dilly had been induced to stay on at the Foreign Office as a peacetime cryptographer, continuing to read the secret traffic of the nation's rivals and ill-wishers, and, occasionally, of its friends. While his work had to remain in secrecy or obscurity, Ronnie was named by the *Daily Mail* in 1924 as "the wittiest young man in England". As a sparkling light essayist he blossomed out, not only in the Catholic press but in columns everywhere. Many of these pieces were not religious at all; they simply established his personality and opinions with a wide public. Ronnie Knox was young in his high spirits, nostalgic in his recall of the lost domain of childhood. His imagery was largely drawn from school prizes, cricket, laundry, drawers that stick, embarrassing moments, pipes, trams and bicycles (unsound arguments "give you a sensation of freewheeling instead of pedalling"). The readers got to know him very well. He told them about his expenditure on tobacco, his income-tax forms, his reading (Herodotus, Trollope, *The Egoist*), none of them quite coming up to the excitement of his first book, Wood's *Natural History*; he explained his objection to flying, and the length of time, as a travelling preacher, that he had to spend in stations—he memorized, quite uselessly, the whole map of Cardiff Docks while waiting at Crewe Junction. Then, in describing a walking tour in the Cotswolds, he passed the camp where in 1914 his friends had assembled in their new uniforms. "A little rain crossed that peopled solitude, and memory rehearsed for me the roll-call of the unregarded dead." This transition to a graver key was beautifully managed, both in articles and sermons.

Ronnie's weekly pieces have suffered the fate of most journalism, but they had long-lasting, perhaps unexpected, effects. Quite casually and straightforwardly, they introduced an exceedingly brilliant person whose reasoning mind was able to accept the contradictions of Christianity. At the same time they showed that a normal, pipe-smoking, income-taxed Englishman, not a Jesuit, not a mystic, no black cloaks, no sweeping gestures, could become a Roman Catholic priest. The *News* and *Standard* columns, with their wide readership, brought very many people to think rather more favourably of God. Ronnie's informal sermons of the 1920s were in much the same style, and as he tried to sort out, step by step, his own difficulties of faith and doctrine, his congregations found—though they did it timidly at first—that it was possible to laugh out loud in church.

The newspapers of the day were obsessed, or felt that their readers were obsessed, with Famous People. That was why Mrs K. had been induced to write her article, and Ronnie was often run as a kind of rival or opposite number to the equally witty, but deeply pessimistic Dean Inge, who claimed that the world after the Great War was "a place where everybody was wanted, but nobody was wanted much." Another use for Famous People, so popular that it amounted to mania, was the collection of their opinions about God—"What I Believe". Everyone was asked, from Bertrand Russell to the excavators of Tutankhamen's tomb. Eddie contributed to this in *Punch* by claiming to have interviewed Steve Donoghue, the champion jockey, and getting the reply: "I have always been conscious, especially at the finish of a race, that Good and Evil are Relative Notions, and Sin is a Mere Negative," while Jack Hobbs is said to have smiled quietly at the scant interest his fellow batsmen took in eschatology. This hit the tone pretty well. Ronnie's task, in the name of authority and orthodoxy, was to take on the writers one by one and to point out their faults in logic.

For this he was reasonably well-paid, and began to accumulate a certain amount of money. His motives were completely unselfish. Ronnie, like all his brothers, was generous to a fault; during his life-time, for example, he gave more than £20,000 to the Converts' Aid Society alone, on condition that nothing should be said about it. Eddie was known in Fleet Street as a soft touch; his sardonic smile was deceptive, any hard-luck story would do. At home Christina tried to protect him, but in vain. Not long after he was demobilized she found him being harangued by an ex-serviceman who had called, uninvited, to read him some verses:

> While you sat here at home
> I sailed across the foam
> And fought with heart so brave
> To keep the likes of you safe. . . .

"I thought he ought to have a fiver," Eddie muttered. "I couldn't have written that poem."

If Ronnie, therefore, was hoping for financial independence, it was for a specific reason. At the back of his mind there still lingered the example of Hugh Benson, who had feverishly written books for money to establish himself as a writer-priest in his own house at Hare Street. Hare Street had been somewhat theatrical and showy. Nothing that Ronnie did after his conversion was likely to be showy, but the idea of a home with some resemblance to the house party with Guy and Harold Macmillan that never took place, a home shared with other congenial priests, a centre for reading and writing—that ambition died hard. And it was particularly tempting at the moment because the daily conditions of his life were becoming unbearable.

Cardinal Bourne had appointed him, as his first post in the Catholic Church, to teach Latin at St Edmund's, a seminary and dullish boys' school in a dullish part of Hertfordshire. The level of the classical forms was low. Bishop Knox had feared that the Romans would make "no sparing use" of Ronnie, and Dilly pointed out that this was the sparing use to which in fact he had been put. Ronnie accepted the appointment with true humility. But he had not realized that he would be required to stay at St Edmund's for seven years.

During the Twenties and early Thirties the Catholic Church in England made a miscalculation, the kind of error which history permits to Rome so that she can resume her majestic progress undisturbed. It was the heyday of the Conversion of England, or Apostolate to Non-Catholics (an awkward word which Ronnie had difficulty in fitting into his lucid sentences). But the task was seen, not so much as the capture of the Establishment as the creation of another one side by side with it, a Catholic model, every bit as good. Power was felt to lie with the aristocracy, public schools, universities, rank and patronage. Right-wing causes were supported everywhere, and the trained intelligence of the Jesuits was directed to organizing a cricket match at Lord's which would be as smart as Eton and Harrow. Cardinal Bourne's great anxiety, however, was for the secular clergy. There were too few of them, and their standard of learning was unimpressive; on all brilliant occasions, the demand was for Benedictines or Jesuits. It was, in the true sense, a Godsend when Ronald Knox, after the death of Guy, no longer thought of joining an Order. As a secular priest at St Edmund's he could be— to quote one of his contemporaries—"a sort of talent scout and a sort of trophy."

Ronnie's duty was to be brilliant, and to advertise the place, socially and intellectually. The idea was quite enough to make him miserable; worse still, St Edmund's happened to be disturbed, as most places of education are at some time or another, by unpleasant feuds. Neither Eton nor Shrewsbury seems to have prepared Ronnie for this. He pined, and his indigestion tortured him. For the sake of good example, he attended the school dinners, where he was faced with mutton stew that tasted of sheep droppings, and a blancmange known as "shape", which, he pointed out, was its only attribute.

But it was years before he complained. Difficult things were the right ones to do, and, as a recent convert, he felt uncertain and humble. ("Whoa! I'm only a convert!" he once said to an Irish priest who was pouring him out a triple measure of whisky.) His colleagues loved him; the boys remembered him as the priest who could balance on a garden roller, and imitate a mouse taking a sip of beer and then going out to challenge the cat. He retreated from the schoolroom to lecture on the New Testament in the seminary. But the days still seemed long.

Ronnie did not fish, and his summer vacation was spent in Scotland, where he was the yearly guest of the Lovats at Beaufort Castle. Lady Lovat was the younger sister of Charles Lister, which made a strong link; she had "gone over" at the age of eighteen, when she had become engaged to the forty-year-old Catholic clan chieftain, Lord Lovat. Her letter to Ronnie on his conversion was one of the most delightful he had.

> I think the first year (or 6 months) after being received are v. difficult—I fluctuated between feeling utterly isolated—or being one of a rather—unsympathetic and *very* dense crowd. I don't know which sensation was worst—Both, I think now—were very superficial but meant a rather long swim against the current—(or is it currant? Scarcely the latter I feel!) . . . asking to be remembered in your prayers—Laura Lovat.

The mixture of seriousness and charm marked Lady Lovat as a true descendant of the Souls. She had utterly transformed Beaufort, restored the gardens, banished the cows from straying into the front hall, and provided a haven for artists and writers. Lord Lovat, who was said to be a patron of every sport and activity except literature, painting and coarse fishing, welcomed his wife's guests as his own. The great Victorian castle resounded with children and relations and with those who came to discuss sport, farming and politics; Ronnie worked apart, in the peace of the library. All the generous chieftain's books were there to be lent; Ronnie suggested that the family motto on the bookplates, *Je suis prêt*, should be changed to *Je suis prêté*.

Another literary guest was the brilliant and wordly-wise Maurice Baring, said to be the original of Chesterton's Man Who Knew Too Much. Baring loved things to be done with an air; Ronnie delighted him by translating a line of Rossetti's, "You could not tell the starlings from the leaves," into Greek and Latin on the spot. At other times they had to speak Umble, one of Baring's several invented languages, in which Dickens's *Old Curiosity Shop* came out as Dumble's *Umble Cumble Shumble*. Lord Lovat did not attempt it.

"By far the greatest scholar in this language," wrote Mumble Bumble to E. V. Lucas, "is Ronald Knox."

Although Ronnie's family wished him to be happy, and understood that he needed a change from St Edmund's, they looked with some misgiving at his gravitation towards grand country houses. Dilly felt that patrons were like the mills of God, and if you were not careful they ground you down exceeding small. Wilfred once again wondered why, if Ronnie wanted to get to know his new church from the inside, he did not apply for a working parish.

Perhaps they did not realize how much Ronnie needed feminine sympathy. He was truly at home in a home. Little habits showed this. An old friend of Ebury Street days, Mrs Baker, recalls how he used to stand by the fire in his long soutane which completely sheltered the cat, so that no one could tell where the purring came from. He understood the day-to-day problems of women, the peculiar diminishment, for example, which a woman feels when her children grow up; he learned that through Winnie and Mrs K. The devotion, too, with which he had picked bunches of flowers for his new stepmother was something he needed to feel, in some form or another, throughout his life.

Eddie and Christina moved back to Hampstead in 1922, to a small Queen Anne terrace house this time, 34 Well Walk, at a rent of forty pounds a year. The village—and Hampstead still felt itself very much a village—was a place of high thinking, plain living and small economies. The steep, charming old streets were full of ham-and-beef shops, old bookstalls, and an amazing number of cleaners and repairers, all helpful to shabby refugees and literary men. There was even a jeweller's where one bead could be bought at a time, for all the Hampstead ladies wore long necklaces. The livery stables had only just turned into a garage, and still called itself a Motor Jobmaster. Poets walked the streets, Stanley Spencer pushed his pramful of painting materials amiably across the Heath, Henry Lamb was living in the top room of the Vale of Health Hotel; his sister Dorothy was now married to Reeve Brooke, an old Corpus

friend of Eddie's. At one end of Well Walk was the wooden seat
which John Keats had sat on, at the other was a pub kept by a man
called Strube, the brother of the cartoonist; it was a haven for journalists down on their luck.

In the winter evenings muffin-men and lamp-lighters came on
their rounds, and Eddie and Christina often had to make their way
down into foggy London, since Eddie was now doing a good deal of
theatre criticism. Theatre-going in the Twenties was of quite another dimension; Owen Seaman went to *The Immortal Hour* twenty-
five times; people lost count of how often they had seen the Lovat
Fraser *Beggar's Opera*; for Shaw's *Back to Methuselah* one had to go to
the Royal Court every night for a week, Christina bravely adapting
the same diamanté dress with scarves and necklaces. Flecker's
Hassan in 1923, with its intoxicating orientalized language, was also
long, though the intervals were short, so that, as Eddie put it in his
review, "the barrier of Procrastination tended to sever the whisky-
and-soda from the lips of Desire." Sometimes there was a show with
Ivor Novello in the cast; Ivor, loyal through the passing years, came
gliding thick with greasepaint into the audience if Christina or her
brother Ned were there, to greet them with his reverberating
"Darlings! you came!"

Neither Ronnie nor Wilfred ever went to the theatre after they
were ordained priest, but both of them retained the Victorian notion of "standing treat" to their nephews and niece. It was a memorable experience to go to Gunter's teashop with Ronnie and Eddie.
Ronnie's shy courtesy made it difficult for him to attract attention
from the waitresses, and his insistence on "doing the most difficult
thing" led him to tackle his meringue with a fork only. While doing
this he began to talk enthusiastically to Eddie about Henry
Vaughan's "Peace":

> My soul, there is a country
>   Far beyond the stars,
> Where stands a wingèd sentry
>   All skilful in the wars . . .

Ronnie, chasing the crumbs, objected to the half-rhyme, *country* and *sentry*, and to the unlikeliness of one sentry guarding a whole boundary. The text must be wrong. Mightn't Vaughan have written

> My soul, there is a fortress
> > Far beyond the stars,
> Where stands a wingèd porteress . . .

Eddie immediately rejected the fortress; it was too menacing; why not a tea shop?

> My soul, there is a caterer's
> > Far beyond the stars,
> Where stands a Gunter's waitress . . .

At the false rhyme, Ronnie half-rose from his chair in agony. The tea was brought, the band played on unnoticed. Other customers stared in amazement. So much did the words and assonances of the English language mean to the Knox brothers.

Wilfred came to Well Walk every Christmas without fail, on the afternoon of the 25th, when the great ceremonies of the Church were over. In 1922 he left Cambridge for two years to help a hard-pressed friend, Stephen Langton, in the East End parish of St Saviour's, Hoxton. The Bishop of London had refused to allow a curate because of the extreme Anglo-Catholicism of the services, and Wilfred served without pay.

He arrived on Christmas Day 1922 in a state of mild satisfaction; as he left the church in his cassock and overcoat a man had shouted at him from a public house: "Them ain't the clothes Our Lord used to wear!" Wilfred had paused, and told him that his remark, as a piece of logic, was based on four false assumptions. He always got on excellently with drunks and small children, because he treated them exactly as he treated rational adults.

In 1923 Wilfred brought with him, attached to the end of a long piece of string, as though he disclaimed all connection with it, a villainous-looking mongrel. The dog had come into church during his sermon, he explained, and "almost in a spirit of criticism, quietly proceeded to die." He had revived it with a saucer of sweet tea. Of course, as he serenely assumed, 34 Well Walk would be its new home, and there it systematically destroyed everything, devouring Eddie's leather gloves, his briefcase, and a new collar which had been purchased for it. Then it escaped, and ran away back to Hoxton.

No other Christmas guest could replace Wilfred Knox. He spoke of what was uppermost in his mind, disregarding the inessential. Chocolates, bought as a practical joke from Hamley's, each one filled with soap and sawdust, were eaten by Wilfred without comment, and indeed without noticing. When the crackers were pulled he accepted his paper hat with interest, but soon forgot it and sat there crowned as an Emperor or a jolly jester, while his conversation drifted away to the commentaries of Philo of Alexandria. What recalled him to worldly matters for a moment was the appearance of the "hard sauce", or brandy butter. This was a matter of close interest to all four brothers. Only one way of making it was acceptable, and that was the Merton College recipe; but then, even Merton had lost the art of doing it, and only old Alice, at Beckenham Grove, could get it quite right. If any one of the brothers had been greedy, if any of them had been discourteous enough to express disappointment, people would not have tried so hard to please them; as it was, the perfect hard sauce became a memory only. Perhaps perfection should be left where it belongs, in childhood.

At the *Punch* office Eddie had now carved his initials, according to tradition, on the famous Table, where every Wednesday the editor presides, and management is only a guest. At the Table, during the post-war years, there was an awkward mixture of nostalgia and impatience. The younger ones back from the front, Eddie, A. P. Herbert, Ernest Shepard, had quick wits, felt the new world coming, were prepared to regret the old, but found the discrepancies funny. Owen Seaman was entirely loyal to the past. He had dispensed with A. A. Milne, an incurable dissident, and remained in the editorial chair, monolithic, refusing change. The cinema and the paintings of the Twenties must not be reviewed seriously, they were a foolish craze; socialism he regarded as active treason. The circulation fell, and *Punch* was becoming a byword for what was old-fashioned and genteel. In 1925 the first issue of *The New Yorker* threatened a new kind of joke, understated and biting, and Ross, the editor, told his staff that he believed *Punch* had some kind of tea party every Wednesday; but Seaman could not yield; *Punch* was an institution, and while institutions remained, the structure of the nation would hold. His staff respected the gallant obsession, but began to wonder whether he had any sense of humour left at all. E. V. Lucas, as the senior assistant editor, thought this might be tested. Why not hide under the table, and, as soon as Owen came in, jump out and surprise him? This was enterprising of Lucas, who was no longer agile; difficult, too, for Bernard Partridge, the senior cartoonist, who, though always genial and obliging, was nearly sixty.

Surprise is one of the only six jokes in the world. Seaman came in, looked round, signalled to the waiter to pull out his chair, sat down, and unfolded his napkin. After a little while the *Punch* staff crawled out, and also took their places. The editor said nothing, and no one ever knew what he thought.

Although he seemed quite impervious to the first hints dropped by the proprietors, Owen might, in time, resign. Meanwhile the staff served him with the protective loyalty of the old Fleet Street. The loyalty was counterbalanced by a guarded cynicism towards the sources of power.

They were touched by the wonderful reassurance which Owen drew from the great Wembley Empire Exhibition of 1924. This, as might be expected, he wanted covered as elaborately as possible. Eddie was sent as reporter, and as illustrator a very good black-and-white artist, the junior cartoonist Raven Hill.

Raven Hill was a friend of Kipling's, though with none of Kipling's subtlety. When Eddie went down to his weekend cottage to discuss the assignment, he was distressed to find the fire being lit with Kipling manuscripts. But Raven was heart and soul in the imperial theme, and, like Seaman, had to be persuaded that there was no disrespect in finding some aspects of it funny.

On 5 March 1924, the two of them splashed through the unfinished streets of the Exhibition. Eddie had never seen such mud since Flanders; some of it was being hastily painted black to represent a Welsh coal mine. In the West African Tropical Village the cutting northeast wind left him almost numb. By May (Seaman wanted every single dominion and colony covered) the weather had changed and was exceedingly hot. Journalists tended to concentrate in Jamaica (which consisted of one bar, serving rum), and later at the Fountain of Eno's Fruit Salts. But Raven Hill was tireless. The world press grew accustomed to the sight of the *Punch* team, both of them in straw hats, Evoe slight and elegant, Raven short and round, pressing on a few steps ahead. The House of War was showing naval battles several hours in length. Then there was the reconstructed Tomb of Tutankhamen to be described, although, as Eddie pointed out, Howard Carter himself had said that words "failed him at the sight". But Owen wanted many thousands of words.

Eddie began to feel the parts of speech float away from him. We wemble. We shall have wembled. Having wembled. Ronnie announced, in the *Daily Mail*, that he intended to be the only man in England who hadn't been to the Exhibition. In August, at the great Pageant of Empire, followed by the Creatures of Shakespeare's Brain ("the Master himself passes by"), Eddie allowed himself to realize that he had almost wembled. Fellow journalists came up to congratulate him. But at the beginning of May 1926 Owen sent for him again. Wembley was to reopen. They could report the whole Exhibition once more.

Eddie, of course, was proud to be a reliable reporter. On the rare occasions when Christina persuaded him to take a holiday in France, he gave "journalist", not "writer", as his occupation on the passport. He keenly appreciated the Fleet Street of the Twenties, still a great power in the land, wilder and more diversified than he had ever known, with sudden mad swoops into respectability. Beaverbrook and Rothermere were in the ascendant; the unemployed, a silent warning, slept out on the Embankment, wrapped in free posters from the *Express* and *Mail*. Beaverbrook took the inspired risk of running a left-wing cartoon alongside a right-wing editorial. There was no chance of *Punch* doing this. Eddie much regretted that they never printed anything by Strube or by David Low.

His own week turned round his regular article. Writers' families, in small houses, suffer greatly. Lack of the right subject sometimes darkened Monday, difficulty in finishing it always haunted Thursday. Like Dilly, Eddie composed well in the bath, and could do nothing without tobacco. At three o'clock the printer's boy came up from the works for the copy (there was no need to type it in those days). Eddie never kept a stock of standing jokes or poems. His pieces, however elaborately worked out, reflected the passing minute. He envied Ronnie's file of sermons, used again and again until they were reluctantly sent for publication. Ronnie replied that ethics were a better investment than culture or politics; they lasted longer.

Ronnie was, perhaps, not quite interested enough in politics; or at least in the social realities behind them. This appeared to be so in January 1926, when he broadcast a comic eyewitness's account of a revolutionary march by the unemployed. The crowd were supposed to be actually attacking Westminster, roasting one of the ministers alive, proceeding to the B.B.C.'s Savoy Hill station and there being lulled to rest by reading the *Radio Times*.

Unemployment was not a very good subject for satire, but alarmism was, and so was the B.B.C. manner of presenting news, which Ronnie, always a good mimic, did well. As soon as he finished, inquiries began to pour in to Savoy Hill, and the B.B.C. was kept hard at work issuing retractions to soothe "widespread discussion and alarm". The Lord Mayor of Newcastle had been challenged to say "what Newcastle was doing in the emergency". Only Scotland stood firm. Newsmen caught up with Ronnie in Birmingham, where he had gone on to preach. He could only say that he had not meant to deceive anyone. He did not dare to add that he had meant to be funny. Humour, as Eddie could have told him, is relentless.

Cardinal Bourne deeply regretted the broadcast. He related it to the struggle against Communism, and the dethroned and persecuted Church of Soviet Russia. It was difficult for him to descend to lesser things. The panic caused by Ronnie's broadcast would, he thought, encourage the Reds. The *Tablet* of 23 January reproved Ronnie for misusing his "sense of fun". The word "facile" was used. "We are sure," the editorial added, "that Father Knox will take our words in good part."

They were remembered against Ronnie, however, when a chance at last presented itself to get away from St Edmund's. The University Chaplaincy of Oxford was about to fall vacant.

When in 1897 the Hierarchy had cautiously allowed Roman Catholic boys to enter the English universities they appointed chaplains to instruct and maintain them in the faith. That was the foundation of the job, which offered great opportunities for the spiritual care of young men, independence of a kind, and privacy for study in the atmosphere Ronnie loved. It was one of the posts which Newman had dreamed of, but which, to his grievous disappointment, had been refused him. It was a chance, too, to work with Father Martindale (just back from leading a delegation of the unemployed to the Vatican), who would be a colleague at Campion Hall.

But would Ronnie's name be considered? Would he remain the victim of the fatal association between cleverness and unsoundness? He knew that some at least of the Universities' Catholic Education Board considered him quite unsuitable. "The Board thinks of me as a radio maniac let loose on Oxford," he wrote, and, to his old friend Francis Urquhart, of Balliol, "Nothing can make me acceptable or business-like. That is a fact which I can't conceal from myself or anybody else . . . if I am really going to be turned down, it would be a kindness to let me know . . . I am trying to be pious about it, but I can't achieve anything better than a sort of Stoical fanaticism."

Urquhart was largely instrumental in persuading the Board that in spite of the broadcast, and in spite of a lack of formal theological training, Ronnie was the right man. Everything seemed set fair. Lady Lovat offered to supervise the move to Oxford, and even to supply a housekeeper. The only trouble seemed to be that the stipend was very low. But Ronnie had already decided what to do about this. He would make ends meet by writing detective stories.

On the subject of the Red revolution and of hireling Communists, if on no other, Cardinal Bourne and Owen Seaman were in absolute agreement. The General Strike he took simply as a war of class loyalties. Raven Hill, always good at sea-pieces, drew Baldwin as a pilot quietly sticking to his job and being congratulated by John Bull as he emerged from a stormy sea marked GENERAL STRIKE, though the rocks of COAL CRISIS lay ahead. Eddie took an oblique approach, and wrote not in criticism of the Government or the Unions, but about the consumers' strikes of the distant future, when, he thought, the blacklegs would be filmgoers, lured into the cinema to see newsreels of themselves going on strike.

Punch never missed an issue, and the paper was distributed, in holiday spirit, in vans marked FOODSTUFFS. Wilfred wrote from Cambridge to say that although anyone of sense must support the miners' claims, he felt a certain envy of one of the Oratory members who had volunteered as an engine driver. None of the Knox brothers, to whom the railways had meant so much, were ever likely to have such a good chance of driving a train.

The political connotations of the General Strike, which Stalin regarded as an important test for the new grand strategy of the United Front, were not the business of the cryptographic department of the Foreign Office. Part of their work, however, was to assist in watching the Russian activities in this country, as suggested by their signals and correspondence.

Neither in the Twenties nor at any other time did Dilly ever give his family a hint as to what he was doing at the office. His work on the Soviet ciphers is a matter of inference, nothing more.

The Twenties were a successful time for Soviet diplomacy in Europe, and in the establishment of Russian commercial delegations, who claimed diplomatic privileges, at least for their senior officers. In New York the delegation was called AMTORG, in London it was ARCOS, which stood for All-Russian Co-operative Society. The capital was provided by the Moscow Bank for Foreign Trade, and the organization did a brisk import-export business. ARCOS ran a banking corporation of its own, had an agency for Crossley Motors, and published a weekly trade magazine. It was subject to frequent unexplained changes of address; from Coleman Street it moved to Lincoln's Inn Fields, and from there to Southampton Buildings. Like all commercial delegations of every nation, ARCOS was engaged in spying. The only questions were, how dangerously, and how much?

The publication of the Zinoviev Letter, whether or not it was a forgery, was followed in April 1925 by the seizure of the entire contents of the British Embassy in Leningrad, which the Soviet Government offered to swap for their "properties" (i.e., confiscated monasteries) in Palestine. This unsuccessful bargaining set the tone of what followed. In May 1926, when *Izvestia* declared that it was watching the General Strike with delight and wonder, at the same time bitterly attacking the British Labour Party, and complaining about British activities in Persia, "where even the water-carriers are not deceived", it was clear that the information war was being intensified. Every section of the Soviet intelligence abroad had its own ciphers and code; all were sent by post or cable, since Russia was far behind in short-wave radio technique. Every Western country intercepted the signals and hoped to break the code. According to David Kahn's *The Codebreakers*, the United States committee which subpoenaed three thousand AMTORG telegrams was unable to get a single word of them deciphered.

Dilly at this period was almost unapproachable, and showed every sign of being at work on an elusive, but closed, problem. The beauty of decipherment is the limitation of the field. There are after all, only twenty-six letters in the alphabet (or, in the post-Tsarist Russian alphabet, thirty-two). Dilly was thinking entirely in letter values. Asked for a good crossword clue to GHANDI he replied quite casually, "seven, eight, nine" (G *and H I*). That was all the word meant to him at the moment.

The governments of the world now began to close down the Soviet consulates and trading posts in their midst. In 1926 the Turks raided the Soviet-Turkish delegation, and made arrests; there were also arrests in Switzerland and Austria, and in April 1927 the Chinese police entered the Soviet consulate in Peking.

In December 1926, after various protests and rebuffs, a Foreign Office memorandum was circulated privately to key ambassadors, giving notice that a breach with the Soviet Union, and a raid on ARCOS, were probable in the near future. On 13 January 1927 Dilly bought himself a new Burberry overcoat, costing £6 10s, and ordered dinner at John Fothergill's rather expensive inn at Thame, the Spread Eagle. These expenses might pass as unremarkable, but with Dilly they could only mean a celebration, and it is at least possible that the Government, apart from any other intention, had agreed, in his own phrase, to "get something from the post office".

At 4:30 on the afternoon of 12 May, the British police raided Southampton Buildings on an ordinary magistrates' search warrant. The editorial staff of the ARCOS magazine, who in January had announced that they were gaining "more opportunities of getting to know the situation of our hosts, the British people," were thrown into confusion. Rather oddly, they printed an issue dated 16 May with a leading article on the raid. We are told that "in the cipher room Comrades Meler and Zudyakov tried to explain to the police that as fundamental principle of right they could not allow anyone to see the ciphers and telegrams," but met with a "harsh rejoinder." The paper then goes on to discuss the market in heavy machinery.

The police were not dissatisfied, because they were able to pick up several "known spies" in Southampton Buildings. Of the confiscated secret papers, most were ludicrous. They found a complaint, for example, that the British Communist Party had made a terrible mess of providing "politically conscious seamen" for the three Russian vessels which remained under the British flag after 1918; they had sent "the refuse of the Labour Party"—some drank, some were good orators but bad stokers, some did no work at all. Such things were hardly worth knowing, but it has been said that a mysterious "missing document" was never found because the police gave proper warning, and ARCOS had time to destroy it. Indeed, the Soviet *chargé d'affaires* encouraged this idea, cabling to Moscow on the 18th: "I consider it expedient for you to publish as a rumour a statement that the missing document refers to the aerial bombardment of a certain European capital."

How was this last message—which must have been in cipher—translated in London? The real prize which Scotland Yard brought back was what the ARCOS leading article described as "the writing machines and all that they had printed". These would give away the general system, even if the specific key was changed. When they realized that the material would not be returned, the Russians appealed to Khinchuk, the head of the trade delegation, to protest on the grounds of diplomatic immunity. The reply was unfavourable. No more numbers of the ARCOS magazine appeared, and the delegation were requested to leave Great Britain.

Our information about Soviet Russia between the two world wars is usually considered to have been good, though it was derived, of course, from many other sources beside cryptography. The question remains: did our cryptographers break the cipher, and provide information which led to the expulsion of ARCOS, or did they fail to break it, but profit from the raid far more than anyone else?

Dilly was promoted to a higher grade—which may have been for a number of reasons—and joined the Wine Society, although he never became, like Eddie, a connoisseur. Olive also thought they ought to buy more land, and in 1929 E. S. P. Haynes acquired for them another small estate, North Dean, let out at a yearly tenancy of £17 10s.

The family felt that Dilly's woodlands were too much for him already. Small accidents abounded with the saws and choppers. Olive's shelves, put up by Dilly, collapsed with the year's preserves. Aunt Ethel, visiting, fell into a deep pit full of brushwood and hurt herself quite badly. There was no real safety at Courn's Wood, just as there was no real warmth, outside Dilly's study.

VII

"The Fascination of What's Difficult"

I F DILLY'S INTEREST IN THE ARCOS AFFAIR can be presented only as a series of disconnected clues, that, at least, is appropriate to the late Twenties, the period of the classic detective novel. The "rules" for these novels were drawn up by Ronnie in 1928, and adopted in 1929 as the Solemn Oath of the members of the writers' Detection Club. The criminal must be mentioned in the first five chapters, and the reader must not have been allowed to know his inner thoughts; only one secret passage is allowed, no unknown poisons, no mysterious Orientals, no lucky chances or unexplained intuitions to help the detective; the detective must "declare" all his clues, so must the "Watson", or uncomprehending friend; and the detective must not turn out to be the criminal. Agatha Christie, although a founder member of the Detection Club, broke nearly all of these rules, and G. K. Chesterton had broken most of them, but Ronnie was happy with their safe dimensions. A game should be an imitation of life's dimensions in which the players themselves can decide when to stop and get off.

Between 1926 (*The Viaduct Murder*) and 1937 (*Double Cross Purposes*) he wrote six detective stories. All of them, even the earliest, were backward-looking. To feel at home in them, you need to be familiar with Bradshaw's railway timetables, canoeing on the upper reaches of the Thames, vicarages, gas taps, and country house parties in which the first duty is consideration for one's hostess. Time has obscured these things, although time may well restore the wish to read about them. The solutions to the mysteries are most scrupulously set out, and page references are given, in case the reader has missed the clues.

As a novelist, Ronnie was not strong on characterization. In 1920, when formidable Aunt Ellen (the college Principal) wrote from Toronto: "I have been trying my hand at a story of Old Canada, and am sending six chapters so that my nephews can put more life and buoyancy into the 'conversations,' " none of them, not even Eddie, was prepared to take on the job. Some of Ronnie's characters he found to hand, just as he used the familiar scenery of Scotland, Oxford and Herefordshire—the convert clergyman, for instance, in *The Three Taps*, or Miss Morel, the lady motor-car driver in *The Body in the Silo*, who was taken from Miss Gompertz. But he was not able to establish a popular detective to carry him through book after book—couldn't even think of a name for him, but opened his *Shropshire Lad* and found:

> In summertime on Bredon . . .
>   In valleys miles away . . .

Miles Bredon, Ronnie's investigator, is a stick. He smokes a pipe and plays patience, as both Dilly and Ronnie did, to clear his mental processes, but without coming to life for a single moment. Yet Ronnie had admirable models—Dilly himself (except that flashes of intuition were forbidden by the rules) would have served, and Wilfred would have been even better, though here the pain of the old association stood in the way; and besides, the figure of the wise, ageless, shabby priest who puts the conventionally-minded to shame had been done once and for all, Ronnie thought, by Hugh Benson and Chesterton; no one guessed how soon Graham Greene was going to drag him out again for *The Power and the Glory*.

Ronnie's six detective stories, which earned him about four hundred pounds a year each, were written in the vacations at Beaumont to supplement his income from the chaplaincy at Oxford. They made it possible for him to bear most of the expenses of hospitality himself, although it worried him that it might establish a precedent and that all his successors might have to find extra money, and perhaps write novels, as well. Although he was still modestly uncertain as to what the job entailed and whether he was the right man to do it, he left St Edmund's for Oxford in the Michaelmas of 1926, with sober expectations of success.

The chaplaincy house at Oxford, misleadingly called the Old Palace, is on the corner of St Aldates. It is a very old place, part of it pre-Elizabethan, with the oak beams that support it—"if anything does," Ronnie said—showing through the plaster. A stream, a tributary of the Isis and once used for a mill stream, runs beneath the whole building into Christ Church Meadows. Different levels, sloping floors and low passages make getting about an achievement; two ancient chimneys go up the whole height of the house, and the drainage system is a study in itself. As a link with the past, the Old Palace could not be improved upon. Bishop King, the first and last Catholic bishop of Oxford, had lived there. As a link with the future, it was less suitable, but Ronnie could not foresee its later metamorphoses, its doors open to down-and-outs and unfortunates, a thriving cafeteria, open debates with all the world's religions. His vision did not extend so far. He saw it as a centre of exchanged confidences, prayer and peace.

It was also a home. Ronnie became a householder. Before that he had always been in school or college, or a guest, or a lodger. In an essay, "Joys of Householding", he described the heady sensation; he was sleeping, for the first time, in his own bed: "I could go out and sell it in a shop if I wanted to." And he could have food because he liked it, not because it was all he would get, or "because it would look so rude if I didn't."

Food, however, depended on a good housekeeper. Mrs Lyons—she never married, the "Mrs" was honorary—was an old family retainer supplied by Lady Lovat, who acted for more than ten years as Ronnie's cook, business manager, almoner, sacristan and clothes-mender. Pious and frugal, refusing to give up work until a few days before her death, she was fiercely protective of all priests, and of Ronnie, of course, in particular. With her, his comfort was assured, that of his visitors rather less so, as Mrs Lyons did not take to everybody. Some were in perpetual disfavour. To these the Old Palace became the Den of Lyons.

The move from Ware was easier than he had feared. He chose the blue chintz curtains himself, or thought he did, for every woman guest, including Christina, was consulted. He stood gazing wistfully out into St Aldates, to see whether people were looking at them, and whether they noticed that there were no linings. The Sisters of Nazareth came with a hand-cart to clear away the junk, and Ronnie took possession, as the chaplain's room, of the long panelled room on the first floor where once again he could sit down on his own fender, with his back to his own fire.

Oxford welcomed him without reserve. One disappointment was the departure of Father Martindale, who had suddenly gone off, with the speed of a whirlwind, and returning only for an occasional sermon to a wider apostolate. Otherwise there were old friends everywhere, and no reproaches at his change of faith. His old college, Trinity, elected him at once to dining rights; this, and the Honorary Fellowship they gave him at the end of his chaplaincy, he felt as two of "the nicest things that ever happened to me".

He proved himself to be a good, if anxious, organizer, better, though less successful, than Eddie and Dilly, who were able by instinct to find others to organize for them. In 1931 he personally raised and gave six thousand pounds for the building of a new chapel. With none of the *folie de pierre* which is the last infirmity of so many priests, he dismissed the architect's Gothic plans and asked for something that "could be turned into tea-rooms later on", as indeed it was. His main object was to find a reliable routine for the household, the chapel and the University societies, which he hesitantly hoped might become a tradition. In "The Whole Art of

Chaplaincy", a document which he bequeathed to his successors, he gives not only a summary of his pastoral methods but a loving description of loose gas taps, frightful draughts and creaking doors which could, surely, have been put right on the spot. The chapel harmonium had not been tuned for thirteen years; a white stole, picked up in the ruins of Ypres, Ronnie would rather have liked to get rid of, but didn't. He did not want to change these things, any more than he changed the position of the picture which was hung upside-down in the passage and stayed like that till 1938. He was at Oxford. This was his home. As a Catholic priest, he felt more deeply united with the medieval foundation which, he now felt, had lost its way for a few centuries—but what did that matter at Oxford?— and to which the Faith had now quietly returned.

Writing to his publisher, Tom Burns, about a collection of chaplaincy sermons, Ronnie explained that he wanted to call it *The Hidden Stream* because of the mill stream that ran beneath the Old Palace. "It is the easiest thing in the world to go down it in a canoe, but I find that my name has become immortal as the intrepid paddlesman who did it. It would draw a parable between this single, unsuspected branch of the Isis and the stream of teaching which goes on at the Old Palace, rather shiftily, quite differently from the main stream of University teaching, etc., etc." By "rather shiftily" he meant what others might call unobtrusively and profoundly. In that spirit he undertook his new duties.

At Courn's Wood, Dilly hacked away persistently at the chalky slopes of beechwoods, and planted several acres of trees himself, a gaunt figure in half professorial, half woodlander's attire, ending in grey flannel trousers tucked into waders.

> Two miles from our sombre home in the Chilterns [writes his son Oliver], across a valley, up a broad bridlepath, then down a meandering track left almost invisible, stood the log-cabin built by my father, in a glade surrounded by ash-saplings and willow-herb. He had built this hut with his own hands, sawing and splitting the larchwood, with relentless energy, all day so long as there was any light, every

Saturday and Sunday through one summer in the early '30s. Here one afternoon I returned from some expedition, to hear the murmur of my parents' conversation. What I heard was disturbing.

My father was talking of the frustrations of life at the Foreign Office, and of the yearnings to return to Cambridge and resume his passionate studies of Greek. My mother was reminding him, low but firmly, of his duty to educate his sons, and of the national importance of his work, and adding, too, that she herself could not bear the thought of returning to the chill wastes of fenland and the inhospitable society of dons.

I didn't dare to shuffle, or announce my presence, but peeped between the cracks of the timber wall. My father was in his shirtsleeves, holding his saw. His pipe lay neglected on the crude windowsill. For once he wasn't wearing his horn-rim spectacles, so that his eyes looked unfamiliarly naked.

This was one of the very few times indeed that I saw him looking as though not in control of his destiny.

The yearning prevailed, even though Dilly had become somewhat impatient recently with the wave of supernaturalism which appeared to be invading King's. Monty James, the scholar of malignant hauntings, had transferred to Eton, but Dilly's old friend, the historian Esmé Wingfield-Stratford, had been receiving poems from the spirit world dictated by Oscar Wilde and Rupert Brooke, while his once rational and cynical tutor, Nathaniel Wedd, was attending séances to conjure up the philosopher Ellis McTaggart from the dead. In 1929, indeed, McTaggart apparently *did* return to a séance in Redhill in the form of a man with a stout walking-stick, which he tried to poke into the ground, repeating "I have loved you all the time"; when Wedd failed to recognize him, the medium told him he had summoned the wrong McTaggart, and declined to enter into any further correspondence. Dilly, in the name of Cambridge, objected bitterly to all this. "Middle age is drifting away," he told Lytton Strachey, and unbelief seemed to be weakening. Yet Dilly, quite rightly, felt that King's would in the end resist the temptations of faith, and the discussion about his future was particularly acute because in 1929 he had challenged fate with another scholarly publication, the Loeb Classical Library edition of Herodas.

This was a condensed edition, presenting many new readings and conjectures, and including fragments of Hipponax, Cercidas and the *Life of Alexander*, which, Dilly characteristically tells us, "was more popular between the 3rd and 12th century in the Greek and Byzantine world than any other book except the New Testament, and is some of the worst poetry ever written." Its childishness should correct, he says, the mistaken notion that the Greeks were intellectuals. He also, in accordance with the scheme of the Loeb series, provided an English translation, skilfully reproducing the metre as well as the sense of the Greek verse:

> But now that there gleam on my head
> White hairs but a few at the edge
> Still does my summer
> Seek for the thing that is fair . . .

However, he only did this if, in his judgment, the original poems were good enough. Herodas himself, like the *Alexander*, did not "pass", so the Mimes appeared translated into prose.

But what prose! There is no trace of what the Loeb editors said to their wayward contributor when they saw this version, designed, in principle, as a key for advanced students. The language of the Mimes is precious, with unpleasant affected archaisms, and an honest translation, it seemed to Dilly, must be the same. Cloistered in his study, with a new, terrifying form of patience which he had invented himself and taught to Ronnie to celebrate his move to the chaplaincy, Dilly worked out his English equivalent to Herodas. "La no reke hath she of what I say, but standeth goggling at me more agape than a crab" is a typical sentence, while "Why can't you tell me what they cost?" comes out as "Why mumblest ne freetongued descryest the price?" Satisfied, Dilly corrected his proofs; he read the reviews, all of which praised the accuracy of the text but considered the translation a complete failure, with indifference. "If I am unintelligible," he wrote, "it is because Herodas was."

Nineteen thirty-one was a year marked out by the Fates for disappointment. The long-dreaded motor-bike accident took place at last, a serious crash, and Dilly's leg was badly broken. Afterwards he always walked with a slight limp, sometimes on tiptoe, sometimes breaking into a jog-trot, to avoid cramp. Laid up in the Acland Home, at Oxford, he expected Ronnie to visit him, and felt disproportionately hurt when Ronnie never came. True, he might have sent a note round to the Old Palace, but "surely one doesn't have to write to one's brothers?" Dilly complained.

A letter arrived from the wife of the distinguished Dutch scholar, also a commentator on Herodas, Professor Grooneboom: "When we hear that our dear Professor Knox is not well, we say to one another that we wish nothing better than that he was among us here." Dilly put the letter away, with the earlier one offering him the chair of Greek at Leeds. If Olive could not face Cambridge, what would she say to the prospect of Holland or a northern University? She had been in the deepest anxiety over his accident, and she loved him dearly. Sacrifice must be met with sacrifice.

Emerging from hospital, he practised walking round the lawn, following the footsteps of a large tortoise to whose shell he had attached a wooden engine on a string. Its trundling could be heard on summer mornings, and in the winter, when it buried itself, the engine was left above ground to mark the spot. Then, partially recovered, Dilly bought an Austin Seven to cover the five miles to High Wycombe station, which gave him exactly time to recite the whole of Milton's *Lycidas*, taking his hand off the wheel now and then to say: "Look! It drives itself!"

Few people were anxious to accept a lift from Dilly; one who did, without the slightest worry, was the artist Gilbert Spencer, Stanley's brother.

After our marriage [he writes], my wife and I took rooms at Mr Rogers the chairmaker, just at the bottom of the road leading up to Dillwyn's home in Courn's Wood . . . [He] always gave me a lift to the station and used to amuse himself seeing how far he could go downhill with the engine off. He also told me that our terminus (Marylebone) was so out of the way that he was pretty nearly the only passenger, which

explained why he was so politely received by the station-master. But
we thought it was his highly important position at the Foreign Office.

Since his early friendship with Henry Lamb, Dilly had always
liked a certain kind of low-keyed, unassertive, but deeply felt
English picture. He did not much care for the large bright Medici
prints which hung in his dining room. It was agreed that Spencer,
who, with a wife and young baby, needed commissions, should do a
portrait. This firm but delicate pencil drawing, an excellent like-
ness, illustrates another of Spencer's remarks: "For an artist, not to
understand someone does not mean not to know them."

In another range of Dilly's sympathies was his Sunday visitor, the
impeccable Professor Lobel. As editor of the "laundry lists", the
Oxyrhynchus papyri, Lobel came down with his fragments and
problems, not so that they could consult each other, but simply so
that they could sit side by side, each in his own Greek world, ex-
changing perhaps half a sentence. The children were overawed, and
hid in the brushwood.

> If Edgar Lobel was the most imposing of my father's friends [Oliver
> recalls], Frank Birch was the jolliest, most amusing and mondain.
> When he came down to Courn's Wood I was slightly ashamed of the
> cold unworldliness of our home, and vaguely conscious that the half-
> bottle of Châteauneuf du Pape customarily provided for visitors was
> not enough.

It was not enough, but Frank Birch produced a magical change in
Dilly. The cold and daunting "Why do you say that?" which was his
answer to anything muddled or inexact, disappeared into the gaiety
which Birch brought with him. Never to be forgotten was Birch's
virtuoso appearance, all but unrecognizable in wig and elastic-sided
boots, as the Widow Twankey in *Aladdin*. It was remarked in King's
that he was the only member of college to appear in pantomime
while still a Fellow. For the occasion Dilly treated the family to seats
at the Lyric, Hammersmith, and the smaller ones sat laughing, half
in terror, as the Widow found a baby mixed up with the washing.
"Quite spoiled, isn't he? Never be the same again!"

Otherwise, Dilly came up to London only for work and cricket, which also worked a transformation. To Oliver,

> an outing to a Test Match was a spree, almost, on which we were alone together. My father's metropolitan manners came as a surprise. To begin with, he took a taxi from Marylebone; unheard-of extravagance. Then he forgot to collect our change at the turnstiles, and waved aside more change for a score-card, in his hurry to watch the game. Such carefree behaviour seemed a far cry from the thrift and sobriety of Courn's Wood.

The fates did not give Dilly a daughter, before whom, very likely, he would have been as helpless as he was without his spectacles. To his niece, confined for what seemed an eternity to a boarding school at nearby High Wycombe, where the girls, although their anatomy made it impracticable, were obliged to play cricket, Dilly was the kindest of visiting uncles. Agitated at having brought her back late in the Baby Austin, which seemed to spring and bounce along the roads like a fawn, he bravely entered the precincts, blinking in the bright light, confronting the outraged housemistress, who said "Rules are made to be kept," with the answer: "But they are defined only by being broken."

For his fiftieth birthday, in 1934, Dilly resolved to entertain his brothers and sisters to lunch. Eddie, when he was fifty, had given an elegant family lunch at the Café Royal; Dilly decided on the Spread Eagle at Thame.

The famous inn was still under the management of John Fothergill, who has described in his *Innkeeper's Diary* his successes as a host, but not the trials of the guests, which increased towards the end of his heyday at Thame. As mine host he still looked welcoming as he stood at the door, a figure left over from the Beardsley era, with copper buckles at his knee, and in chilly weather wearing a sealskin cap made out of his mother's muff. His grand manner remained, but dining at the Spread Eagle had become unpredictable. There were long delays, and Fothergill had barred off all the lavatories in the house, so that guests had to pick their way through the long wet grass of the orchard to relieve themselves, often pursued by vindictive bees, said to have been brought from Hymettus.

Dilly made an anxious host, though Fothergill was apparently ready to honour them, and bowed over Christina's hand with the strange compliment, "Madame, I admire your teeth." You did not order on these occasions; Fothergill provided. After they had sat some time, he returned bearing in his own hands a small dish of perfectly plain boiled potatoes, with an explanation which only he could have given: "You must not think I would insult you by serving anything with them."

When poor Fothergill departed to Market Harborough ("a Midland desert not fit for a pigsty," he wrote to Eddie), Dilly entered a farewell verse in his private notebook:

> Long the Spread Eagle host has ranked
> His very privy sacrosanct;
> Now all things shall be free to use,
> Nor need we mind our pees and qs.

But relaxations, even unsuccessful ones, were not so characteristic as an intense concentration and withdrawal, when, as Olive told her son, "your father is miles away." "It was years after his death before I knew what he did," Oliver said; "to his work he referred not at all, any enquiries in that respect being met with the dismaying device of total silence."

During the Thirties, finding that smoking and patience were not sufficient as alternative tranquillizer and counter-irritant to the active mind, Dilly suddenly produced a new way of writing poetry. A devoted reader of *Sylvie and Bruno*, he particularly valued Lewis Carroll's notion that "if you have a long tedious evening ahead, why not store up the useless hours for some other occasion when you need extra time?" The hours spent at Naphill dinner parties seemed now to be turned to account in the fastnesses of the study, from which he emerged every now and then with a poem in his hand. These were, perhaps, an attempt at wholeness, that is, at uniting the two sides of himself, the relentless "Why do you say that?" with the unpredictable visits of intuition.

The rules, Dilly claimed, were transparently simple; each line must end with a word of the same form, but with a different vowel, the vowels "of course" coming in their proper order, a, e, i, o, u, or the equivalent sounds in English. One of his earliest examples was:

Just look at my father	A
And mother together!	E
I fancy that neither	I
Would very much bother	O
If rid of the other.	U

Irrelevant proper names could not be allowed. Wanting a more difficult rhyme-word, he had tried:

> And waiting in a sad row
> For the head-waiter, Pedro,
> The inmates of the hydro
> Longed for their tea and cod-roe,
> And talked of Wilson (Woodrow).

That wouldn't do, Dilly thought. The situation was improbable. There was no *rationale*. Why should they talk about Woodrow Wilson? Might they not, however, have been driven mad by the Peace Treaty? And after all, why not write poetry about food and drink? Why should a life spent in eating and drinking be considered baser than a life devoted to sex? Sex, it was true, was a kind of communication with other human beings. But then, drink helped one to forget them.

It was suggested to him that the Pentelopes, as he called his five-line verses, were an acquired taste, that not very many people would appreciate them, and that (like Gerard Manley Hopkins) he was making poetry too difficult to write. And it would be almost impossible, under these new rules, to convey emotion. About whom or what? Dilly asked. Why do you say that?—Well, for example, A. E. Housman had recently died. What epitaph could be appropriate for him, except, "They told me, Heraclitus, they told me you were dead . . ."?

The pain and restraint, the hesitation on the part of the messengers which the repetition in the first line suggests, surely these couldn't be expressed under the new "rules"? It turned out that Dilly *had* done so, on the very morning that he heard of Housman's death:

> Sad though the news, how sad
> Of thee, the poet, dead!
> But still thy poems abide—
> There Death, the unsparing god
> Himself dare not intrude.

He agreed that it would scarcely do to show this condensed version to his brothers. It was put away in his tin box, where the pile of Pentelopes grew, awaiting the day when the new system would be acclaimed as the easiest and most obvious form of reducing poetry to a game.

Two years earlier than this, in 1934, a wave of intense depression had led Dilly to try and make over the whole of his wooded estates to King's. It would have been an ingenious solution.

> My dear Dillwyn [Maynard Keynes had replied], the college is in fact already in the timber business on a certain scale, and is not unduly unsuccessful, but there are great difficulties in the way of the college going in for it on a large scale. But all this does not mean that we should not like you to come up and talk about it.

Once again, the appeal of Cambridge was strongly heard. Nevertheless, in 1936, for the first time, Dilly began to refuse his invitations to Founder's Feast. The reason was simple; the dinner was noted, even among Cambridge colleges, for its hospitality and its fine wines, and, in consequence, for the occasional indiscretions of the guests. These, to be sure, were heard by Kingsmen only, but the time had come when Dilly could not risk even the hint of a shadow of a reference to what he was doing. He had started work on a new problem.

The importance of this problem was the cause of his erratic behaviour, the sudden gloom and exhilaration, the obsession with the obstinate five vowels of the alphabet which emerged in the queer poems. His department was face to face with difficulties far beyond the imagination of Room 40.

Since the end of the Great War every government which had something to hide, and could afford to hide it, had been in the market for an electromechanical system of encipherment which would avoid repetitions, and so make the old methods of solution through letter frequencies almost impossible. During the Thirties, cipher machines were patented by the ingenious which generated their own alphabets by the million, printed or indicated the letters, and could be put into reverse to decipher them for the receiver. Each type had its advantages—compactness, ease of operation, accuracy. France, Italy, and later the United States, chose the Swedish Hagelin. The Soviet Union had its own. Germany bought the Enigma. The keys, the settings and the method of operation were all secret. It was the business of the Foreign Office's Department of Communications to solve Enigma and, later, the Enigma Variations.

At the beginning of the Thirties Wilfred was quite alone at Oratory House, except for the daily visits of Mr Smith, the gardener. But in 1933 he was joined there by Dr Alec Vidler. The arrival of this great priest, theologian, and natural administrator and organizer, a man whose horizon widened year by year, was of untold value to Wilfred, always fortunate in his friends. A certain shyness had held him apart from the University. An Oxford man to the very depths, he felt doubtful of his reception in the bright windswept fenland city. He had no access to the University libraries. Students came to consult him, he was supremely at ease with the fruit-pickers, but he was seen very little in the colleges. As a scholar, he was a member of the New Testament Seminar conducted by F. C. Burkitt, but he seemed almost afraid of social distractions. Alec Vidler put an end to all this, drew him out and dusted him off, induced him to take steps to get his Doctorate of Divinity, and introduced him to the heads of colleges. He was pleased when Wilfred was invited to give the University sermon (although, owing to the rapid, quiet delivery, not many people could hear it), and delighted when he was made a Canon of Ely. At a deeper level, he confirmed Wilfred's vision, in the true spirit of the Good Shepherd, of a universal Christianity, with total authority, but without sectarian bitterness. Then he introduced him to the work of Reinhold Niebuhr, whose social ethics, based on his experience in industrial cities, made a direct appeal to Wilfred; only, by temperament, he could not quite admit this at once, but let several months pass before saying that he had found Niebuhr "quite interesting".

His natural tendency to broadness of spirit could be judged by his services on the Committee for Christian Doctrine, which met during those years to find a basis of common doctrine for the whole Church. No Roman Catholics attended, but Wilfred was invited as a representative of Anglo-Catholic opinion, which, it was thought, would mean extreme Conservatism. Many were disconcerted when he spoke out in favour of the tolerance of birth control and civil divorce. If his first draft manifesto had gone out, he told his old friend Stephen Langton, "it would have produced the headline 'ANGLO-CATHOLICS CALL FOR CONTRACEPTIVES' (*Daily Mirror*). Then we should have cut some ice. Thine, Wilfred."

The strength of this came from Wilfred's serene inner certainty. When faith was discussed he was the most consistent and even conservative of them all. On the essential beliefs of Christianity he was as firm as a rock, nor did he care if most people, or indeed if everyone, found them too difficult. "At the end of the day, God is still where He was." But on the necessity of recognizing the human needs of this world, Wilfred was also firm.

As a matter of fact the Committee's summing-up, when it eventually appeared in 1938, was greeted in the daily press as CHURCH SAYS SEX NOT EVIL. The report, in consequence, sold surprisingly well, and the Committee had to school themselves to patience and hope that their painstaking summary of the faith would make its way in time.

Ronnie, for his part, analysed the report in several despairing articles. "Nobody who reads it can fail to be impressed by the goodwill of the signatories," he wrote, "or by their learning in certain fields. But their whole conception of faith differs so completely from ours, that no bridge of understanding seems, at present, to be possible. There is nothing to be prayed for except a revolution in their whole method of thought."

When Dilly came over on his increasingly rare visits to Cambridge he usually saw Wilfred, paid a visit to the Oratory, and told his brother that he could no longer be surprised by the vagaries to which Christianity led. Yet he was not quite unsympathetic to Wilfred's studies, because they were concentrated on the one saint whom Dilly could tolerate, the recklessly determined St Paul, to whom nothing was impossible.

If *Meditation and Mental Prayer* is the most accessible of Wilfred's books, where his speaking voice can still be heard, *St. Paul and the Church of the Gentiles* is the one by which fellow historians and theologians remember him. In it he set out to reconstruct the mind of the Hellenized society of the first century, when Jew influenced Greek and Greek influenced Jew under the uneasy Roman peace. The Gospels were not the only biography produced in the first century, nor was Paul the only man who wrote letters. Only by understanding the climate in which they were written can we hope to estimate whether they are true or not, and Wilfred is scrupulous in not doing this for us. "The fact of Paul's experience may have been no more than an illusion, but for him it was a matter of immediate certainty. It followed from this that nothing else mattered." Each chapter then explains a different aspect of the Greek religious and philosophical notions which Paul had to use and to adapt by hook or by crook, if anyone in Corinth or Ephesus was to be got to listen to the truth. Wilfred's knowledge of the sources, from classical literature to magical papyri, went deep and wide and has rarely been equalled. He knew his own Greek world, that is, as well as Dilly and Headlam knew theirs. Through all his weight of learning, it emerges unmistakably as a place of fear, craving for either a practical guide or a magical formula, and dominated by the power of the stars, in which, we are reminded, Paul himself believed, when he set out to fight against them in their courses.

Wilfred's work is scholarship for scholars, but, in his approach to it, he never forgot those who were not. The widening gap between theologians and anyone else to whom Christianity might be of interest was of great concern to him. "If we read a great deal of theology," he said, "we shall need a great deal of faith." The Gospels and Epistles were disintegrating in the devoted hands of twentieth-century structural analysts. Christ was left with no Life, and St Paul with very few Letters. The popular religious best sellers of the Thirties took no notice whatever of these developments, and Wilfred was shrewd enough not to despise them. H. V. Morton's tour of the Holy Land, *In the Steps of the Master*, a consistent best seller, treated every place and event in the Gospels as simple fact. It was followed by the equally popular *In the Steps of St. Paul*. But if Morton were to write "In the Steps of the Theologians", Wilfred said, we should pretty soon find ourselves in the desert.

Once again, this did not mean that he had any idea of compromise, which would have been false to his character, and totally false to his vocation. There is only one truth, but he believed it was the business of scholars to preserve it and defend it.

In the summer vacations, Eddie and Wilfred still met in the Welsh Border country, but now they fished not the Arrow, but another tributary of the Wye, the Lug. They shared (unequally) the rent of a thatched cottage in the very small village of Knill.

Knill is at the bottom of a valley, and memory associates it always with summer heat, sheep standing stuffily in the high bracken, the fumes of cider apples, and a haze of warmth at the farm where the enormous featherbed, in the room sometimes let out to visitors, almost suffocated them. A team of cart horses stood ready for the fields or to pull an unwary motorist out of the ford, which ran across the road to join the stream. Mr Davies, the farmer, was of course not idyllic but practical. As the years passed he sold the team, inspected the sheep from a Ford van, and replaced the thatch on the cottage with slates. But in the 1930s the thick straw still projected over the eaves, raucous with birds and insects. In Wilfred's small room, known as the "prophet's chamber", the chirping and rustling were deafening. Downstairs, magpies' nests fell down the chimney, and rabbits invaded the vegetable garden which Wilfred had carefully laid out.

It was felt that he needed looking after when Eddie and Christina were not there, and this was undertaken by Mrs Moses, the wife of the water-bailiff on the Lug. George Wozencroft, the head gardener from the big house, Knill Place, came to work at the cottage in his spare time, not without some clashes with Wilfred over the direction of affairs in the tiny garden. They understood each other perfectly. When Wilfred's unmanageable dog Tim flew at Wozencroft, fastening his teeth on his old stained moleskin breeches, Wilfred watched dispassionately. "Your dog's chewing the seat of my trousers, Canon." "So I see; I don't feel tempted to follow his example." In fact, no dog would have been a match for Wozencroft's moleskins.

In the tiny village church, cared for by Mrs Davies, Wilfred took duty for the incumbent, who had a scattered parish. His sermons are still remembered there, although they were not always well adapted to their listeners. Once, when he was ill, the sermon was entrusted to a lay reader, who had to begin, in the soft Herefordshire accent: "We read in Plotinus . . . "

In the 1920s Eddie had been asked by a reporter what he would like to be. He had replied—a Prince Archbishop (enjoy yourself in this world, absolve yourself for the next), or a Tartar, riding thirty horses a day, and making butter by swinging milk in a goatskin bag at the saddle, or, perhaps, a potboy at the Mermaid Tavern with a good memory. But in 1931 he became an editor; he was offered the editorship of *Punch*.

The hints to Sir Owen Seaman that it might be time to quit the stage had at last been understood. For some time he had apparently thought that the Company Chairman must be talking of himself—

"Surely you're not thinking of retiring, Lawrence?" This was his mind's defence against the unacceptable truth that his twenty-six years' pastoral care of the paper and of the Conservative Party must draw to a close. His sense of loss was a measure of the standing of *Punch*. In spite of recent criticisms, to be editor of *Punch* was still to be "King of Fleet Street".

Certainly Seaman could never have wandered round the office, as Ross did round *The New Yorker* after the markets crashed, asking: "Are we important?" and demanding the answer: "No, we're only a fifteen-cent magazine!" As the day of his retirement drew closer, Seaman published a depressing poem (15 July 1931) to "Mr. Punch on His Ninetieth Birthday", addressing Punch as "Master and Friend", and praising him as "changing not his style" and holding fast to standards proven long ago, no matter

> If we grow old and go our ways
> For you will still be there
> With other service at your call.

Eddie was to be the "other service", receiving the formidable bequest of a paper which had apparently become a semi-religious institution. In November 1932, when Seaman presided at the Table for the last time, he prepared a Valete card giving his apostolic blessing to "the friend and colleague who succeeds me." Jokes were neither mentioned nor thought of. Still, Eddie, at the age of fifty-two, could feel that he had reached the top of his profession. He had reversed his father's bitter disappointment when he had failed to take his degree, and he had justified the confidence of Christina.

The details had been settled on a weekend at Littlecourt, the Agnews' country home; Eddie was to get £3,000 a year, inclusive of his contributions as "Evoe", with thirty guineas extra for the Summer Number and the Christmas Almanack. The position would be reviewed in ten years, and, for the first time in the history of *Punch*, there would be an editorial pension. He was not offered, neither did he expect, any travel or entertainment allowances, a car, a flat, or a staff of copy editors to do the day-to-day work. An editor in

1932 went straight to his desk, dealt personally with the contributors and the printers, and put the paper to bed himself.

There had been other aspirants, not to say disappointed claimants, for the job. One of the first to write, with his usual good grace, was A. A. Milne ("I am indeed *very* glad")—then, when paragraphs appeared about the new appointment, an astonishing number of congratulations, and of jokes about a new Seaman at the helm, came in from England, Europe and America. Old Uncle Lindsey struck a warning note. "I fear that there may be a great deal of extra work, and going into and receiving society." To a true Evangelical, such things were perilous. Rudyard Kipling wrote:

> As to Punch—I've seen him . . . in all sorts of out-of-the-way places where he represents England in all its varieties to men who, because they are far removed, see and remember it more keenly . . . it is perfectly true that he has become urbane, which he was not, even as late as the sixties (see files), or thirty years back, when he used to whack me on the head on general principles. But he can bite quite hard enough when he likes . . . only give us subscribers every shade and detail of our queer facing-both-ways national outlook on all things; and when the wind changes, as it will in the next few years, stand by to allay the panic. To which you will justly answer: 'Who the deuce made *you* an Editor?' But I never was. I was only a sub-editor and, of course, in that capacity, thought I knew more than my Chief. You may have noticed that all subordinates do.

This was good advice and Eddie tried to follow it. Most tributes, including his election to the Athenaeum under the alarming Rule B, for people of special eminence, he took "simply as something due to the position of the paper, nothing to do with me."

The new *Punch* offices, built in 1930, were still in the narrow canyon of Bouverie Street, but were now seven floors tall, with lifts and red carpets. The statue of Mr Punch looked down from its niche above the world of the Press. Eddie, as well as several of the artists, had warned the management that the figure was not correctly scaled to be seen from below, but it went up, the stomach looked far too prominent, and the building became known as the Paunch Office. In Eddie's view, the whole place was rather too grand and serious.

He had a staunch friend in the enormous ex-sergeant-major who presided in the entrance hall. On the third floor was Advertising, where Jean Lyon, Raven Hill's wife, reigned undisputed. The income from space had long since exceeded the revenue from sales, and the third floor was a place of fierce, puritanical power. Miss Lyon charged high, but it was a long while before she would allow advertisements for alcohol in *Punch*, even though the paper kept its original 1841 cover design, which showed the red-nosed hunchback decidedly the worse for drink. Any editor had to begin by standing up to Jean Lyon, and Eddie, in his courteous way, did so successfully.

The fourth floor was Editorial, with windows looking straight across the street into the *News of the World*, so that you could watch the "Rape Committee", a group of solemn-looking executives bending over the sex-outrage stories for next Sunday. The *Punch* furnishings were also solemn, of good quality, like those of the *Queen Mary*. Eddie occupied the traditional swivel chair. The handsome wastepaper basket, however, caught fire so often in the first few weeks (he smoked cigarettes now instead of a pipe) that the sergeant-major replaced it with a metal one.

Eddie settled down to edit his paper. As soon as possible he selected his own young assistant staff, finding the most loyal of assistant editors, Humphrey Ellis, who had come to the job from school teaching, and was the author of *Assistant Masters: Are They Insane?* Among the old hands, Eddie was most at home with the artists, who made an agreeable link with the past. Bernard Partridge, still the senior cartoonist, had acted with Henry Irving, and had been Bernard Shaw's original Sergius in *Arms and the Man*. He never said much, and yet half an hour's conversation with him was enough to show how vain it is for modern actors to attempt Shaw or Wilde. George Stampa, the artist of London's street life, had helped the boozy Phil May in and out of his cabs. Ernest Shepard, whose airy, graceful drawings seemed to blow across the pages, had been trained at the Royal Academy Schools in 1896. W. Bird, the Irish artist, who could give, within the tiny oblong of an ass-and-cart joke, the whole atmosphere and the distant horizons of County Sligo, was in fact Jack Yeats, the poet's brother. Eddie appreciated these links with the past, the paper's and his own, knowing that human beings, like wines, have their vintages. He loved *Punch*'s history, and, quite deliberately, was the last editor on Fleet Street to call the illustrations "cuts", a reminiscence of the old days of wood engraving. But Eddie was also an accessible editor, anxious to find and encourage new talent.

An early reaction to his appointment was a wild rush of aspiring contributors and illustrators. They were desperate, times being hard. The seasons, for free-lance humorous artists, were divided into spring (courting couples), summer (misadventures of campers and hikers, bathers attacked by crabs), autumn (jokes about fog and slipping on fallen leaves), winter (people falling through the ice). A rumour had also gone round that the new editor would consider rather broader jokes; portfolios never before opened in the *Punch* office were furtively brought out. All these callers were dealt with patiently. The overmatter was already an accumulation, left by Seaman, of hiking and skating jokes. As to sex jokes, Eddie, like his contemporary Ross of *The New Yorker*, decided that the time would come, but was not yet.

He was, however, as has been said, a seeker and finder, particularly on his own chosen ground of fantasy and poetry. He pleaded with Ernest Rhys, the editor of Everyman editions, to support modern poets, having discovered at the Poetry Bookshop that "only Eliot is bought at all." He sought out, with some difficulty, the short-story writer A. E. Coppard, whose indefinable moonlight oddness appealed to him, as though reality had slipped one notch or more, or, as Coppard put it, "some essential part had been detached from the obviously vital part." Rowland Emmett, whose drawings showed the latent poetry of old engines and old steamboats, he put under contract for as long as he could. The reviewing of cinema, books and theatre, and the Parliamentary Reports, all came to life for the first time under the new editor.

The effect of this kind of thing on the readership is best illustrated by the matter of the Hippo Joke. In July 1937 *Punch* printed a
drawing by Paul Crum, which showed, in a few lines, two hippos almost submerged in an open swamp, miles away from anywhere; one
is saying to the other: "I keep thinking it's Tuesday." This joke
proved a breaking point for many subscribers, while it rallied others.
"We are told that a sense of humour is the greatest gift of all," Eddie
wrote in *What Life Has Taught Me*, "yet I find that everybody has it."
"Sir, I flatter myself on my sense of humour," he quoted from the
Hippo correspondence, "but neither I nor any of my friends can see
the point of the joke at the bottom of page 173. We are still trying
hard, but if we do not succeed in a few days, we shall give up the attempt." Another says, "DEAR SIR—I can boast that I know a good
joke when I see one, and as soon as I looked at the bottom of page
173 I burst into such a roar of merriment that the whole house
shook. When my friends had seen it we made such a noise that the
neighbours threatened us with violence, and the police were called
in." Nevertheless, the total circulation of the paper continued, as it
did throughout his editorship, to rise.

Eddie brought *Punch* forward, gently, apparently casually, into
the twentieth century. He saw competitors rise, and sometimes fall;
The Humorist, which, when *Punch* still sold at a shilling, boldly ad-
vertised itself as "1s worth of humour for 6d"; *The New Yorker*, with
which friendly relations were always maintained; the short-lived
Night and Day, started in imitation of *The New Yorker*, shipwrecked
over a libel case brought by the employers of Shirley Temple. *Punch*
was a survivor. Eddie loved the paper, understood it, worried over it,
stayed up half the night at the Mount Pleasant works arguing with
the head printer, Mr Goby; ideas for it came to him at any time,
often in the middle of the night. Praise or blame, although he might
not show it, affected him deeply.

When you employed one of the four Knox brothers, you got absolute integrity. No one was printed in Eddie's *Punch* because they
were a friend or relation or because they had tried to offer him a
favour. On the other hand, beginners were sure of his attention.

Impossible to forget his own early days, when it was an anxious matter to lay out money for a cab to the *Punch* office. It was this quality
of true politeness which struck D. H. Barber, a hopeful contributor,
who in 1933 was a young man of twenty-five, living over a fried-fish
shop and "at the lowest ebb of my fortunes".

> When two more little articles had been accepted I bought a new suit
> at the Fifty-shilling Tailors and a ninepenny cigar, and frittered away
> another ninepence on a taxicab from Ludgate Circus to Bouverie
> Street to call on the Editor. In those days I thought it gave a man a
> wealthy and aristocratic air to arrive in a taxicab. All this vast ex-
> penditure, of course, was quite unnecessary, for there never lived a
> more unsnobbish or unvulgar man than 'Evoe', or a man who placed
> less value on externals.
>
> The *Punch* office seemed to me unnervingly palatial. I tottered
> across a marble vestibule to a graceful wide staircase, up which I
> marched in nervous bravado, cigar in mouth (it had of course long
> gone out). Large paintings of past editors in great gilt frames glared
> down at me. I knocked tremblingly at the Editorial door, and a quiet
> voice bade me enter. The room seemed as big as St Paul's Cathedral,
> and a thinnish man sat behind an enormous table-desk.
>
> I sank, perspiring freely, into the chair to which he waved me, and
> blurted out gruffly:
>
> 'Meeting you, sir, is rather like meeting God!'
>
> He smiled gently.
>
> 'Any resemblance,' he said, 'is purely coincidental.'
>
> He was no doubt very busy, and had I been self-assured and dressed
> by Savile Row he would probably have given me five minutes, but
> because I was gauche and poor and nervous he gave me forty, and
> gently led me on to talk about myself, which is everybody's best sub-
> ject . . . He gave me tips about the best length to write, and suggested
> some ideas. I think he liked me, and personally I left him feeling that
> I now really knew how gentlemen behaved on business occasions.

Barber also perceived that his editor was at heart a poet, and
"poets think in terms of centuries, not of years or even decades,"
but, as a wit, Eddie was politically minded. On two issues of the
Thirties, the paper was adamant. When the economic situation

showed a hint of improvement, *Punch* urged the case of the unemployed, and steadily, remorselessly, and at one time unfashionably, it
attacked the dictators. In the April of 1933, when he was still settling into the editorial chair, Eddie's senior cartoon showed Hitler
as a fool on All Fools' Day, smashing the windows of Jewish shops,
and in May Bernard Partridge produced a fine design of Hitler tread-
ing the Jews underfoot, although the management, who liked everything made very clear, thought the words ANTI-JEWISH CAMPAIGN
ought to be written across the sky.

Sometimes, sitting in El Vino's with a friend of long standing,
Johnny Morton, "Beachcomber" of the *Express*, Eddie would agree
that humour had had its day, because the state of the world was such
that nothing was too absurd or too unpleasant to come true.

The atmosphere of the *Punch* office had radically changed.

> It became casual, deliberately rather slapdash [says Richard Price in
> his *History of Punch*], a place for long conversations on any subject
> under the sun, for a good deal of snoozing and reading and day-
> dreaming. Sometimes there would be nobody in it, everyone being
> at a club or a pub or away in the country. Press night became an
> agony. Week after week it seemed impossible that the Editor would
> ever get down to the proofs. A lengthy dinner was given by a small
> dining-circle collected in order to prevent Evoe from disappearing
> altogether. Then suddenly he would get down to work and the paper
> would appear for another week . . .

Casual as he was, Eddie had the quality without which an editor
is nothing: flair. He was able to find new contributors, and having
found them, to give them their heads. The convenient modern
practice of commissioning nearly the whole paper in advance would
have been as unacceptable to him as canned wine. A good deal of
Punch was still dead, and he knew it; he had to consider the older
readership. But he created a new climate in which good jokes could
arise spontaneously.

> Evoe's strength was in creating this atmosphere among his immedi-
> ate colleagues, the younger men who loved him, appreciated his gen-
> tleness and kindness, found his company stimulating and enjoyed

his odd, oblique humour. He was often infuriating: the urgent article was hidden under a pile of papers, the decision required a month ahead was given when it was really too late so that a solution to the problem had to be fudged, and the major issue was left undiscussed while some fascinating by-way was explored at great length. As an Editor, Evoe had the defects of his qualities . . . But on looking back one can see beside the old growths, new growths, something *Punch* had not seen for many years . . .

When Seaman went, *Punch* did not look like having a future. If Evoe's editorship had not left behind it something healthy and capable of growth, no amount of galvanising and altering would have saved the paper (changing a paper is traditionally in Fleet Street the penultimate stage before going bust).

Sometimes Eddie lost his temper. This was an alarming family characteristic. To the younger brothers, trained as priests, it happened less often, but it did happen. Ronnie was more likely to be incensed by breakdowns in transport, which he felt was invented, after all, to work for him. Wilfred was partly drawn to the character of St. Paul because the saint's temper was so bad; and Alec Vidler thought that Wilfred needed grace to control *his*. Both Dilly and Eddie, when they encountered dishonesty or meanness, or simply at times when they were struck by the inveterate hostility of things, razor blades and collar studs in particular, could sweep clean, like a volcano. They never raised their voices; they jingled the money in their pockets, and with quiet concentration proclaimed the pointlessness of existence in a society where such idiocy could flourish; then their office staff would withdraw, their families would disappear for the time being; even Dilly's dog James, even the witless Tim, would hide in terror.

Nobody's feelings were ever permanently hurt. In Eddie's case it was truly said that those who knew him best loved him best. That was proved, if proof was ever necessary, in 1935, when, only three years after his appointment as editor, he had to face the greatest mortal blow that could be imagined for him, the loss of Christina.

In 1933 they had moved from 34 Well Walk, where they had had so much happiness, where the floors were uneven and the children had grown up and there was not quite enough room for anything, to a large, dank, charmless house in Regent's Park. There was no garden. Neither of them much liked Clarence Terrace, neither of them wanted to leave Hampstead, but, as Uncle Lindsey had said, the editorship meant more going into society and receiving it, and they thought the move necessary. However, they had not given many dinner parties in the tall rooms overlooking the park when Christina began to suffer from her final illness. Like Eddie's mother, forty years before, she was moved from one nursing home to another, finally to the south coast. In the summer of 1935, she died.

It was many years before Eddie could bring himself to mention her name directly, even to his own son and daughter. At the time, he asked the proprietors of *Punch* for a short leave of absence, and an understanding that he would not be writing any funny pieces for the paper that year.

Even on such a wretched occasion as Christina's funeral, it was a memorable thing to see all the four brothers together. Wilfred took the service, Dilly, who rarely entered a church, stood in silent misery at the back, Ronnie, who had not been to an Anglican service for nearly twenty years, knelt in the aisle. Those who saw him, not cut off from the human grief around him, but totally absorbed in communion with God, felt that they had seen prayer manifest.

There were other losses. In January 1937, Mrs K.'s calm voice was heard on the telephone in the desolate house in Clarence Terrace: "Please tell Mr Knox that his father died ten minutes ago." Almost to the last the Bishop had carved at his own table, with hands so palsied that the silver knife-rests shook and danced, but never making a mistake; in his study, a last book exposing the errors of Newman was in preparation. He died as he lived, a stout warrior. Mrs K. remained, to all appearance, as tranquil and unhurried as when she had entered in her diary: "Finished the *Antigone*. Married Bip." As the four brothers came away down the leaf-strewn drive, Dilly, in his anxious stammer, suggested that perhaps she did not feel much at all; "one has to be glad of that." The others disagreed,

Ronnie in particular, but what and how much she felt, they could not tell. Mrs K. returned to the companionship of poor Ethel through the long winter evenings.

Almost exactly a year earlier George V had died. Preaching at Oxford to his student congregation, asking for their prayers for the dead king, Ronnie told them that he did not want to depress them, or to draw obvious lessons about the shortness of human life. The death of a ruler did not mean much when you experienced it for the first time. "It is different," he added, "when you can remember a small boy in an Eton collar and jacket who helped to line the road when Queen Victoria took her last journey to Frogmore, and that boy was you; can remember an undergraduate in his fourth year who woke up one May morning to hear the bell of St Giles tolling for Edward the Seventh, and that that undergraduate was you. Like the women in Homer, who wept not for Patroclus but for their own griefs, you regret the passing of your own life in the passing of a king."

It was a curious fact that to the youngest brother the past meant most. At the age of forty he deliberately began the process of turning himself into an anachronism, not by admitting defeat, but by politely rejecting most of what he saw around him. At the time of his conversion to Catholicism, G. K. Chesterton had written to Ronnie about his sense of lost innocence: "I am concerned about what has become of a little boy whose father showed him a toy theatre, and schoolboy whom nobody ever heard of." These were not Ronnie's worries. He knew, only too clearly, where his childhood had gone. It was still with him, too much so, at times, for his own comfort.

The chaplaincy, from which he had hoped so much, had proved, by the mid 1930s, a disappointment. He was disappointed, that is, not with Oxford, but with himself.

It was not that he had expected the undergraduates to be like those he had known before the war. In their memory, he still passed every Armistice Day "in decent quiet and solitude, rereading a pile of letters, scrawled in violet pencil." The letters were Guy

Lawrence's. Such a generation would not return, but Ronnie made
no comparisons. He regarded himself, he said, as medieval rather
than middle-aged, a man who refused to fly or go to the cinema and
whose idea of the last really good invention was the toast-rack.
Oxford, of all places, was prepared to tolerate such an attitude.

In contrast, he had one of the most agile minds and one of the
warmest hearts that Oxford was ever likely to know. And yet although the twelve years of his chaplaincy became, in their own way,
legendary, very few recalled him as ever looking quite happy.

His state of mind could not be properly judged in Lent, when he
gave up smoking his pipe, and was described by Eddie as looking actually pale green with suffering. But spring, even when Lent was
over, was a trial. March was the cruellest month. "Yes, the term's
not being so bad now," he wrote to Ethel, thanking her for one of
innumerable knitted grey scarves, "but we're just getting those early
crocus days when the sun starts shining and one always feels rather
cheap. At least I do." This was as early as 1928, when Ronnie was
forty, and when the reviewers, as he pointed out, had ceased to say
that he "showed promise", and mentioned with apparent surprise
that Evoe of *Punch* was his elder brother, "as if I hadn't spent most
of my early years fetching his boots for him." His indigestion made
it impossible for him ever to drink brown sherry again. In serious
matters also he paused to take stock.

He felt, as Bishop French had so often done, "an unprofitable servant", believing that he had lost the secret of encouraging young
men in their faith. To make himself accessible (since he could not
face having a telephone) he followed an unvarying routine; every
afternoon, rain or shine, he could be found walking in the Christ
Church Meadows; after four, he was always in his room, waiting, in
case anybody wanted to call. That was the time for giving advice,
but "I am conscious," he wrote in "The Whole Art", "that all
through my time here I have failed in this duty, owing to shyness
and fear of saying the wrong thing." Four generations of Oxford undergraduates remembered things otherwise, but, in retrospect, this
was how they seemed to Ronnie.

What went wrong? Or what made him think it had gone wrong?

To begin with, it was not altogether a successful idea to take in lodgers at the Old Palace. The plan arose partly from Ronnie's generosity—he made no profit at all—partly from the embarrassing request by certain Catholic parents, that their sons (like Sebastian Flyte in *Brideshead Revisited*) should be kept an eye on. It was never clear to him why so many of the lodgers grew restive. It didn't strike him as awkward that he had installed both the baths in one bathroom, but only one could be filled at once. Again, after dinner parties, Ronnie frankly hoped that guests would leave by ten. "From ten, when the house has to be locked up (if there are lodgers) by proctor's orders, I have not encouraged callers. This may be quite wrong; Fr Martindale once expressed himself surprised that undergraduates did not drop in to call at an hour when, he assures me, they are at their most communicative. But we have not all the same talents."

Supervision of the unwilling was a torment. So, too, were the slight rejections which seemed to outweigh all his fame and success. Whole days passed, sometimes, without a caller. His nephews and niece were now, at intervals, coming up to Oxford, but even they were elusive. Winnie's eldest son, a brilliant philosopher at Trinity, tactfully declined an invitation to a canoe trip upriver because it appeared to him a waste of time to tie up under the willows without what was called in the Thirties "some female". And yet Ronnie was such a familiar sight on the river that every reach of the Isis must still expect to see him, in semi-clerical white shirt and black trousers, at ease in the summer moments when the passage of time, which oppressed him, seemed suspended. "Mint and meadowsweet and lying hay blended their scents in that most delicate of all mediums, the smell of clean river-water," he wrote in *The Footsteps at the Lock*. Just as Wilfred and Eddie fished the Arrow, with a discriminating love of the water itself, Ronnie stirred the ripples and reflections of the Isis. Many who did not go with him, finding what seemed to be better things to do, regretted it later. But Ronnie, they felt, was an Oxford institution; he would always be there, there would always be another summer.

In his chaplaincy sermons, Ronnie was hampered by feeling him-

self obliged to give a continuous course of Catholic apologetics, beginning with the five frowsty and unacceptable classical "proofs" of
the existence of God. He did his best to vary them, but confessed
that he was grateful that revelation had been granted to mankind to
back up the "proofs", particularly when (as often happened nowa-
days) he woke up at four in the morning and was unable to get to
sleep again.

His personal conferences, on the other hand, were full of denun-
ciations of the idleness, drunkenness and spiritual slackness of his
charges, their poor attendance at chapel, their pose of languor,
"about as attractive as a piece of wet sponge," and, as the Thirties
advanced, warnings that they were unlikely to find employment and
that they would be members of a second-class nation. These remarks
were called "Ronnie's rockets" and were, he complained, expected
from him and largely ignored. The trouble was that the students of
the Thirties were preoccupied with three subjects: sex, travel and
European politics. Shyness and his own scrupulous purity of mind
made him avoid the subject of sex whenever possible. Travel he considered (as all four brothers did) an overrated activity, and would
greet returning undergraduates who wished to boast about the opera
at Salzburg or an expedition to Tibet with the question: "Let me see;
which country are you boring about now?" Politics he avoided, believing that his business was with the spiritual debate of the twentieth century. Even there, the fashionable language was alien to him.
W. H. Auden's remark that in detective stories only one is guilty, all
the others innocent, but that in the Thirties all were guilty, and
only the crime was uncertain, seemed to Ronnie nothing but an escape into vagueness.

How effective he could have been as a political speaker was
shown in the early days of his chaplaincy, when he was invited to
Glasgow to speak at the Peace Rally of 1928. He arrived to find a
crowd of two thousand troublemakers, some Communists, some
Protestants, waiting, as the police put it, to get at him. The organiz-
ers were anxious for him to leave, and Ronnie decided to stay. "I am
so little accustomed to being taken seriously," he began, "that I

never anticipated my presence would make trouble." He had consented to speak about peace because it seemed to him the only worthy response to the sacrifice of the dead. "Progress may have softened all other human relationships; war it has only made more destructive." And the row going on outside only confirmed what he had wanted to say anyway; that a peace movement could never be sectarian. "It takes all sorts to make a world," he told them, "even my world."

But at Oxford—where, as the years advanced, he was still the most brilliant speaker at Union debates, and increasingly, like other monuments, something for passing visitors to have seen—what had happened to his cure of souls? "Roughly nothing," he considered, "that's the trouble. What I find depressing is just the averageness of it all." The attendance figures at mass remained much the same, or slightly less. There were no notable scandals, no notable gains. What was it his duty to do? Even the springs of his writing seemed to be drying up, and yet, he wrote to an old friend, "It's difficult to get over the feeling one was meant to write." Ought he to go? He waited (for ever since childhood he had attached great importance to such things) for a sign.

A pattern which a novelist would have hesitated to invent now showed itself in Ronnie's life. In 1930, when he had gone on a Hellenic cruise with Lady Lovat, he had remembered not the siege of Troy, but his friends who had died at Gallipoli. Now, in 1937, on another cruise to the same haunted coasts, he found a new friendship to revive his hopes. Ronnie, in spite of a wistful leaning to unpopular causes, had always wanted to do things with somebody else—to reform the Church of England with Wilfred, to dedicate himself side by side with Guy Lawrence, who had written "You must be quick and become a priest," and, in these last years, to find some sort of way into the minds of the hundred and fifty young men in his charge. All these beginnings had been checked in a way that Ronnie accepted with humility, and yet he felt an emptiness, "an air that kills". He went on the cruise because his doctor had thought that, after several heavy attacks of flu, it might do him good. He was to lecture on classical civilization to the comfortable passengers (uneasily remembering that Father Martindale had refused to do this, and had gone into the boiler room to say mass for the stokers); he had no expectation at all of enjoying himself. There are no second chances in life, but Ronnie came very near to one on that summer voyage, when he became a close friend of Lady Acton.

Lady Acton was a strong-minded, handsome young woman of twenty-six, the granddaughter of one of the most high-minded of the Souls, and the daughter of Lord Rayleigh, a scientist and agnostic. She had shown her independence of mind when, at the age of twenty, and against family opposition, she had married the eldest son of an old Catholic family, Lord Acton. Five years after her marriage, and not till then, she decided to receive instruction. She had been introduced to Ronnie, and joined a family party on this particular cruise with the idea of getting to know him better before he undertook any formal preparation. Within the first week the two of them were deep in an exceptional and particular friendship, spiritual, intellectual and emotional.

For Ronnie it came as a totally unexpected blessing which it must be wrong to waste. For the other paying customers on the ship, who had expected to make the acquaintance of the famous Monsignor and hear him make witty remarks, it was something rather more than a disappointment to find him spending all his time with Lady Acton. They could not tell how much he needed to be needed—this was exactly his trouble at Oxford—how much he wanted inspiration, or what it meant to him to have the company of a sympathetic young woman. Perhaps, indeed, only Winnie ever realized that. "There was that terrible break in 1914," she thought, "when I was in Edinburgh having babies. I knew he missed me, and letters couldn't be the same." She understood in what sense his heart was empty.

"The fact that [Lady Acton] was remarkably attractive while he was now approaching his fiftieth year might so easily have become a source of spiritual trouble to him and of embarrassment to her," wrote Father Thomas Corbishley in *Ronald Knox the Priest*. This was impossible, however, with two sensitive people so much more scrupulous on their own behalf than their friends could ever be. In his struggles to bring home to his hearers at the chaplaincy the Proof of the Supreme Excellency of God, Ronnie had spoken of "the pull of human love, which points to something beyond it." That was what he felt now. Both of them confided in the wisest Benedictine they knew, who was human enough to feel a mild irritation with the excessive anxieties of both of them. He advised them to pray more, to forget about other people's experience and theory, not to rationalize what they felt, and to take themselves as they were before God, without fooling themselves. Painfully Ronnie became convinced that, for once, it was not necessary for him to do the most difficult thing. Lady Acton was received into the Church in April 1938, while he became, for the time being, almost completely absorbed in this new friendship.

According to Evelyn Waugh, Lady Acton, during the course of the cruise, threw a copy of Ronnie's last detective story, *Double Cross Purposes*, overboard, together with her lipstick. (Ronnie disliked make-up; he sometimes described young women as "really pretty, without paint." Wilfred and Dilly were easily deceived into not noticing it, while Eddie had no objection to anything that made women look well.)

It was the sign of a pact. The detective stories (to which Ronnie's bishop had also objected) were to go, because he was to undertake in future only what was worthwhile. He had the exhilarating sensation of being persuaded to do something he very much wanted to do anyway. Lady Acton confirmed his half-formed decision to leave the chaplaincy, and, certain of her sympathetic encouragement, he told her what it was that, in late middle age, he hoped and dreamed to write—a new translation, for Catholics, of the entire Bible.

Once again, it was a task in which Newman had been frustrated, and one which, ever since his conversion, had been particularly close to Ronnie. The Authorized Version had been his birthright, although he had lost it. Couldn't one—in his own words—"produce something decent" which Catholics might love and remember in something of the same way? Generous always, he hoped to give part at least of the inheritance of his childhood to the Church of his adoption.

The official Roman Catholic text was the Vulgate; in 1526 the Council of Trent specified that it must be used for all public readings. There followed nearly seventy years of frenzied editing by the Vatican—at one point Cardinal Sixtus was reduced to sending out correction slips to be pasted over earlier mistakes—to establish the Sixto-Clementine version, without variant readings. The Catholic English translation was the Douai, made in exile by William Allen, an Oxford scholar who could not accept the Elizabethan Settlement. Allen's work had much of the beauty of the King James version and was closely related to it, but because he "presumed not to mollify the hard words, for fear of missing the sense of the Holy Ghost" (the Lord's Prayer, for instance, appears as *Give us this day our supersubstantial bread*), there was need of revision; this was undertaken in 1750 by the saintly Bishop Challoner. To replace Douai-Challoner, or even to suggest replacing it, seemed a bold step, with its long ancestry and touching association with the Catholic exiles—the last annotation on *Come Lord Jesus* is a prayer for their return to England—it was dear to the hearts of millions. Or was it, Ronnie wondered, only the thought of it that was dear? Did anyone read it much, in private, at all? He had noticed that when, as a visiting preacher, he asked the Parish Priest for a Bible to verify his text, "there was generally an ominous pause of twenty minutes or so before he returned, banging the leaves of the sacred volume and visibly blowing on the top." If that was so, might it not be replaced by a version that brought out the meaning—which Douai, particularly in the Epistles of St Paul, notoriously didn't—which would be in "timeless English", and, though he would never have claimed this himself, equally beautiful?

But, if the scheme was accepted, why not bypass the Vulgate and translate directly from the Hebrew and Greek manuscripts? St Jerome had access to some sources which are now lost, but we possess many others which he knew nothing about. These texts are a matter for international scholars, who have divided the manuscript copies of the New Testament alone into five "families", on which forty years' work is but a day; every word, for example, must be checked against its use in the Greek papyri as they come to hand— Professor Lobel's "laundry lists"; it was in fact in these lists that the word ἐπιούσιος was found in an ordinary household account-book and finally established as meaning "daily" and not "supersubstantial" bread. From other translators the reader asks for illusion, but from the Bible-translator he wants truth. He must know "what the Bible really says". The Vatican had acknowledged this, and while Ronnie was at the Old Palace, the English Westminster Version, taken directly from the manuscripts, was being prepared under the editorship of a Jesuit, Father Cuthbert Lattey. This was for scholars, and was not authorized for public use, but the way was open for a clean start, a twentieth-century popular Catholic Bible which would challenge the newest and most accurate Protestant versions.

But Ronnie stuck to the Vulgate. Any new suggestions, after a close study of the originals, would have to go into footnotes. His own need was not for freedom, but for authority, and, as a convert, he felt he should never presume too far. Undoubtedly his diffidence over the matter lost him a great opportunity.

His brothers were somewhat surprised to hear of Ronnie's new venture. "A bad text," Dilly remarked, "and he doesn't know very much Greek." "Or theology," Wilfred added, "except what I've taught him." And indeed, from their point of view, he did not. Their criticisms were in no way unkindly meant. They were proud of Ronnie, but they did not really consider him a scholar.

By 1938, however, the project was accepted in principle by the Hierarchy, though they felt he should have the help of a committee. Their next and most unwelcome proposal, that he should return to St Edmund's as President, was easily circumvented. He would need seclusion, protection and peace, and Lady Acton, catching enthusiastically at the idea, offered all these. Ronnie could come to Aldenham, the family seat in Shropshire, as chaplain. Outside his duties, and his preaching engagements, his whole time could be given to what Cardinal Hinsley (who had succeeded in 1935) called "the great work of the pen-apostolate". In arranging matters, Lady Acton, like Lady Lovat, showed herself a true descendant of the Souls. She was confident of finding a cottage and a housekeeper for him—Ronnie, as Eddie pointed out, was the only member of the family, apart from Ethel, who never in his whole life had to wash up a teaspoon for himself—and he would be free from the tedious routine of everyday.

Unquestionably Ronnie became somewhat obsessed at this time with the details of the household at Aldenham. The younger generation of Knoxes could not quite reconcile his spiritual force with the continual discussion of "carriage folk". They felt he was in danger of getting a little like one of the recurrent characters in the glossy period films of those days, a clerical figure shyly entering the salon—"Why, Abbé Liszt, have you been writing anything new?" All this was quite unfair. They did not understand the priestly life, and underestimated the amount of happiness necessary to someone of fifty. As usual, Winnie understood him best. "I wish I could make this clear," she wrote after his death; to her he was still "the hopeless romantic", even the small boy who had played at Caves in Arabia, and now needed, above all things, rescue and retreat.

Whatever misgivings his family might have, they could not fail to recognize the unique quality of the book which Lady Acton inspired him to write, and which he finished in 1938—his last Oxford book, his farewell, indeed, to Oxford—*Let Dons Delight*. It is dedicated to her, as the friend who gave him heart to begin again.

Of everything he wrote—and he lost count himself of the titles—this was Ronnie's favourite book. Its framework is a dream, taking us back through time in the Senior Common Room of Simon Magus, a college ironically named after the magician who tried to bribe St Peter. The changing styles of English conversational prose have surely never been better imitated than here, as the centuries pass, and the generations of dons discuss and comfortably disagree. But the true spirit of Oxford is seen to rest with the Catholic recusants, who leave her to go into exile. From 1588 to 1838, from the days of Tudor persecution to the days of Newman, these exiles go reluctantly. "You have reproached me, Mr Provost," says Mr Lee, a martyr of 1588, "for that I go lightly overseas; do you think that I have not understood what thing it is that I leave behind?" Three centuries later Newman's converts remember the walks and gardens of Oxford "only as better things—no, not better things, though more companionable things." It was time, also, for Ronnie to go. He had resigned the chaplaincy, and only Nuffield, he thought, could be happy in Oxford without a job connected with the University. But one could not take leave without a long look backward.

In *Let Dons Delight*, the college Fellows, over their port, always predict wrongly. "You will not teach the potato to grow in Ireland," and, in 1788, "The Frenchman will not revolt." But in 1938 the scientists and materialists left in the Common Room are saying: "The next world war is scheduled to break out next July, isn't it?" Ronnie, presumably, trusted that they would be wrong once again.

In the autumn of 1938 he was ready to transfer himself to Aldenham. "I am leaving Oxford," he told the new generation of undergraduates, "because the conditions of life give me no time to do the job the Hierarchy, in their great kindness, have entrusted to me." "Whoever comes after me," he adjured them, "don't let him feel as lonely as at times you have made me feel."

After the Munich Conference and the abandonment of Czechoslovakia, Eddie wrote, for the Christmas of 1938, with a sense of bitter humiliation, a "Hymn to the Dictators":

> O well beloved leaders
> > And potentates sublime,
> We come to you as pleaders
> > Because it's Christmas time.
> Illustrious banditti,
> > Contemptuous of our codes,
> Look down to-day in pity
> > On democratic toads.

All the systems evolved by human beings for living on this earth were now shown to be either delusory, destructive, sadly outdated, or at risk. Wilfred, realizing that when war broke out Oratory House would probably have to shut down, wondered where his duty would lie. Dilly was not well. Cancer was suspected, and he had already had a preliminary operation. Without much comment on this, he returned to his office, and to Enigma. He had the advantage of knowing exactly what he was supposed to be doing. But so far he was getting nowhere.

VIII

The Uses of Intelligence

AT THE BEGINNING OF 1939 Dilly was still working in the Broadway. His health was not much better, if at all, since his operation, and he appeared to live entirely on black coffee and chocolate. To the casual visitor the office would have appeared disorderly, even though it was tidied by a girl assistant, but the chaos was restored at the end of every day by Dilly, like Daedalus in his own labyrinth. A brilliant young Oxford mathematician, Peter Twinn, who was recruited to the Department in February, found to his dismay that Dilly was not prepared to offer any explanation at all of the working system. Worse still, it turned out that the girl assistant, who went about her routine so calmly, did not understand anything either; she had given up, she said, but thought it best not to say so. The trouble, of course, was not that Dilly would not explain, but that he thought he *had*. "Mightn't it be a good idea . . ." and "Why do you say that?" were, surely, enough to cover everything? At four o'clock every afternoon Dilly suddenly left the office to drive himself perilously home to Courn's Wood. The regulations of the Foreign Office had to give way to him. In contrast to Ronnie's deep need for authority, Dilly recognized the need for rules only in ritual (poetry, cricket, emendation of texts), not in what he thought of as the rational conduct of his own existence. To Newman's, and Ronnie's, question, "Can a kingdom have two governments?" Dilly would have replied that it could have as many as it had individuals. He reappeared at any time he liked in the very early morning, made coffee, and resumed his work where he had left it.

His section was at present concentrated full time on the solution to Enigma, the enciphering system which had been selected by the Nazi Government in the 1930s and now distributed as standard issue to the German forces. The Enigma machine was a harmless-looking object, not much larger than an office typewriter, which was offered, not very successfully at first, on the open market by its German promoter. It was one of a number of similar machines which had been patented between the wars.

Enigma enciphered by means of three turning discs, or rotors, made of rubber, and about four inches across. Round the rim of each of these were twenty-six brass contacts, which corresponded to the twenty-six letters of the alphabet, but were usually given their numerical values. Each of them was wired, through the thickness of the rotor, to a contact on the opposite face, which in turn passed the current through the crossing and re-crossing wires in the other two rotors. At each contact, the original letter which was being transmitted changed into another one. In addition, after each encipherment the rotor turned one notch, bringing a completely new arrangement into play. After it had turned twenty-six times, the second rotor began to turn—one notch for every twenty-six notches of the first one, giving 676 possible positions. Enigma also came supplied with two spare rotors which could be substituted for any two in the machine, so that if all five were used in every possible order they could produce eleven million different arrangements of the alphabet before returning to their original positions.

To send a message the operator simply typed it on the keyboard, and it eventually emerged as a series of numbers, which were lit up by a row of small lamps at the output. At the other end, the receiver could put his machine into reverse, so as to read the message *en clair*.

Enigma

Hinged lid with windows for reading
rotors set to the "key of the day"
(*seen here in raised position*)

Rotors
(*Walzen*)

Inner
power-supply
switch

Lampboard
(*Glülampenfeld*)

Keyboard
(*Tastatur*)

Plugboard
(*Steckerbretf*)

Plug connections
(*Steckerverbindungen*)

A BOVE IS A LATE-MODEL Enigma with a QWERTY "typewriter" keyboard (described on page 247). Though the order of letters on the keyboard changed during the war, the basic look and mechanism of Enigma did not. In the photograph, the three turning discs, or rotors, are clearly visible. Not visible is the internal mechanism of the larger message-scrambling unit. On the left-hand side of the rotors is a stationary entry wheel (*Eintrittwalze*), which received the keyboarded message and sent an electrical current through the variously wired rotors (described on page 222); on the right-hand side is a stationary "reflecting" wheel (*Umkehrwalze*), which, once the current had passed through the rotors, scrambled the current and advanced the rotors. The optional plugboard allowed for further levels of encipherment. The standard-issue Enigma was housed in a wooden carrying-case, rather like a 26-pound portable typewriter. It ran on an internal battery, but could be connected to an outside power supply.

If the message had always begun at the first position of the first rotor, the decipherers might not have found their task too difficult; but it might start anywhere. Every Enigma operator had in his secret drawer a selection of red, green and blue spools and an instruction book. Every twenty-four hours he was given a new "key of the day", expressed in colours and numbers, telling him how to set his machine to the *Grundstellung,* or starting position. There was a separate indicator which registered the day's setting in three small windows, to avoid any possible discrepancies.

The Foreign Office had supplied its department with an old commercial Enigma, costing about £2,500, from which they could study the general mechanism, but no more than that. Further progress was almost impossible without enormous quantities of material in cipher, a reasonable amount in clear (not forthcoming), and an example of the current German setting instructions (also not forthcoming). With these it might be feasible to start the laborious mathematical task (they had no computers of any kind) of marking in at least a few of the connections between the maze of wires.

Enigma could never be "solved" in the ordinary sense, but the millions of alphabets could be reduced to the few possible ones for each day, and these could be solved by trial and error. However, even to begin work it would be necessary (1) to read the setting instructions, which were given, as has been said, in letters, figures and colours; (2) to wait until the setting indicated that only the first rotor would be turning; this meant that though every letter enciphered had to pass through rotors two and three, these last two rotors at least would be standing still; (3) to get hold of messages sent while only the first rotor was turning, and their complete equivalent in clear; and (4) to wait again until the same letter occurred twice in the first twenty-six letters of the cipher text. For example, if the clear text message started with the word AACHEN, the first A might register as Z, and C might also appear as Z, although the first rotor would have turned two spaces, producing a completely different alphabet.

This lucky find could be expressed as two equations by letting numbers stand for letters (A = 1, B = 2, C = 3, etc.,) letting $h(n)$ be the unknown displacement of the nth letter on the first rotor (the displacement is the number of places in the alphabet which the letter gains or loses as it passes from one contact to another), and letting k be the displacement on the last two rotors (which must be the same in each case since these rotors have not moved and the output was in both cases):

$$1 + h(1) + k = 26$$
$$3 + h(5) + k = 26$$

Here, $h(5)$ occurs instead of $h(3)$ in the second equation because the rotor has moved on two places between the encipherment of A and C, and for convenience it has been assumed that the first rotor starts at setting A. Subtracting one equation from the other, this gives

$$h(1) - h(5) = 2.$$

Information of this kind will help the cryptographer to work out, in time, all the contacts on the first rotor. But even this first step towards recovering the arrangement of even one rotor is impossible unless he knows the order of the letters on the keyboard. The order makes no difference at all to the operator, but considerable difference to the solver. A random keyboard (on which, for instance, A might be not the first but the twentieth letter) would mean adding another factor into the equation so that it would take very much longer to get a simple result like $h(1) - h(5) = 2$. Once, however, he knows the order of the keyboard he can make allowance for it, and proceed as before.

The Enigma keyboard which the Germans were using was, Dilly thought, certain to be random, as this would make for much greater security. But the different ways of arranging twenty-six letters come to 403,291,461,126,605,635,584,000,000.

The Foreign Office Communications Department were not the only, or even the first people in Europe who were trying to solve Enigma. The Germans had been manufacturing their version (called the *glühende Chiffriermaschine* because of its glowing lamps) since 1926, and they had tried it out on manoeuvres on the Polish border. Some of the early models proved unreliable. Polish interceptor groups frequently recorded *Maschine defekt* and even *Maschine kaput*. Others, particularly Mark 2, were too heavy for rapid transport. Eventually the Germans reverted to Mark 1, combined with an automatic device which printed the signal either in clear or in code.

The liaison between the Poles and the French Deuxième Bureau in the years before the war was excellent. Here the key figure was General Gustave Bertrand, then a major with the Services de Renseignement, who was particularly well able to get on with these brilliant, suffering and heroic people. For their sake, he admitted, he readily sacrificed his health, drinking away long evenings with them, bottle for bottle, when vodka was the only remedy for despair. London was not in the confidence of the Poles, but Bertrand, who had a delicate sense of honour, was prepared to share any results they might give him with his British allies. He had, also, the advantage of a defector from the Chistelle (the cipher room at the German Defence Ministry), whose motive was very simple—money—and who was able to supply a number of valuable documents; among them were the servicing instructions and manuals for the machines, and tables showing the changes of key, which at that time operated monthly. When, in 1934, this useful agent lost his job, Bertrand knew a good deal about Enigma, but not the *ventre de machine*, its exact internal construction. His next idea was to obtain a list of all the workers in the German firms manufacturing Enigma, in the hope of finding a contact, but this proved impossible. The machines were assembled in special workshops under the direct supervision of the Abwehr. Furthermore, in September 1938 the Nazis modified the system by introducing interchangeable rotors.

In January 1939 Major Bertrand arranged for a group of British technicians to visit Paris, and gave them one of the last legacies of his secret agent, a message sent on Enigma, both in clear and code. It dated from before the modifications; still, it was precious. But while the Department of Communications were still considering it the Poles succeeded in reconstructing the current Enigma. With only the specifications for 1931–34, which have already been described, they managed to build a working model, a good deal larger than the original, but still only half a metre square.

In July 1938 an invitation arrived to a conference, this time not in Paris, but in Poland itself. The British deputation was to consist of Commander A. G. Denniston, Dilly's superior since the days of Room 40, a Naval Commander from the Admiralty and Dilly himself. At Courn's Wood the two boys, neither of whom had any idea what their father did, were amazed to see an Admiral in full uniform sitting in the draughty dining room. What could he want? Two weeks later, the deputation flew to Warsaw.

Major Bertrand had the delicate task of creating a friendly atmosphere. The English party were booked into the Hotel Bristol, and that evening he took them out to the celebrated Restaurant Crystal. Here the Naval Commander ate and drank too much, Denniston remained discreet, and Dilly, in Bertrand's words, appeared "*froid, nerveux, ascète*", scarcely touching the numerous courses, and concentrating only on the matter in hand. The next morning they went to the "house in the woods"—the secret radio and intelligence station at Mokotov-Pyry, a few kilometres from Warsaw, hidden underneath a concrete shelter and almost invisible, among its thick surrounding trees, from the air. The Poles were waiting at the bottom of a flight of damp steps. After the best Bertrand could do by way of congratulations and introductions, they gave a demonstration of their model.

Dilly had been working for the past twelve months on the problem of the sequence of letters on the Enigma keyboard. Now he was told what it was. It was ABCDEFGHIJKLMNOPQRSTUVWXYZ.

Dilly's reaction was characteristic. He was furious. It was a swindle, not because he had failed to solve it, but because it was too easy. Games should be worth playing. The keyboard was, it turned out, not a significant factor at all. During lunch, which was taken at the Restaurant Bacchus, and at which the Naval Commander was actually sick from overeating, Dilly sat hunched in his loose-fitting suit, unresponsive and groaning slightly. He only just rallied sufficiently to make a polite farewell.

He was deeply grateful to Bertrand, but he was outraged. A problem which had been presented to him as too difficult had turned out to be too simple. He intended, however, never to make the same miscalculation again.

When Poland was invaded in September 1939, Bertrand succeeded in evacuating both the Poles and the reconstituted machines to the Château de Vignolles, where he had his hands full not only with a heavy and dangerous routine but with British liaison officers "authorized to know all", who complained that they could not get a decent cup of tea. In spite of this, he sent the Foreign Office a model of the machine. In July 1939 he had met Dilly briefly in London when he came over to arrange a system for the exchange of information; this was vitally important, because Enigma made 4,789 changes of key between the occupation of Poland and the invasion of France.

In 1939 the Department of Communications was moved down to Bletchley Park in Buckinghamshire, which was given the name of Station X. Bletchley was selected simply as being more or less equidistant from Oxford and Cambridge, since the Foreign Office remained faithful to Blinker Hall's principle of recruiting dons as cryptographers. As it happened, Bletchley was also an important railway junction, and it might have been expected that the tracks, gleaming in the moonlight, would make a good target for enemy bombers—in fact the R.A.F., before the development of radar, used them for a "steer"—but this disadvantage was outweighed by its convenience for professors. Confidence was justified. Although many of the personnel, accustomed to the lecture room, spoke openly and much too loudly, and on one occasion a quantity of secret decodes were brought in from the ordinary rubbish heap, the secret was kept, and Bletchley never suffered a severe attack from the air.

The house itself was a large Victorian Tudor-Gothic mansion, whose ample grounds sloped down to the railway. It had been much done up by Sir Herbert Leon, a prosperous merchant, and the panelled, crocketed rooms had been fitted with majestic plumbing. The perimeter was wired, and guarded by the R.A.F. regiment, whose N.C.O.s warned the men that if they didn't look lively they would be sent "inside the Park", suggesting that it was now a kind of lunatic asylum. There were passwords for entry and exit, but Dilly could never remember any of them, or where they were kept.

Lodgings had to be found for the cryptographers in Bletchley, which was still a little railway town, so that the wives of engine drivers, cleaners and shunters now had billeted on them an unfamiliar Elite. The small front parlours were taken over by very advanced bridge games, and experts in symbolic logic worked out on a sliding scale the exact amount everyone should pay for cocoa and biscuits. Before long chess-players were recruited to the department, and the champions, Alexander and Golombek, demonstrated the romantic and classical styles of chess. These were intellects at play. Those who solved problems in the bath, however, were at a loss, because few of the billets had bathrooms. Even before rationing there were grievous shortages of pipe tobacco and copies of *The Times* in Bletchley, and the corner newsagents developed a serious power complex. Then, gradually, hotels and country houses were taken over for the higher administrative grades.

Dilly himself always slept in the office, going back to Courn's Wood once a week. His driving was worse than ever. His mind was totally elsewhere. Fortunately he drove slowly. "It's amazing how people smile, and apologise to you, when you knock them over," he remarked.

In time the buildings inside the Park walls extended into blocks of huts and cafeterias, and by the end of the war the personnel numbered more than seven thousand, increased by observers and liaison men and important visitors in uniform. With all this Dilly had nothing to do. At first his department consisted of ten people, though these included, besides Peter Twinn, two very brilliant and sympathetic young women, Margaret Rock and Mavis Lever (now Mrs Batey). They were accommodated in a small cottage overlooking the old stable yard.

He would, however, need more ciphering clerks—not the vast numbers which eventually made the Treasury complain that "Bletchley was using up all the girls in the country," but still, a section of his own. Into this task Dilly entered with quite unexpected enthusiasm, and when the assistants arrived down from London with the files they were surprised to find him surrounded with pretty girls, all of them, for some reason, very tall, whom he had recruited for the work. The girls took from four to six months to train, though this was not undertaken by Dilly, who never trained anybody, but by a capable and understanding woman, Mrs Helen Morris. They worked on the equations in three eight-hour shifts, and when Dilly wanted to speak to them or to the punch-card operators who registered the encipherments as dots, he would limp across from the cottage, often in his grey dressing gown, indifferent to rain and snow, to tell them his new idea.

The cottage suited Dilly, though it had disadvantages. The walls were coated with whitewash, which rubbed off on visiting admirals who were seen to brush their uniforms furtively. The two downstairs rooms were connected by a cupboard, which Dilly frequently mistook for the door. His voice could be heard inside, resounding hollowly. To get his hot bath he had to go to a special hut adjoining the main buildings. But the isolation was precious and he could have coffee with real milk, supplied to him by a lady who lived nearby, and kept her own cow.

The invasion of France had changed the nature of the work completely. When the Germans crossed the border, Bertrand moved his organization from pillar to post, and by a heroic effort kept it functioning even when the French Higher Command was giving up. It proved impossible, however, to transfer the "factory" out of France and he entrusted some of the best of his Polish cryptographers to a *passeur*, who was to smuggle them into Spain across the Pyrenees. This man sold them to the Nazis. Meanwhile the Germans, on the eve of the invasion, had begun to work a completely new version of Enigma, a new setting programme, a new keyboard, a new arrangement of wires. All the solutions had to be started again. The Department of Communications temporarily "went deaf".

Dilly's particular corner of the work was the Spy Enigma Variation. This was not used by enemy agents in the field—the machine was too heavy to carry about easily—but by the German Embassies in neutral countries and in the occupied zones. As a problem, the Variation was crucial, because the traffic, if it could be read, told not only the enemy plans but what they knew and did not know, or mistakenly thought they knew, about ours. The Variations used by the German Army, Navy and Air Force were assigned to different departments, or "huts", which, as the war went on, required expert administration and an automatic routine to handle the enormous volume of material. This did not interest Dilly, who was not an organization man. Possibly he would not have adapted to computer-based techniques, but then he was not a technical man either. He was, essentially, what he had been in Room 40, an idea-struck man.

He could, for example, look at a mass of cipher text and pick out unerringly the parts that might be of help towards a solution and therefore should be tried first. There is no rule for doing this; it is a matter of instinct, though instinct, Headlam always said, is the natural way of discovering what happens. The "way in" they were hoping for in 1940 was through the indicators, that is, the date and number at the beginning of each signal, which could be solved in time by trial and error, and the padding, or nonsense words, which were used to fill up a message; these were issued to the German cipher clerks in lists; one of them was *Rosengarten*, which surely must have taken Dilly back twenty-odd years or so to the *Rosen* of Schiller.

The mechanical work was done by the tall girls, and largely consisted of solving equations and of arranging and rearranging the dots which represented the transpositions of letters, until every alternative likely or possible in a message sent at that time and place had been tried. They had elementary devices to measure the displacements, invented by the Department, and known as "creeping subtractors". To describe the groupings, and perhaps to amuse the patient clerks, Dilly invented a special language, "beetling", "lobstering", "if one cow can cross the road so can two" and so on. Combined with his hesitant way of speaking, this made decipherment, to the outsider, seem quite as unintelligible as the cipher itself. American observers who came for a briefing were unable to make head or tail of their notes; beetles, cows, lobsters . . . They asked if they might see the working papers, and, after some search, were shown the backs of some old envelopes. They wanted to know the office routine, but there wasn't any.

Dilly had written on things with purple ink, which faded, or with a blunt pencil, and when everything seemed to be going reasonably well he had taken his staff out and treated them to the best dinner that the Seven Bells public house could provide. Perhaps all this sounded like the deliberate holding-back of information, but it was not. There was no further explanation to give.

Occasionally the terrible Knox temper would blaze up, and then Dilly's language was cutting and intemperate. This was particularly the case if he thought that anyone at the Park was using the war to promote a business career. Otherwise his kindness was unfailing —at least to the women, for it sometimes had to be pointed out to him that he should be kind, also, to men. Hadn't one said the right thing? You haven't said anything; you haven't spoken to him at all for two weeks. And Dilly would lope out again, to redress the wrong.

As the months went by the Park, like any other human society, began to find a communal life; the cryptographers danced, and skated on the lake, and there was cricket, though Dilly no longer bowled his slow spinners. The Local Defence Volunteers he did join, and his staff thought it was lucky that no live ammunition was issued, but here they were wrong. Dilly, in spite of his poor eyesight, was a very good shot.

There were old friends at Bletchley, among them the inscrutable

Frank Birch, who had rejoined the Department, and had the distinction of being one of the few people ever to refuse to employ Kim Philby (he turned him down on the grounds that Bletchley would not be able to offer him enough money). Dilly also made new acquaintances, and became particularly fond of the young genius Alan Turing, who was responsible for expressing the solutions and possibilities in mathematical form. Turing's vagaries were worthy of the high standard of Bletchley. Doubtful of the future of sterling, he had wheeled away two ingots of silver bullion in a pram and buried them as an investment, but later he could not remember the place, and they are still lying unclaimed beneath one of the post-war housing estates of Bletchley. As early as 1937 he had suggested a "universal computing machine" and had showed that there were mathematical problems which would not be computable; he was largely responsible for devising a way to read the settings of Enigma. During his idle moments, however, Turing had worked out the likelihood, on the data the Department had so far, of a complete solution. The odds were more than 50,000 to one against.

The Spy Enigma cipher texts piled higher and higher, still without any significant way in. One day a huge sack of torn and burnt papers came in, salvaged from a German vessel, and Dilly amazed the staff by the eager skill with which he pieced them together. He telephoned for colleagues from Cambridge, who hurried over to help him. In spirit he was back at the British Museum, among the papyri.

Although he had now added mushrooms and gruel to his strange daily diet, the old stomach trouble was recurring, and he never felt really well. His solicitor, E. S. P. Haynes, had said that dentists were to blame; obviously Nature intended all animals to die as soon as their teeth dropped out, whereas human beings insisted on living on, to experience intolerable illnesses. Dilly liked to refer systems back to Nature, though he himself would be hard to fit into any hypothesis of biological survival. To and fro he drove to Courn's Wood, reciting choliambics or *Lycidas*, determined that whatever happened he would survive long enough to see the solution of Spy Enigma.

———

Not long after the outbreak of war, Wilfred, as has been explained in the last chapter, was homeless. When Edward Wynne had been offered the Bishopric of Ely he had consulted the O.G.S., as their rule required, and Wilfred had told him that, "on the whole, you'd make less mess of being a bishop than anyone else I can think of"; and after Wynne's departure he was in the unfamiliar position of having material possessions to give away—he was able to send the new Bishop the forks, spoons and crockery which he had bought himself for the Oratory. Of course, this did not mean that Wilfred was any the less a member of the O.G.S.; indeed, in 1941 he was elected Superior, and the impression he made on the brotherhood was as clear as Eddie's upon *Punch*. But in 1940 he was faced with Ronnie's recurrent problem of where to go next.

Wilfred could live anywhere; but if the house in Lady Margaret Road had outlived its usefulness, it meant leaving his garden. A tenderness for the plants you have raised from seed and the earth you have turned over a thousand times seems one of the most allowable of earthly attachments. House and garden, however, went to the Franciscans, and subsequently to the Lucy Cavendish Foundation for mature women students.

A suggestion came from Pembroke. Meredith Dewey, the chaplain, had volunteered to serve with the Navy. Wilfred was asked to take his place for the duration of the war.

Cambridge was preparing for what was called "the emergency". The college gates were blocked with sandbags, treasures were sent away, the Director of the Fitzwilliam, a bachelor, had fifty invalid women quartered upon him. In March 1941 Pembroke itself went up in a blaze which started in its R.A.F. Initial Training Wing, and the New Buildings stood roofless for about a hundred yards. Wilfred, arriving with his old bike and his old clothes, gave a valuable sense of continuity with the past. In a few weeks he had taken over the gardens. They were given over to the wartime cultivation of vegetables, but he managed to retain enough ground to construct a rockery.

He was to teach theology, history and logic to the undergraduates. Many of these were short-course students, soon due to join the forces, and hoping if they survived to return to Cambridge. They needed all the care that he could give them. "Examiners found that they could recognise his pupils," Canon Dodds has written, "both by the direction of their interest and by a certain freedom of approach; possibly the less able men found him somewhat puzzling."

It was the old story: Wilfred took getting used to. This was particularly the case for the young men whom he took down on reading vacations to Knill. The fishing had now become a syndicate of Eddie, Wilfred and Bishop Wynne, Wilfred retaining the right to debit any sums spent on beer for Mr. Moses, the water-bailiff, "in order to reconcile him to the idea of the syndicate." Wilfred caught about a hundred and fifty trout a year, and grew a large quantity of potatoes, some of which he sent to Eddie in London as "swill for the trough". Bishop Wynne, with all the latest equipment, caught little.

To the young men, the "rules" of the cottage seemed odd at first. The fire, for reasons of wartime economy, might not be lit till four o'clock. One former student (Canon Murray MacDonald) recalls "having the temerity to light it in the morning. A note was placed on the fireguard restating the rules: not before four." The trout which Wilfred caught were cooked by Mrs Moses and handed out in rotation: "If it was your turn you had it, like it or not."

> He somehow communicated with everyone a deep love from a broken unloving man . . . Looking back now one realises how deeply he had been hurt, how much he longed for simple affection, how nervous of it he was, and how he hid behind his wit and apparent tartness. The last time I saw him, I wanted to give him a simple parting gift for all that he had done for me. I saw a reproduction of a map of the Radnor-Hereford border. I knew that he would have been too embarrassed to have received it from me, so I left it in his rooms with a note. I was amazed how delighted he was to have it, not simply for what it was but that somebody had given him a present.

In point of fact Wilfred was given many presents, though each one seemed to amaze him, but this is a very perceptive account, for it shows, what the writer could not guess at, the enduring pain at the loss of his brother. Others who came to Knill were able to break through the nervousness. Horace Dammers, the present Dean of Bristol, felt only his affection, helpfulness and ingenuity. Wilfred confided in him "that he had a recurrent nightmare of sitting in a small boat in the middle of a large lake with his brother Ronnie, while the latter attempted to convert him to Roman Catholicism." This was perhaps as far as Wilfred cared to go on the subject; on another occasion, up on the shoulder of the hill near Offa's Dyke, Wilfred pointed to a man in the far distance, aiming a shotgun, presumably at a rabbit. "If that was murder, we should be the only witnesses," he told Dammers, and he invented on the spot, with great precision, the plot of a detective story. One evening he informed the young men that he was writing a book on ethics in two volumes: Part 1, Respect to the Clergy; Part 2, Any Other Virtues. Some of them believed this at first, but not for long. "He was the sort of man," says another correspondent, "who understood every natural joy and sorrow that we could feel at that age, but couldn't find his own collar stud." This, however is a misapprehension, because Wilfred never had any collar studs; he used a paper clip.

As always, he put his pastoral work first. As the short-course students passed rapidly through their University year, Wilfred, for many of them, was the only senior member of the college they really knew. For some of them, this odd figure was their abiding memory of Cambridge. Every year he asked every student in Pembroke to tea, and went on asking, at the risk of a snub, until the invitation was accepted; his lists were like the elements of a game, indeed, of an elimination tournament. And the young men did come, though the majority were not sure why.

Wilfred's standards of tea-giving were high, having remained unchanged since Edmundthorpe. There had to be two cakes, one "fancy", the other a plum cake, with one slice already cut to put visitors at their ease. As rationing grew stricter—the shortages were even worse in Cambridge than in Bletchley—Wilfred could be seen, tattered, persevering, often half-freezing, in the dawn queue outside Fitzbillies, the famous cake shop in King's Parade. His guests must be honoured. Some people had their own "arrangements" with the shop, but Wilfred would never have dreamed of such a thing.

Letters from Service personnel on every front recalled his heroic patience in the queue. Tobacco was sent from Mount Carmel, butter and sugar ("to lighten the task of providing those teas") from New Zealand, plants for the rock garden from Hong Kong. Someone had found a copy of *St. Paul and the Church of the Gentiles* in Rawalpindi, on the way to the North-West Frontier. Living in barracks on four shillings a day, they "kept sane" by writing, and appealed for help when they felt hopelessly alone, or "contaminated by the filth of the world". All of them would have liked to get back, if only for a day, to the tobacco-choked atmosphere of the chaplain's rooms on Staircase M. They had not realized—one of them not until he had his arm and half his side blown away—how much they would miss Cambridge.

Dammers, now a gunner in North Africa, wrote in 1943 that he felt discouraged, but

> I feel as soon as you read this that reinforcements will come pouring over the ether (or whatever the medium for such things is) and meanwhile I must try again. In all seriousness this kind of life makes it difficult for feeble people like myself to keep contact with God and sometimes I feel deeply ashamed of myself. On the other hand I feel a sort of instinct (whether right or wrong I don't know) against forcing myself to such contact. I feel it should come naturally and get a bit miserable when it doesn't. Presumably I share all this with hundreds of thousands of others but there it is, I feel that an effort of some sort is required but am not quite clear about what. We are now allowed to recount our battle experiences. Mine are negligible. On the whole I enjoy action. One's faculties are extended and one has little time to think, while performing one's technical duties, what a beastly business it is to direct masses of high-explosive against your fellow-men whose most earnest desire is to do the same to you. The only unpleasantnesses are occasional lack of sleep . . . and when one is shelled or bombed or machine-gunned from the air . . . Even so the danger is I imagine less than that involved in bicycling fast down King's Parade twice a week.

By no means all the correspondents cared anything about religion, but Wilfred saw to it that they cared about *something*. "Much worse than drifting," he thought, "is letting others drift."

The attendance in chapel, which a priest watches as carefully as an editor watches the circulation, went steadily higher. Wilfred's methods were a curious mixture of briskness and spirituality. There were no concessions. Students were not asked to "brighten up" the services. He believed that a sermon should never last more than ten minutes; every minute after that bored the listener and undid the work of two minutes, so that after fifteen minutes you were, so to speak, preaching in reverse and ought logically to have a deduction made from your pay. He was no more audible than he had ever been, but relied on people to make the effort to hear his rapid, often cryptic sentences.

He could make an impression, quite unconsciously as always, on those who did not know him at all. Mr Iain Mackenzie writes:

> As an undergraduate of Fitzwilliam House, reading for Part 1 of the English Tripos between 1944 and 1946, I used to go at least once a week in term to Pembroke College for supervisions from Mr (later Professor) Basil Willey. Quite often, when passing the porter's lodge at Pembroke, one had to stand aside for an elderly cleric wheeling out his bicycle. He always looked straight in front of him and seemed entirely oblivious of the presence of others; but I was conscious enough of an inner strength in him to find out who he was, and although I never met him, I know that these very small contacts helped me to grow in the Christian faith.

Probably Wilfred was only going to snap up the last cake at Fitzbillies. But as a true evidence of his character this would make no difference. There are very many ways of bearing witness. When he was told that prayer was wish-fulfilment, or a compensation device, Wilfred never contradicted; he said he did not particularly mind what it was called; it existed.

But only a very few of his friends knew that during the war years he had to pass through a "black night of the soul", no less painful to a Christian because so many have experienced it. At one point he could not even repeat the Lord's Prayer with any sense of its meaning. Then the ordeal passed, and he came out into clear daylight again.

Once a year, without fail, Ronnie came over from Aldenham to have dinner with Wilfred in Pembroke. The High Table were disappointed on these occasions by his silence. He was not on his own ground, and was haunted by a Cambridge memory of 1937, when a visiting professor had leaned towards him with the remark, "Well, Monsignor, I haven't heard you say anything very witty yet." The meeting provided a sort of competition in clerical shabbiness, as the brothers' black suits grew nearer to absolute incoherence. Wilfred's cassock was almost green, Ronnie's collars so much too big for him that it was difficult to imagine when they could have been bought. "Clothing coupons" were issued to them, as to everyone else, during the war; but they gave them all away.

In going to Shropshire, Ronnie was returning to the Border country which they all loved, Housman country, the "blue remembered hills". With Lady Acton's eager patronage, he had begun to draw up schemes and headings ("for I cannot work without headings") for the immense task of Bible translation. Contentment, as being too easy, almost "cheating", always made Ronnie somewhat anxious; however, it was not to last long.

One thing he had dreaded in leaving Oxford had been the possibility of a convent chaplaincy. "There are two kinds of nun," he told Evoe, "those who do you much too well, and those who do you terribly badly." So far he had not had to face either for any length of time, but, at Aldenham in 1939, a convent came to him. The Sisters of the Assumption, who had a girls' school in intensely respectable Kensington Square, decided, like many other establishments, to evacuate them to the country until the threat of air raids was past. They began to arrive, the nuns, fifty girls and their luggage, at the beginning of September.

Ronnie therefore became for the duration of the war a convent chaplain, with board and lodging, but no pay. He still travelled tirelessly as a preacher; the trains still ran, unheated and blacked out; the 10 a.m. to York, which Ronnie believed was the foundation of the whole British railway system, still left King's Cross every morning. One of the restrictions which he had made for himself was that he could visit members of his family only if it could be fitted into his official engagements. His "plans" were sent out in all directions, on postcards, in his fine handwriting.

Aldenham changed. As in the days of the Crusades, the wartime ladies of England ruled their homes and farms much more rigorously than the men who had gone to battle. The land must produce food; Aldenham produced, principally, root crops and pigs. The "plans" were now entered in Tildsley's Farm Diaries, and Ronnie, who could not help learning things by heart, took a morbid pleasure in knowing, for example, that the Maximum Grant for Field Drainage, Other Than Mole Drainage, was £7 10s. But he could not feel that he was of much help on the farm. His indigestion grew worse; his nose was red, his fingers blue with cold, emerging from woollen mittens. Lady Acton had necessarily to make the most economical use of space after the convent had been housed, and there was only one smallish room left for her own farm accounting and Ronnie's work; the table had to be cleared for his meals. At no time did he have a secretary. All the typing, retyping, packing, posting (but Ronnie was good with string), all the filing, indexing and proof correcting, he did for himself.

Many people who have never read his version, or indeed any version, have come to respect Ronnie as the man who tackled the Bible single-handed. This, though it was the way that suited him best, was not what had been originally intended. The terms of the commission, imprecise though they were, required Ronnie to work with a committee, under the chairmanship of the Bishop of Lancaster; one of the members was Charlie Martindale, who wrote to his father in 1939: "I expect to emigrate to Oxford and can quietly help Ronald Knox in his translation of the Vulgate . . . He was sure he could not get me as assistant. Now he has got me." Cardinal Hinsley had hoped for a joint version from these two eminent scholars.

Martindale, however, found that "all [Knox] wants me to do is to make a paraphrase of the most obscure passages in St Paul and St John." He did not object to this, but he was busy, the committee rarely met, and Ronnie departed to Aldenham.

The Cardinal was doubtful whether somewhere "within easier access to libraries" would not have been more suitable. Ronnie seemed to be taking on the almost impossible. Newman, after all, had only hoped to be the editor of a team of Bible translators. Wilfred never trusted his own Hebrew, but relied on Dr Loewe, the Cambridge Lecturer in Rabbinics. Dilly had all the resources of the British Museum and of King's. Ronnie, in the depths of Shropshire, had to entrust all his consultations over minute shades of meaning to the uncertain wartime post. And at his elbow, so to speak, stood the lively new Protestant translations and the only too well remembered Authorized Version, learned by heart with Uncle Lindsey, as unwelcome to him now as it was to Dilly, but impossible, while he could still think and breathe, to forget. He reminded himself that the Authorized Version was never really authorized at all, certainly not by Parliament, but this did not help him.

Ronnie did not have Newman's musical ear, nor his pastoral touch with ordinary people, but as a translator he was sympathetic, fastidious and reverent. Possibly, as Belloc once suggested, he was "insufficiently coarse". His object was still to produce a Vulgate which could be read aloud with pleasure and which English Catholics, perhaps for the first time, might study together at home. "Our first job is to make them love it. If they don't love it, they won't read it."

He was a wordmaster, but the words of the New Testament cannot be made servants. On a single phrase, consolation may stand or fall. Is the angels' message "Peace on earth, good will toward men" or (as in the Vulgate) the much more grudging "Peace on earth to men of good will"? The question turns on whether a Greek noun is in the nominative or the genitive case. Wilfred, who was consulted, argued convincingly for "good will toward men", but Ronnie felt obliged to stick to the Vulgate. The problem was to come up time and again. What did Jesus say to Mary Magdalen, in the mysterious early morning appearance in the garden? Was it the traditional "Do not touch me", suggesting a spiritual body beyond our comprehension, or "Do not cling to me thus", suggesting an earthly one? Footnotes and commentaries can modify, but no one reads them, least of all those in search of comfort.

During the next few years Ronnie was to meet many discouragements. The Hierarchy had approved his work, but persisted in feeling that he ought really to be doing something different. He was urged first of all to go on a propaganda trip to the United States ("In so far as I am justified in making a decision, my answer must be No. [The Ministry] is thinking of a much younger R.A.K., who in 1917 might have been of some use"); then to go back to Oxford to counteract what his bishop called "the confounded left-wingers and pro-Russians". This task was taken on by his old friend Vernon Johnson, who became chaplain to both men and women students. Ronnie emerged from each of these proposals like Christian escaping from By-Path Meadow. If he had been ordered to go, he would of course have obeyed, but, with an amazing fund of quiet obstinacy, he demurred and survived.

The convent school, meanwhile, had become a source of real happiness. The nuns he always found intimidating, and he never managed to identify the Sister who darned his clothes, but the girls became, first teasingly and then deeply, attached to him. They were an easier generation than his own highly strung nephews and niece. Schoolchildren have a large tolerance of age, little habits, out-of-date slang, where they can detect sincerity. It was for the Assumption girls that Ronnie wrote his popular *Creed in Slow Motion* and *Mass in Slow Motion*. They show him at his best just where Dilly was at his worst—in the art of clear explanation.

He wrote these things easily; most of his strength had to go into the Knox Bible. It mattered to him in every possible way that the Church should approve of it. At the end of the winter of 1939 he submitted a draft version of passages from St Matthew's Gospel for the approval of his committee. To his dismay, Martindale raised sixty-four objections to the first chapter alone.

The impetuous Martindale had wanted something quite different. Knowing Ronnie's ear for style, he had hoped for three Gospels distinct from each other, "making the reader feel the real delicate difference between the naive Mark, the cultured Luke, the rather stiff Matthew." At the same time it must be right for dockers, miners and soldiers. Ronnie had proposed to write in decent, timeless English, but there was no such thing as a timeless language, and what did "decent" mean? Were dockers decent?

To disagree with Martindale, and on this subject above all, was agonizing. But events took an unexpected turn. Martindale, who really wanted to devote himself to the wounded and dying, reluctantly accepted an invitation to lecture in Copenhagen. Two days later the Germans invaded; he was trapped and interned, and had to spend the next five years miserably checking his engagement book to see where he should have been on that particular day. Ronnie's friends, and even the nuns, were disposed to look on this as a blessing, but they were wrong. Martindale, though he was as quarrelsome as St Jerome himself, had the authority that was needed. Without him, Ronnie was driven back on to his own strength of will, and perhaps he asked too much of it.

He was most at ease with the Epistles of St Paul, which, many Catholics agree, he made intelligible to them for the first time. In September 1941 he was finishing 2 Corinthians, when the Bishop of Southwark, who had at last found time to look at the draft of St Matthew, reported that he didn't like it: "It is a complete change from what we have used so long." This criticism, with its implication that any new translation ought to be exactly like the old ones, was almost too much for Ronnie, and he offered his resignation. The Cardinal, however, having routed the Bishop, persuaded him to go on.

Sometimes he missed his family intensely. "Brother is the man to stand by brother," he wrote in answer to a correspondent. "If I went on the rocks, I have three brothers and two sisters to keep me out of the workhouse." During the London air raids he worried about Eddie. In the green heart of Shropshire the bombing seemed remote, and yet it arrived every day in the news columns of *The Times*.

The air raids, however, had a mildly stimulating effect on Eddie. "With casual courage," wrote his assistant editor, Humphrey Ellis, "he took to wandering about wherever the bombs fell thickest, with a bottle of whisky in his pocket, looking for people who needed it."

He had agreed to stay on as editor of *Punch* until the war was over and a younger man could be found. He was now most happily re-married, to the daughter of his friend Ernest Shepard. Mary and he were living in a flat in St John's Wood; when the first bombs fell there Eddie was opening a bottle of claret for his guests, and the blast was close enough to make the cork jump straight out of the bottle. Eddie stood among the débris, corkscrew in hand, quietly in-terested: "If one could rely on its happening regularly . . ." London itself, absorbed in air-raid precautions, he saw as

> A city of painstaking pupils and earnest instructors
> (And everyone's craters the largest of all in the land),
> A lemonless onionless city with female conductors
> On Manchester buses half lost in the wilds of the Strand . . .

The suburbs, however, were transformed, with gaping open spaces, and wild flowers growing out of the rubble. Mary kept hens and grew marrows in the derelict garden behind the Air Raid Wardens' Post. E. S. P. Haynes, who also lived in St John's Wood, and whose house in 1941 was the only one left standing in his road, could be seen every morning, defiantly swimming naked in the emergency water-tank. Rose Macaulay, an old friend of all the Knoxes, drove briskly about, fascinated by the ruins, comparing them to Babylon and Pompeii. Foxes appeared among the rubble, and kestrels soared overhead; it was more difficult than ever to get to the office by half past nine, or even by ten.

Eddie caught exactly the Londoner's characteristic reaction of enjoyable gloom, the conviction that those at the top were perfectly safe and doing very nicely, the perverse determination on business as usual, even if there was very little business to do. He had been to the same barber for twenty-eight years, and the barber's shop was still open to cut his hair. Then there was his old friend and tailor, Dodson, who wrote to him in October 1940:

> Dear Sir—No doubt you are wondering what has happened to your two suits, I had them well in hand last week and the coats and waist-coats are ready for fitting, but the two pairs of trousers are somewhere in a heap of rubble, the remains of my trousermaker's workshop. The result of a Hun Souvenir which arrived last Saturday morning. The workman and his helpers escaped by a miracle with not bad injuries but are all in hospital.
>
> Part of my trouble is that there is not enough material now available for another pair of trousers and for either of the suits. There is just a chance that the trousers may be saved. I hope also that you will be indulgent for the delay, your obedient servant, William Briston Dodson.

An Edwardian by temperament, Eddie created an Edwardian loyalty. The suits, with two pairs of trousers each, were ready by November. And, of course, Dodson and his philosophic trousermaker, who recovered in hospital, were right; imperturbable daily work meant sanity.

The proprietors of *Punch*, like many others on Fleet Street, had planned to evacuate if things got much worse. The Round Table was sent down to the country to be kept safe. An emergency office had been acquired in Manchester, or, failing that, the United States offered hospitality. One American well-wisher was ready to print *Punch* at his own expense, but, in the event, the paper stayed in Bouverie Street. Eddie arrived one morning after a fire raid to find that the offices had been smouldering all night, but were still intact. "A cord was drawn across the top of the street, with little paper notices attached showing the new addresses of the periodicals which had been bombed out. They ranged from *The Economist* to *Little Dot's Playbox*." He would have liked to smoke, but it was not allowed, too much gas was escaping from the broken mains. He had to go straight up to the editorial floor to sort out the week's jokes.

The senior cartoon remained as the paper's serious comment on the progress of the war, and Bernard Partridge was on duty, drawing as meticulously as ever, but with even fewer ideas. "It falls to the lot of the Editor to suggest the subject, and when the staff of the paper is greatly depleted and printing arrangements more difficult, there are not as a rule many other ideas." And *Punch* still had to gamble with destiny. The paper had, as always, to be locked up for the printers by Saturday morning, and by Monday a new country might have declared war, or an Empire might have fallen. Mobile warfare is the nightmare of weekly editors.

> Uncertainty as to what was going to happen in North Africa, and afterwards, perplexed our cartoonists every week, and at last I was forced to have a Lion ready, a Lion reproduced and plated, a Lion in mid-air, a Lion without attachments, in the act of leaping upon Europe, and ready to be run into the paper at the last moment, whenever and wheresoever it might happen to spring. It ought to have been accompanied by the Eagle and by the Canadians too, but this we could not guess or judge until the full news of the attack on Sicily was made known. As it was, after wavering about Pantelleria, I was obliged to telephone at the last moment (a Saturday morning as far as I remember)—'Release the Lion.'

Eddie did not drop the cartoon for the simple reason that the readership liked it and wanted it. In the irrecoverably strange atmosphere of June 1940 countless letters of the simplest kind of appreciation came in response to *Punch*'s picture of a single aircraft, flying out to the attack into a darkened sky. Even at this point of danger, it mattered very much that *Punch* should appear every week.

In the article which is quoted above, Eddie says nothing about his personal commitments; it would never have occurred to him to do so. In 1942 Mary's brother was killed in action on convoy duty, and his own son disappeared, for four years, into a Japanese prisoner-of-war camp. Eddie, in W. S. Gilbert's bitter words, was "paid to be funny"; that was his business, and he never regretted it, but it was a difficult business at times.

Eddie knew that Dilly was tired, and suspected that he was ill. He suggested a holiday at the cottage at Knill, but Dilly had to refuse; he was bound to his trance-like alternations between Bletchley and Naphill.

Early in 1941, he had a new idea. It was not, apparently, the result of calculation, but came into his mind like a visitor, as ideas had come to him at Cambridge, making him stand absolutely still in the middle of passing traffic. Like everyone who does this kind of work, he had been concentrating on one problem at a time, then relaxing by changing to another one. At the moment he had returned to the question of the order of the letters on the Enigma keyboard, which, of course, had been changed completely on the new model. Now it struck him that perhaps he had been looking at things the wrong way round. Enigma was usually described as being "like a typewriter". Suppose, on the contrary, a typewriter was like Enigma? The typewriter keyboard reads QWERTYUIOP . . . Out of the many millions of millions of ways of arranging the alphabet, mightn't this be the right one?

It was. He had hit on the first significant "way in" to the Spy Variation. Once the keyboard was known, it was possible to work out the displacements so rapidly that in February the shift workers, sitting round a model many times larger than the real machine, and using material several months old, knew that they had a breakthrough. Dilly was not there when the first deciphered text began to come through in clear. It was his day off, and he was at Courn's Wood. This first signal read: "The garden wall is broken down"—evidently a code message, and "typical romantic rubbish" from the point of view of the Department, whose attitude to all Secret Services, whether German or Allied, was one of tolerant paternalism. Nor was Dilly at all distressed at missing the occasion. What mattered was that his idea had proved useful.

How useful? It has been estimated that it cut short the search for a solution by six months; no one can estimate the value of six months in 1941. The solution, in turn, is thought to have played an important part in at least three crises:

1. The battle of Matapan (March 1941), when Admiral Cunningham had warning that the Italian fleet had ventured out of harbour and saw his chance to damage it decisively, but had to keep up the appearance of unpreparedness while he brought his destroyers to at short notice; credit for spotting the Italian cruisers had to be given to the Fleet Air Arm, so that the Enigma source would not be compromised. Dilly on this occasion wrote a poem for the Department, "When Cunningham Won at Matapan", introducing the names of all his girls; Mavis (Lever) rhymed with "rara avis", and Margaret (Rock) with "target"—not a good enough rhyme for a Knox brother, but all this doggerel came from the heart.

2. The search for the *Bismarck* (May 1941), when the battleship disappeared during the middle watch until eleven a.m. on the 25th; at this point the Admiralty received information which made them tell our pursuit forces to "act on the assumption that the enemy was making for Brest."

3. The anxious matter of the Malta convoy (April 1942), when the U.S. aircraft carrier *Wasp* undertook to bring a cargo of Spitfires through the Straits of Gilbraltar, and it was essential to find out, through the signals of the German agents in Spain, whether the secret of the convoy had been kept or not.

Churchill paid a visit of congratulation to Bletchley. Once again, Dilly was not on duty, and once again this left him unconcerned. He admired Churchill, but did not consider him discreet, and he felt that, if the work at Bletchley was not to be compromised, it might be better if as few details as possible were known to the Former Naval Person. He would, admittedly, have liked his staff to receive some credit for the work they had been doing for so long and so patiently, but he understood, as did they all, that credit might very well not be possible.

In 1942 Dilly was threatened with a second operation for cancer.

He was admitted to hospital. Eddie, the only person who could understand him completely, arrived to find him smiling sardonically over a book called *The Art of Dying*. They took turns in reading each other passages, just as in the Birmingham schoolroom they had read each other Smiles's *Self-Help*. Dilly did not want the operation; his considered opinion was that a human being ought not to be turned into a bit of plumbing; the place for taps was the sink. He had also been looking, in a detached way, through the burial service, and, unexpectedly, through the Epistles of St Paul, in particular 1 Corinthians 15, which is a discussion of the resurrection of the dead. Of what use was it, St Paul asks in this chapter, "to fight with the beasts at Ephesus," if, at the end of it, he did not know he would rise from the dead and live again?

After he had got back home to Courn's Wood, Dilly asked his niece to come and see him, to discuss the possibility of a job at Bletchley. "You don't share the family pretence of not understanding mathematics?" he asked anxiously. It had to be a pretence, since mathematics, after all, consisted only in seeing what was there. But was it a pretence when he said that he didn't understand music? That was a totally different matter, Dilly said. Music was simply a conspiracy to make certain loud and less loud noises, to prevent other people from thinking. Returning to the subject of the family, he added that he would not mind seeing rather more of them, as he was going to die. All expressions of sympathy were brushed away. "It will give me something to do," he said.

He had not forgotten the Pentelopes; one of them he considered as his epitaph:

> A wanderer on the path
> That leads through life to death,
> I was acquainted with
> The tales they tell of both,
> But found in them no truth.

Dilly was aware, when he said that he needed something to do, that he could not do much more in his department, but he was too

ill to give up the habit of cryptography, and too loyal to stop working if there was even the slightest chance of being of use. At last he
could not make the journey to Bletchley any longer, but stayed in
his study at Courn's Wood, working on a small, isolated difficulty in
the Italian cipher, with the tactful help of Margaret Rock. Pain produced fantasies, and he would send over to Bletchley elaborate suggestions for solutions which his staff scarcely knew what to do with.
Olive nursed him devotedly. These two people had loved each other
for twenty years without being able to make each other happy. They
would have given the world, now they were at the point of separation, to understand one another. But Dilly's nerves were on edge.
Even the dog James, now very elderly, could not be tolerated in the
room. Still an iron discipline held.

> It was not in his nature to be daunted [writes his son, Oliver] . . . By
> this time eighteen or nineteen years old, I was given compassionate
> leave to be at home during his last days. He had just been awarded
> the C.M.G. It has been explained to my mother that security con-
> siderations precluded his being given some more illustrious honour.
> Far too ill to travel to London, he deemed proper receipt of the hon-
> our to be a duty; he insisted on dressing and sat, shivering in front of
> the large log-fire, as he awaited the arrival of the Palace emissary.
> His clothes were now far too big for him, his eyes were sunk in a grey
> face, but he managed the exercise all right. 'Nothing is impossible.'

The decoration was sent over to the Department, since he felt it
was theirs as much as his. Dilly did not leave his room again. Ronnie
came over from Aldenham; he slept on a made-up bed, praying,
waiting, as a priest, to see his brother out of this world. Dilly, though
hardly conscious, could hear him. "Is Ronnie still out there bother-
ing God in the passage?" he asked.

The end came a few days later, on 27 February 1943. In the *Times*
obituary Maynard Keynes described his old friend as "sceptical of
most things except those that chiefly matter, that is, affection and
reason." Without ever reconciling these two, Dilly had gone, unwa-
vering in his disbelief, into what he believed was endless darkness.

"Yesterday's news came to draw us all closer . . ." Ronnie wrote to his sister. "What a happy family life we've had really, though so scattered in these last years. No feuds, no scandals, and the youngest turned fifty-five before the circle was broken."

Broken it was, however, with a mortal shock to the whole structure.

IX

1945–1971

Endings

"HE WHO TRAVELS IN THE BARQUE of St Peter," Ronnie once said, "had better not look too closely into the engine-room." This was particularly the case when the mechanism had to be put gently into reverse.

His translation of the New Testament was finished on St Jerome's Day, 30 September 1942. It was three years since the Hierarchy had commissioned it, and they might have been expected to authorize it at once. They hesitated.

Extracts from St Paul's Letters, printed in *The Tablet*, had been a success. "The fan-mail," he wrote, "does lead me to hope that my version of the Epistles gives some glimmering of what it's all about." A trial edition, strictly for private reading, not issued to booksellers, barely announced in the Press, sold over 9,500 copies in advance. Subscription was by postcard, and Ronnie allowed himself to feel mildly exhilarated. The farmworkers at Aldenham grew used to seeing him, even more often than usual, tramping across the fields to collect his post. It was encouraging that a lot of the cards were evidently not from his usual book-buying public, not, in fact from people who would ordinarily feel it was worth while to lay out ten shillings on a book; but they wanted his Bible.

The next step was to submit the trial edition to the Bishops for their approval. Their meeting was delayed by the air raids until the autumn of 1944. By this time they had all received their copies from the Archbishop of Westminster, with a questionnaire: would they be prepared to see the Knox Version made official? If not, what about the profits? It was made clear that in no case would Ronnie make any profit beyond the £200 a year he had been allocated for the work, but, if it went ahead simply as a private venture, the Church would lose a valuable copyright.

The replies were not altogether encouraging. "Regrets matter being rushed" (this although it was two years since the New Testament had been finished) . . . "Seeks opinions everywhere. Has not read much yet" . . . "Many favourite quotations spoilt by R.K." . . . "I am not prepared to sanction the translation for public use in Church. I have prohibited its public use here." Only Shrewsbury and Middlesbrough were wholeheartedly in favour. Some had "no strong feelings". The whole could be construed as a grudging majority vote in favour, but, as poor Ronnie said, people kept asking him "Have the Bishops authorized your N.T.?" and he was obliged to answer "Well, sort of."

Would an *Imprimatur* from himself, just to show there was nothing against it, do for the time being, the Archbishop of Westminster wondered, instead of a full authorization? Here the machinery of the Barque could be seen in action. Ronnie's reply is a classic in the literature of disappointment. In the third paragraph of his letter he brought out what, after all, was the crucial point; Protestants would say: "Father Knox should have known the Church of Rome better by now. He would have been wiser to stick to detective stories."

It was not the habit of the four brothers to show enthusiasm about their own work. That would have gone contrary both to their real modesty and to the Edwardian habit of understatement, the habit which called the massacre of the Somme "a show", and an expensive lunch at Simpson's "something to eat". Ronnie had long ago lost count of his published titles, and only hoped that no one would ever have to undertake his bibliography. But he did care about his Bible. "He was very sensitive," wrote Douglas Woodruff, the editor of *The Tablet*, "if anyone criticized the most contentious of his renderings," and he felt rather uneasy himself at the reflection that a long study of the Holy Scripture should result in "this unreasonable streak of touchiness". But perhaps only Ronnie, at this juncture, would have called his touchiness unreasonable.

He had consulted the widest range of scholars he could, and his New Testament, after all these collations, was entirely his own, in his own living language, sober, lucid and civilized, conservative in many ways—he kept "thou" and "thee"—but quietly moving. It was not, perhaps, a people's Bible; a contributor to *The Tablet*, H. P. R. Finsberg, commented that "not all of us know Latin, and some of us, alas, are not gentlemen." In America, as Ronnie well knew, there was a voice of criticism which accused him of scribbling "a flip-throughable improvement on the Divine Revelation." But it was an exercise in humility to read these opinions, and Ronnie said that on his deathbed, if he found he had no enemies left, he intended to forgive his reviewers.

His New Testament finally appeared, officially authorized, in October 1945. It was published by Burns & Oates, who had stood loyally by him, and it began to sell at once. Over the next twelve years or so the royalties earned for the Hierarchy came to about fifty thousand pounds.

Ronnie hoped that the Knox Version would hold its own for at least fifty years. He died before seeing it replaced by competitors— the great Jerusalem Bible, prepared by the Dominicans straight from the ancient texts, and the Revised Standard Version, which at last, in the long troubled history of the Church, has proved to be a Bible acceptable to both Protestants and Catholics. Both these translations looked to the future, and Ronnie's to the past, but that does not take away the value of his struggle against the recalcitrance of languages and of Bishops, his "Nine Years' Hard", or the new ground which he broke when he persuaded English Catholics that the Bible was there to be read.

Working doggedly away at Aldenham, he had made very little comment on the progress of the war—"politics aren't at all in my line"—but early in August 1945, when news came of the destruction of Hiroshima and Nagasaki, it seemed to him that if the Church was going to make no official pronouncement—and he waited several days for one—then, surely, "one might write something". In *God and the Atom*, a long essay rather than a book, with less clarity than usual but a great deal of feeling, he made one of the earliest protests in print; he did not question God's providence, but whatever possibilities nuclear energy might offer for good or evil, we had missed one of the greatest opportunities in history in dropping the bomb, instead of "showing what we might have done and not doing it".

Extracts from the little book appeared in *The Tablet* and it was published in November, but it did not "take". In a letter to Winnie, thanking her at Christmas for yet another gift of home-knitted socks, he noted sadly that "my atom book hasn't had any reviews at all that I've seen; but I suppose it will be unloaded on the sort of people who just ask for a 'book,' knowing that the one they want will be out of circulation." It fell flat because it was not what he was expected—not really what he was "supposed"—to write, the fate of all long-established authors. The family were touched by his resignation and alarmed by his low spirits as he faced another winter of penetrating draughts at Aldenham.

In 1946 the three remaining brothers and their two sisters were together at Beckenham Grove when their stepmother died. Mrs K. had defied the passing years, straight as a ramrod, her white head held high. She had been one of the last private customers of the Bank of England; mounting the steps in her black cotton stockings, and with her large black umbrella, she had continued to cash her small cheques, with the air of one who is used to good service. Now she was gone there had to be a sorting-out of books and furniture, since Ethel would have to stay on, and the maids intended to run 18 Beckenham Grove as a sort of discreet boarding-house. Ronnie had the chance to recover his copy of Wood's *Natural History*. He sat reading the anecdotes, all of which he professed to believe, aloud: "When cut grass is given to giraffes, they eat off the upper part of it, and leave the coarse stems, just as we eat asparagus." He was lost in rediscovery. Later it appeared that, unlike Bishop Knox, who had cut Ronnie out of his will, Mrs K. had bequeathed her small property equally. What was the best thing to do with the legacy? A characteristic idea, at the same time romantic and reserved, struck Ronnie. The cousin who, fifty years before, had courted Mrs K. had fallen on hard times, and Ronnie had always believed "that there might have been something in it" if the Bishop had not come along; so he arranged, in total secrecy, to make over the money to the old man he had never met.

In the spring of 1947 the Actons, discouraged by the difficulties of peacetime, decided to emigrate. The nuns had already left Aldenham. Now the house would be closed down for the time being, and the chapel, perhaps, for ever. "This is to mention the fact that I'll be uprooting from here in the autumn," Ronnie told Winnie, "because the Actons are moving lock stock and barrel to Southern Rhodesia . . . This place will be off the map after September. It's all rather depressing, and would make up well into a novel if it weren't too like *Brideshead*."

This last remark—that of a writer who has, perhaps rashly, given away his material—showed that Ronnie wanted to try something new. Houseless, he began to look around him. What about Crewe? There, at the great rail junction, the living reality of the cold print of Bradshaw, he could take trains in all directions to see his family and friends. So many of his analogies had started there. "When a traveller gets out of the train at Crewe," he had written, meditating on the subject of loss through death, "has he left the train, or has the train left him? There are two points of view. To his fellow travellers he has become merely a smell of stale tobacco. On the other hand they have become for him only a row of dimly remembered faces." Or there was Hugh Benson's Hare Street, which belonged now to the archdiocese of Westminster, but was seldom used. The old dream revived. Perhaps he could rent it, and Vernon Johnson, who was retiring from the chaplaincy, might come and share it with him. Winnie wanted him to come to Edinburgh. In spite of failing eyesight she had continued to write—even when she was induced to rest in a nursing home she had sat up all night and written a novel about a nursing home—and Ronnie had been her unfailing literary critic, as well as her tender counsellor in every difficulty. But all these schemes came to nothing. In October 1947 he went, as chaplain and paying guest, to old and dear friends, the Asquiths, at Mells, in Somerset.

Under the original arrangement at the Manor House Ronnie was to pay eight guineas a week and his wine bill. "But of course," he wrote, "one doesn't know how an arrangement like that will work out, and may terminate on either side when I reach the end of the Old Testament." In the event he stayed at Mells for the rest of his life, and was made so comfortable that the Evangelical conscience, which was his inheritance, was troubled; he wondered whether it was more demoralizing to enjoy comfort, or to take it for granted.

> Going away and leaving Mells
> Is five and twenty different hells . . .

one of his occasional poems begins. "It's a very unexacting place," he told his family with relief, "everybody wearing what they've got on, and not being taken out to see farms." He was living in a circle of Conservative Catholics, near Downside Abbey, he was warm all the year round, and felt part of a family. And the tradition of the Souls was maintained in the lovely old house and village, for Mrs Raymond Asquith, who had invited him to come, was the daughter of one of the most famous of them all, Frances Horner, the patroness of Rossetti and Burne-Jones.

Dilly was no longer alive to comment on his younger brother's last move from one grand house to another, but he would have agreed that it made him happy. "The three great appetites of our nature," Ronnie had written, "are our love of pleasure, our taste for power, and our craving for human affection." The first two meant less and less to him, the last persisted at the close.

If it hadn't been for Mells, or "a perch somewhere", Ronnie, as he dramatically put it, would have been faced with sleeping on the Embankment. Both his life and Wilfred's had touched before on this hardest test of their vows, the renunciation (while the birds of the air have nests) of a settled home. At Pembroke, when Meredith Dewey came back from service with the Navy, Wilfred was uncertain of his place in the college, but the difficulty solved itself; he continued as chaplain, Dewey became Dean. He examined Wilfred's chapel accounts, which were accurate in total but quite inexplicable in detail, with some amazement. Then came the problem of the garden, for Dewey was also a gardener, but he was resourceful, and "in order," he told Wilfred's niece, "to avoid the spectacle of two clergymen throwing snails at each other, I divided the rockery in half."

Wilfred's last years at Pembroke opened with a notable triumph, when in 1945 he bet R. A. Butler a bottle of claret at High Table that Labour would win the election. The Labour victory gave him as much satisfaction as his one or two honours—the Doctorate of Divinity in 1945, and in 1948, a Fellowship of the British Academy. *St. Paul and the Church of the Gentiles*, which had been published at the worst possible time, in 1939, was being considered at leisure now by English and German theologians, and for a short popular *Life of St. Paul* he was given, to his amazement, £400—he was less pleased when, in the *Times* list of best-selling books of the year, it was attributed to Ronnie. In the meantime he was writing something else, but that was a matter of loose notes, crammed into the drawers of his desk. He always wrote straight onto the typewriter, and never discussed work in progress.

In 1946, as Superior of the Oratory of the Good Shepherd, he conducted their annual retreat. They knew him, he told them, too well not to realize his own lamentable failure to live up to the ideals by which their life should be governed. But he wanted to say something about forgetfulness of self, not as a means of salvation—"salvation can never be more than a by-product of the main activity of our lives"—but as something necessary for its own sake. "We think of ourselves as so many billiard balls, moving up and down an infinite table, charged with the duty of avoiding collision as far as possible." But avoidance of collision is not enough, compassion is not enough, even sharing is not enough. We need to be able to think of ourselves as nothing. "After all, it should not be so difficult." But it *is* difficult. And Wilfred recalled a remark of St Francis de Sales, that if our self-love dies half an hour before we do, we shall have done well.

It seemed strange to think of Wilfred, of all people, suppressing his individual personality. "There has never been anyone like Father Wilfred," wrote Canon Henry Brandreth, "and it is impossible to believe that there ever will be. It would be absurd to regard him as a typical member of the Oratory or of any other society to which he belonged . . . yet he sacrificed his own interests and inclinations on its behalf with a wonderful steadfastness." Only in this way can the free self sacrifice self-love, and still remain free.

The only one of the four brothers to retire—though this, of course, is not the same thing as stopping work—was Eddie. At 10 Bouverie Street he regarded himself, when the war ended, as a caretaker. For him, the joke was played out, though not his sympathies or his connoisseur's interest in the ironies of life. Some of these were pleasant—when Oxford, for example, made him an Hon.D.Litt., half a century after he had gone down without his degree; and in any case, he never tired of observing the remedies which were offered to society, even when he declared he could no longer quite understand them. He wrote, in valediction to his own brain

> O idle and incorrigible cranium,
> Why do I fill you up
> With facts about art and economics and uranium,
> You poor inverted cup?

You lumber-room of nonsense, you rag-bag, you emporium
    Of left-off remnants, you receptacle of hay,
What did you do with those lectures about thorium
    I lent you the other day?

Is there any limit to the number of notorious
    And beautiful people, you sieve, you net,
Whom I pass into your keeping, illuminate and glorious,
    And you forget?

In a world where obviously everything worsens
    Cannot you remember overnight
The names of thousands of self-sacrificing persons
    Who are putting it right?

Mary and he had bought Grove Cottage, one of the oldest small houses in Hampstead, close to the edge of the Heath, and marked on earlier maps as the Two Pigeons Inn. The freehold gave them the right, if they cared to exercise it, to graze a donkey on the Heath, many old friends within reach, and the ballerina Karsavina for a neighbour. Eddie was at once in demand for every kind of local committee; "I am welcome on them all," he observed, "because I never say anything," but long practice at the *Punch* Table had taught him to effect a good deal without many words, and it gave him satisfaction to think that he had helped, through one committee and another, to add an acre of common land to the Heath. The air of the hill village suited him as it had always done. "He seemed in good form, I thought," Ronnie reported to Winnie, "and dodging the traffic remarkably well for a man who always stops in his tracks when a remark occurs to him."

The Tatler asked him to write their Book Page in succession to his friend Elizabeth Bowen, and for some years he continued to go down to the Table on Wednesdays, bidding a gradual farewell to Fleet Street. It was a source of pride to him that his son, safely returned from prisoner-of-war camp, was making a name for himself as a Far Eastern correspondent. But, although Eddie had long ago foretold the post-war difficulties of his country, he had hardly counted on the disappearance of the magazines and dailies, one after another, or, eventually, of the *Punch* offices being sold. Still, the paper was tough, and survived.

> *Vogue la galère!* [Beachcomber wrote to him] A fig for melancholy! For is not the merry maid May here, with the east wind in her breath, her gift of sleet, and promise of snow? And is not the cobalt bomb, with a warhead crammed with deadly germs, on its way? What a world it is—but how lucky we are to remember what it was once like.

Fleet Street, in its turn, missed "Evoe". Stories accumulated about him, many of them associated with the journalist-haunted pubs and wine cellars of the quarter. On one occasion, when a few of the *Punch* staff were having a late drink together, the barmaid looked with curiosity at Eddie's neat dark overcoat, dark hat and impeccably rolled umbrella. "What do you do for a living?" Eddie folded his hands on his umbrella and looked down at the ground. "I live by my wits," he said. And that was true enough.

By the Christmas of 1948 a first grandchild had been born, but the acknowledged guest of honour at Grove Cottage, as always, was Wilfred. There were frosted decorations on the table that year, which momentarily caught light from a candle. Wilfred looked on serenely. He was warned that "the snow was on fire". "So it is! How uncharacteristic!"

It was for the last time. At the end of the year Wilfred, who had been suffering, like Dilly before him, rather more pain than he admitted, underwent an operation. For the Christmas of 1949 he could not leave Cambridge, and was the guest of the Master, S. C. Roberts. The question of "hard sauce" with the pudding, absolutely necessary to the festival, arose. Wilfred was on a rigorous diet. "I don't know if any man has eaten hard sauce with rice pudding before," he wrote, "but a man can try."

In January he told Eddie that he had urged the medicine men to remove their stray ironmongery (which he compared to the grape-scissors which Aunt Fanny had always kept on the table at Edmundthorpe), so that he could come up to Hampstead, "but," he added in a postscript, "an unexpected setback." The whole business of being looked after, of giving so much trouble to the nurses, distressed him much more than the pain, which he referred to, when it grew intense, only in one short letter: "O Lord, how long?" There were long spells of unconsciousness, and he could not read his Daily Office, or open the letters that poured into Addenbrooke's Hospital, some of these from Hoxton, and even from Stratford. "Do you remember the old East End 'Wish yer well'?" Stephen Langton wrote. "Well, I do, I do."

Ronnie came up to Cambridge and stood, looking hollow and shrivelled with cold, totally miserable. "Can't I buy him anything?" he asked. "I seem to have plenty of money." Since Lady Acton had gone to Rhodesia, there was no one to make him invest it. Perhaps champagne? But Wilfred's condition defeated earthly generosity. On 9 February, he died.

So many students wanted to get into Pembroke Chapel for the memorial service that there had to be a ballot for tickets. It was hard to envisage life in college without their tattered chaplain.

Meredith Dewey gave Eddie a list of Wilfred's possessions. The only "good" things had been a scarlet gown, which really belonged to the Bishopric of Ely, and an oak desk, which really belonged to Pembroke. The sofa, rather decrepit, might be worth three pounds, the typewriter "was not a very up-to-date machine, I think". His clothes were left to the Franciscans, his books to the college. Dewey also asked Eddie to come to Cambridge as often as he could. "The resemblance," he wrote, "is consoling."

In extreme illness, Wilfred had written, the soul "fetches its prayer", as the body fetches its breath. Those who had been with him had seen this. He had also written that we should be wrong to think of eternity as static, and, in consequence, boring. Why should we not go on, through all eternity, growing in love and in our power to love?

The scattered papers in the drawer turned out to be towards a draft of a book on the sources of the Synoptic Gospels, and the interrelationship between them. This was anything but a fashionable subject. The prevailing scholarly method was "form criticism", which analysed the Gospels into a series of exemplary narratives improvised by an undefined body, the early Church, to meet the political and moral needs of the first century. The question was no longer "What did Jesus teach?" but "What kind of awkward situations led the early Christians to invent these stories?" The idea that the Gospels might be meant to give any kind of real picture of Christ's life on earth, or that they drew on contemporary sources, or in fact had any sources at all, had receded far into the background. Wilfred, of course, had studied *Formgeschichte*, but found it unconvincing. His knowledge of Hellenistic literature made him certain that the Gospels were not folk tales but spiritual biographies, and that each was written, not by a harassed committee, but by an author. Beyond this, as always, he uncompromisingly faced the larger question: by what right do we teach children that Christ was born in Bethlehem if we do not believe it?

He was attempting to go back, therefore, to the Synoptic problem in its classical form. Whoever the writers called Matthew, Mark and Luke really were, they must partly have taken their information from each other, partly had independent material of their own. Can we deduce what that material was, and where it came from? Some of his ideas on the subject had already been presented to his colleagues in Cambridge, the rest was in notes, and nothing was complete. The obvious fate of these papers seemed to be first of all a dusty file, and then oblivion. But the most distinguished of Wilfred's pupils, Henry Chadwick (later Regius Professor of Divinity at Cambridge), came to their rescue. At the cost of much hard work he sorted them out and collated them; they were published in two volumes by the Cambridge University Press. Wilfred Knox, therefore, turned out to be even more fortunate than Walter Headlam.

After Wilfred's death, Eddie gave up fishing the Arrow and the Lug. In 1959 he was invited by the University of Cambridge to give the Leslie Stephen Lecture; they wanted him, as a kind of memorial, to speak about Wilfred, but he found that he could not do it. "Mortal things touch the mind," but even Virgil had not been able to explain them any farther than that. He offered, instead, as a subject the Mechanism of Satire.

Eddie's own humour came partly from sheer love of words. A spontaneous pun-maker, who once started an address to the Omar Khayyam Society with the words "Unaccustomarkhayyam to public speaking," he knew that this talent should be kept within limits. It had made him more critical, for instance, than most people of *Ulysses*, because he thought that Joyce had no one to tell him that puns could become a dangerous habit. Real humour, Eddie thought, lay not in ingenuity but incongruity, particularly in relation to the dignified place which man has assigned to himself in the scheme of things.

That was what he wanted to tell his audience at Cambridge. He divided classical satirists into two classes—fierce men starving in garrets, and renouncing popularity and circulation to dwell in tubs, and calm good-livers "who tell amusingly the kind of truth that no one has ever denied." But for the present century the right spirit, he believed, was self-satire, the ability to see humour in the constant small defeats of life, and "the power to be startled by nothing, however extravagant." The subject, in the end, turned out to be more relevant than it had seemed, as anyone could have told who had heard Eddie and Wilfred laughing together.

The eldest and the youngest brothers, left as survivors, had not altered their relationship since the days at Aston. Eddie still marvelled at the prodigy. It was not that congratulations or honours had changed Ronnie, who received them gratefully, but always quite naturally. At a private audience with the Pope to mark his appointment (in 1951) as Pronotary Apostolic, he chatted for half an hour about the Loch Ness monster, in which His Holiness was much interested. But, to Eddie, Ronnie still seemed to need both protection and a certain amount of keeping in order. This, by and large, was his attitude at public celebrations.

On Ronnie's sixtieth birthday his friends invited him to a dinner, at which the nostalgic atmosphere was rather agreeably sharpened by Evelyn Waugh. To Ronnie's niece, who wanted to leave early to look after her baby, he snapped: "Children! Nonsense! Nothing so easily replaceable!" Everyone must stay. Ronnie himself spoke appropriately of the past, pitying those who had not known the years before 1914, "the golden age of the liberal professions". Eddie said a few words, recalling that Ronnie had been literate since the age of eighteen months, and since then it had been "increasingly difficult to do anything about him".

A much grander occasion was the luncheon at the Hyde Park Hotel, under the presidency of Cardinal Griffin, to mark the completion of the Knox Bible. This title, as Ronnie said, seemed to admit him to the company of Pullman, and Hoover, and the Earl of Sandwich, as someone whose name would be remembered only by a product. It was also the moment for him to pay tribute, which he did most generously, to all who had helped him and all who had sent in suggestions, though he couldn't resist thanking, in conclusion, all who had been kind enough not to send any. Nothing was said about his moments of discouragement. But the occasion was a little marred because no ladies were asked. This was not by Ronnie's wish, but there was "feeling", and the ladies organized a separate luncheon, at the same time, in an adjoining room. So the Knox translation sailed out, to the very end, on stormy waters.

Lady Acton, in particular, was much missed, but in the spring of 1954 Ronnie had received an invitation to visit the Actons at M'bebi, their farm in Southern Rhodesia. For this quite exceptional venture outside England he kept a travel diary. Quite deliberately, he rested his mind by referring new impressions to the old. "The longer one lives, the more one's pleasures are conditioned by memory." The palms were like photographs in missionary magazines, the giraffes like illustrations in Wood's *Natural History*, and on the coast at Chwaka, on the way out, "the natives have exactly those principles of punting which I learned from Julian Grenfell in 1907." All his energies were saved for renewing old kindnesses with old friends. From this point of view the visit was an unqualified success; "[Lord

Acton] said, just before we parted, that it was wonderful being able to pick up life exactly where we left it six years ago." But Africa did not impress him as a possible place of retirement. It seemed to him, like Greek democracy, "built up against a background of slaves," and it was too hot. On his return ("getting into a train at Paddington," he noted thankfully), he came up to London and spent an evening at Grove Cottage. The brothers exchanged few words about the expedition. "Well, how were the Actons?" "Very well; rather anxious to prove that it was a good thing to live in Rhodesia." "And is it?" "It won't be."

Later on that evening, when the brothers were discussing books, Ronnie said tentatively: "Evelyn Waugh writes quite decently, don't you think?" This was high praise. Ronnie (like Eddie) had been approached by several publishers to write his autobiography, a kind of continuation, that is, of *A Spiritual Aeneid*, but he was not making much headway. If anyone was to write about him, and he supposed it might come to that, better have someone who wrote quite decently.

The idea of an autobiography became merged with another project which he had set himself, as soon as his translation of the Bible was finished. He wanted to justify the existence of God to the reason—to show that it is unreasonable to deny God. Unless this was done conclusively, the reason could not be regarded as immortal; if it denied God, it could not survive death. Here, as Ronnie admitted, he was directly challenging Pascal, who had called on reason to recognize its own shortcomings, and to admit how much it depended on the body, and how little it knew in comparison with the heart. In defiance of Pascal, he turned back to the five classic proofs which had made so little effect on his congregations at the chaplaincy, and particularly to his favourite, the third, the Argument from Contingency. This, he thought, was one that occurred naturally to every man as he passed his sixtieth birthday. "Few of us are so unimaginative as to pass a milestone of that kind without giving a thought to the question, 'If my first birthday hadn't happened, what then? . . . That I exist, I cannot doubt; that my existence belongs to me, is in any way part of my nature, I cannot intelligibly maintain.' We know that we are different from, say, characters in a book. By what means, then, are we projected into the world, an actuality?"

And yet, even as he tried to plan out his apologia, he was not quite satisfied with it. Reason, after all, was not enough—he wanted his readers to feel "a glow of assent", like the disciples on the road to Emmaus. The proof must be "humanized", and this returns him to his own experience. "This is an old man's book," he wrote, by way of a preface, but old men, after all, have experience, and have some idea of how human minds work. An old man "has not changed his point of view, but he has begun to understand the other man's . . . if I may use words in a grossly unphilosophical sense, what he demands now is not so much truth, as reality."

But as Ronnie struggled with these new ideas, so much broader and more tolerant than any he had let himself express before, in either the Anglican or the Catholic Church, a doubt assailed him as to whether he could do it. His book exists only in the opening fragments and the preface, which were printed in *The Tablet*. He had never considered himself good at apologetics. Anyone who came to him for them, he used to say, was at the wrong counter. And besides this, the winter of 1956 found him unaccountably tired. Perhaps somebody else, better qualified or more hopeful than himself, would persevere with the book he would never finish. *Exoriare aliquis.*

Ronnie was the third of the brothers to struggle against cancer—in his case, cancer of the liver, which meant increasing spells of nausea and weakness. Not having been told exactly what was wrong with him, he asked Winnie if she could come away with him to Torquay, to try the effect of sea air, but she could not afford to do so, and money matters were always too delicate between them for him to offer to pay. Evelyn Waugh and his wife volunteered to accompany him instead. A large hotel in an expensive seaside resort seemed a curious choice for a sick man who could scarcely eat, walk, or read with comfort, and Waugh found time hanging heavily on his hands, but he was, at least, able to collect some material for the biography he had now agreed to write. On his return to Mells,

Ronnie, who was noticeably weaker, celebrated mass in the chapel for the last time at the beginning of June.

Like Eddie, Ronnie had been asked, as an honour, to give a public lecture—the Romanes, which is delivered in the Sheldonian Theatre at Oxford. The subject was to be "On English Translation", and Ronnie, having accepted the previous autumn, was determined, although by now he found speech difficult, to deliver it. The date fixed was 11 June 1957. He came up to Oxford and stayed the night at Worcester, as the guest of the Vice-Chancellor, J. C. Masterman. Worcester is near the railway-line, and his friends were afraid he might be disturbed by the noise of shunting, which went on the whole night through. But Ronnie slept well. "Trains, to me, you must remember, are music," he said the next morning. Later in the day the doctors gave him an injection which it was hoped would carry him through. He was allowed to sit down, without taking part in the formal procession, and wait with his typescript in front of him while the audience crowded in—an Oxford audience, the one he knew best of all, and had known for a lifetime.

> When he appeared [Father Corbishley wrote], even those who had seen him quite lately at Mells were shocked to see the way in which the ravages of the diseased liver had stained his face an almost brilliant yellow, set off by the whiteness of the collar. The Vice-Chancellor entered. The lecture began.
>
> We held our breath for the first paragraph, wondering if we should be disappointed . . . We need not have feared. The voice, gentle as ever, yet clear and strong, began. All the old magic was there. Ripple after ripple of laughter ran through the theatre, to be hushed to silence as his argument developed . . . It was a triumph of literary criticism; still more it was a triumph of simple human courage.
>
> We almost forgot that he was under sentence of death, until the calm, serene voice quoted, as an example of exact and faithful translation . . . the rendering by William Johnson Cory of a Greek epigram:
>
> > They told me, Heraclitus, they told me you were dead,
> > They brought me bitter news to hear, and bitter tears to shed.

> I wept when I remembered how often you and I
> Had tired the sun with talking and sent him down the sky.
>
> And now that thou art lying, my dear old Carian guest,
> A handful of grey ashes, long, long ago at rest,
> Still are thy pleasant voices, thy nightingales, awake;
> For Death, he taketh all away, but them he cannot take.

A second opinion on Ronnie's condition was scarcely necessary, but he was anxious to know how much working life he had left. He went straight on from Oxford to London, where Harold Macmillan, now the Prime Minister, had arranged for him to stay the night at 10 Downing Street; Sir Horace Evans was to make an examination the next day.

> My Romanes lecture went absolutely all right, but I was doped [Ronnie wrote to Winnie], and I came back quite flattened out. Sir Horace Evans fully supports Dr Williams' diagnosis—I asked him whether he'd reckon my expectation of life in weeks or months, and he said months . . . so I think on the whole my lines have fallen in pleasant places . . . Harold Macmillan saw me off at the station himself, and the station-master took off his hat to me twice before the train left.

The Prime Minister had wished him a comfortable journey. "It will be a very long one," Ronnie replied.

In the few weeks of consciousness he had left, he wrote with painful clarity to his friends to wish them goodbye, sometimes mentioning his condition quite casually, towards the end of the letter. Not all of them by any means were Catholics, and some he had not seen for years. He made one or two small requests, knowing that this would make the letter easier to answer. He told the Church of England rector of Mells how intensely cold he felt, even though it was the height of summer, and asked if he would lend him his heavy cloak. All his correspondents, of whatever faith, were asked for their prayers—*oremus invicem*—let us pray for one another.

As to his remaining brother, he wrote to him, with the last of a lifetime of family understatements, that "some kind of a sentence seems to have been pronounced." There was no need for more, they understood each other too well.

Ronnie died on 24 August 1957. A few days later, Eddie got a letter of sympathy from Rose Macaulay, that sharpest-tongued, but kindest-hearted, of writers. She said that she knew how he felt— "like a survivor from a shipwreck". For her, the world was much impoverished. Like many others, she had been glad to feel, while all four brothers were alive, that one need never be very far away from a Knox.

Bibliography

(other than titles by the Knox brothers themselves)

1. BIOGRAPHICAL

Basileon: A Magazine of King's College, Cambridge 1900–1914. Facsimile edition, with an introduction by Sir Charles Tennyson (1974).

Birks, Rev. Herbert: *The Life and Correspondence of Thomas Valpy French* (1895).

Bone, James: *The London Perambulator* (1925).

Brandreth, Canon Henry: *The Oratory of the Good Shepherd: An Historical Sketch* (privately printed, 1958).

Brittain, Frederick: *It's a Don's Life* (1972).

Caraman, Fr Philip, S.J.: *C. C. Martindale: A Biography* (1967).

Clinton-Baddeley, V. C.: *Aladdin: or, Love Will Find Out the Way*, with additional material by Frank Birch (1931).

Corbishley, Fr Thomas, S.J.: *Ronald Knox the Priest* (1964).

Dewey, Rev. Meredith: Obituary of Wilfred Knox. *Pembroke College Annual Gazette*, No. 24, December 1950.

Eyres, Laurence: "Some Edmundian Memories". *The Edmundian*, Autumn 1957.

Fothergill, J. R.: *An Innkeeper's Diary* (1933).

Fowler, J. H.: *The Life and Letters of Edward Lee Hicks, Bishop of Lincoln, 1910–19* (1922).

Harrod, R. F.: *The Life of John Maynard Keynes* (1951).

Hassall, Christopher: *Rupert Brooke: A Biography* (1964).

Haynes, E. S. P.: *A Lawyer's Notebook* (1933).

Headlam, Walter: *Letters and Poems*, with a Memoir by C. H. Headlam (1910).

Knox, Rt. Rev. Edmund A.: *Reminiscences of an Octogenarian* (1935).

Lansbury, George: *Socialism for the Poor: The End of Pauperism* (1909).

Leslie, Sir Shane: *The End of a Chapter* (1916).

Lindley, Sir Francis: *Lord Lovat: A Biography* (1935).

Lovat, Laura: *Maurice Baring: A Postscript* (1947).

McDougall, D.: *Fifty Years a Borough: The Story of West Ham* (County Borough of West Ham, 1936).

Mosley, Nicholas: *Julian Grenfell: His Life and the Times of His Death, 1888–1915* (1976).

Peck, Lady Winifred: *A Little Learning: or, A Victorian Childhood* (1952).

———: *Home for the Holidays* (1955).

Price, R. G. G.: *A History of Punch* (1957).

Ribblesdale, Lord: *Charles Lister: Letters and Recollections*, with a Memoir by His Father (one chapter by Ronald Knox) (1917).

Simpson, Maj.-Gen. Charles Rudyard: *The History of the Lincolnshire Regiment 1914–1918* (1931).

Speaight, Robert: *The Life of Hilaire Belloc* (1957).

———: *Ronald Knox the Writer* (1966).

Spencer, Gilbert, R.A.: *Memoirs of a Painter* (1974).

Usborne, Richard: *A Century of Summer Fields 1864–1964* (1964).

Waugh, Evelyn: *The Life of Ronald Knox* (1959).

2 . HERODAS

Arnott, W. G.: "Walter Headlam and Herodas". *Proceedings of the African Classical Association*, Vol. 10, 1947.

Kenyon, F. W.: *Classical Texts from Papyri in the British Museum* (1891).

———: *Palaeography of Greek Papyri* (1899).

3 . CRYPTOGRAPHY

(a) General

Kahn, David: *The Codebreakers: The Story of Secret Writing* (1966).

(b) Room 40, 1914–1918

Birch, Frank: *Alice in I.D.25* (a satire on life in Room 40) (privately printed, 1918).

Fraser, Lionel W.: *All to the Good* (1963).

James, Sir William: *Alfred Ewing: The Man of Room 40* (1939).

_____: *The Sky Was Always Blue* (1951).

_____: *The Eyes of the Navy: A Biographical Study of Sir Reginald Hall* (1955).

Marder, A. J.: *The War at Sea: From the Dreadnought to Scapa Flow* (1965).

(c) The ARCOS Incident

ARCOS (All Russian Co-Operative Society): "Police Raid on the Trade Delegation". *Inostrannoye Torgovoye Obozreniye* (Review of Foreign Trade), 16 May 1927.

Dallin, David J.: *Soviet Espionage* (1955).

Documents on British Foreign Policy 1919–1939, ed. W. N. Medlicott, D. Dakin and M. E. Lambert, Series IA, II and III (1970).

Documents Illustrating the Hostile Activities of the Soviet Government and the Third International Against Great Britain (White Paper, 1927).

(d) Enigma

Bertrand, General Gustave: *Énigma, ou la plus grande énigme de la guerre 1939–45* (1973).

McLachlan, Donald: *Room 39: Naval Intelligence in Action 1939–45* (1968).

Turing, Sarah: *Alan M. Turing* (1959).

Index

a devout child, 24
at Edmundthorpe, 26–28
at Summer Field, 34–35
precocity, 38, 39
happiness at Eton, 34–35, 43, 44–45,
  78
trip to Germany, 51
attracted to Tractarianism, 52
leaves Eton, to Rome with brothers,
  67–68
at Balliol, 67, 76
offered brilliant career, 77
"a romance", 77–78
ordained as Anglo-Catholic priest
  (1912), 92
Chaplain of Trinity, 92, 94–95, 131
opposes modernism, 96–98
"a personal person", early intense
  friendships, 108–110, 121–122
influence, 109
tutor to Harold Macmillan, 109–110
"stakes his soul", 110
affection for Guy Lawrence, 110–111
teaches logic through card games,
  113–114
master at Shrewsbury (1914), 119,
  124
distressed by doubts, 121–123
and by Guy's conversion, 121
and by loss of friends in war, 121–122
"The Parting of Friends", 124
at Room 40 and M.I.D.7, 129, 140
painful disputes with father, 130–131
resigns from Trinity chaplaincy, 131
at Oratory, 133, 141, 195, 258–259
"numbed" by Guy's death, 142
ordained as R.C. priest (1919), 143
"the wittiest young man in England",
  165
early essays, 165–166
dreams of congenial home, misfit at
  St Edmund's, 167, 217
in disgrace over broadcast, 176–177
appointed to Oxford Chaplaincy, 177
makes ends meet with detective
  stories, 177, 182–183, 253
at the Old Palace (1926), 184–185,
  211
Hon. Fellow of Trinity, 185
disappointments at Chaplaincy,
  209–212

revived by Lady Acton's friendship,
  214–215, 217–218, 239, 240, 256,
  265
leaves Chaplaincy, plans Bible translation, 215–218
moves to Aldenham (1939), 219
"Nine Years' Hard" on Knox Version,
  early difficulties and discouragements, 239–244
at A.D.K.'s deathbed, 250–251
Knox Version, later difficulties,
  252–255
N.T. authorized and published
  (1945), 252, 254
protest over Hiroshima, 255
low spirits, homeless again, 256
to Asquiths at Mells (1947), 257–258
sadness at W.L.K.'s death, 262
60th-birthday dinner, 264–265
completion of Knox Version, 265
to Africa (1954), 265–266
"proving God", his last apologia,
  266–267
cancer (1956), 267
last Mass in Mells Chapel, 267–268
Romanes lecture (1957), 268, 269
death (Aug. 1957), 270

CHARACTERISTICS:
authority, ideal of, 91, 97, 131
balance, sense of, 168
brilliance, 166, 168
"carriage folk", attitude to, 77, 218
"doing the most difficult thing",
  171, 239
dressiness in early life, 93
and later shabbiness, 239
happy, affectionate nature, 33, 77
and later melancholy, 209–210
"hopeless romantic", 218
mimicry, 42
modesty and politeness, 212
nostalgia for the past, 165, 209
"plans", importance of, 240
power of prayer, 269
river, love of, 211
sympathy, need for feminine, 170
truthfulness, 17
unmusical, 154
unpopular causes, devotion to, 52,
  212–213
unselfishness, 45, 166, 256

Manchester Guardian, 68, 72, 73, 132
Manilius, 83
Mansfield, Katherine, 144
Market Harborough (Leicestershire),
    192
Marsh, Edward, 64
Martindale, Charlie, S.J., 122–124,
    177, 185, 211, 214, 240–241, 243
Masterman, J. C., 268
Matapan, battle of, 248
Maurice, F. D., 50
May, Phil, 104, 105, 202
M'bebi (Actons' farm in Rhodesia),
    256, 265
Meler (Soviet emissary), 180
Mells (Somerset), 257–258, 267–268
Menin Road, 139
Meredith, George, 49, 165
Merton College (Oxford), 10–11, 15,
    173, 261
Mexico City, 134
Middlesbrough, Catholic Bishop of, 253
Miles, Eustace, 72
Milne, A. A., 105, 173, 201
Milner-White, Eric, 152
Milton, John, 189, 233
Modernism, 96–97
Mokotov-Pyry (Poland), 227
Moneymore (Co. Derry), 3, 4
Moore, George, 43
Moore, G. E., 59, 60
Moore, Temple, 30
More Hall (Gloucestershire), 114
Morris, Mrs Helen, 230
Morris, William, 32, 33, 43
Morton, H. V., 198
Morton, J. B. ("Beachcomber" of the
    Daily Express), 206, 261
Moscow Bank for Foreign Trade, 178
Moses, Mr., 235
Moses, Mrs., 199, 235
Mount Carmel, 237
Muggeridge, Malcolm, 153
Munich Conference (1938), 219
Murry, J. Middleton, 144
Muscat, 19, 21, 65

Nagasaki (1945), 255
Naphill (Bucks), 247
National Insurance Bill (1911–12), 91
Nazi Government, 222, 226

Needham, Joseph, 154
Newcastle, Lord Mayor of, 176
Newman, John Henry, 9, 52, 76, 87, 88,
    94, 124, 132, 177, 215, 222, 241
News of the World, 166, 202
Newton, Ethel. See Knox, Ethel Mary
Newton, Horace (Bishop Knox's father-
    in-law), 30
Newton, Professor (Cambridge), 56
New Yorker, 174, 200, 202, 203, 204
New Zealand, 237
Nichol, Robertson, 72
Niebuhr, Reinhold, 196
Nietzsche, F. W., 50
Night and Day, 204
Nixon, J. E., 82, 124
North Africa, 237, 246
North Dean (Bucks), 181
North Manchester Preparatory School,
    68
Nottingham, 145
Novello, Ivor, 104, 171
Nowell, A. T., R.A., 147
Nuffield, Lord, 219
Nugent, George, 4

Oberammergau Passion Play, 93
Observer, 71, 105
Offa's Dyke, 236
O.G.S. See Oratory of the Good
    Shepherd
Old Palace (Oxford Catholic
    Chaplaincy), 184
Omar Khayyam Society, 264
Oratorians, 123
Oratory (London), 133, 141
Oratory of the Good Shepherd,
    150–153, 258
Oratory House (Cambridge), 153–154,
    234
Orthodox Club (Oxford), 90
Oxford, 8–11, 15, 43, 45, 46, 67, 68,
    76, 102–103, 109, 173, 184, 261
    See also Balliol College; Corpus
    Christi College; Merton College;
    Old Palace; Trinity College
Oxford Magazine, 97
Oxford Movement, 87
Oxford Union Society, 94–95
Oxyrhyncus papyri, 65–67, 101, 190

PENELOPE FITZGERALD

The Blue Flower

Winner of the National Book Critics Circle Award

With an introduction by Candia McWilliam

The year is 1794 and Fritz, passionate, idealistic and brilliant, is seeking his father's permission to announce his engagement to his heart's desire: twelve-year-old Sophie. His astounded family and friends are amused and disturbed by his betrothal. What can he be thinking?

Tracing the dramatic early years of the young German who was to become the great romantic poet and philosopher Novalis, *The Blue Flower* is a masterpiece of invention, evoking the past with a reality that we can almost feel.

'A masterpiece. How does she do it?'   A. S. Byatt

———

PENELOPE FITZGERALD

Innocence

With an introduction by Julian Barnes

The Ridolfis are a Florentine family of long lineage and little
money. It is 1955, and the family, like its decrepit villa and
farm, has seen better days. Only eighteen-year-old Chiara
shows anything like vitality.

Chiara has set her heart on Salvatore, a young and brilliant doctor who resolved long ago to be emotionally
dependent on no one. Faced with this, she calls on her
English girlfriend Barney to help her make the impossible
match.

'Witty and moving . . . not just about Italians in love but of
living and loving for all humans'   *The Times*